Illustrated C

Leor Zolman

R & D Publications
Lawrence, Kansas 66046

R & D Publications, Inc.
Suite 200
1601 West 23rd Street
P.O. Box 3127
Lawrence, Kansas 66046-0127

Trademarks:
The C Users Journal, R&D Publications, Inc.
UNIX, AT&T Bell Laboratories.
XENIX, MS-DOS, Microsoft C, Microsoft Corporation.
Borland C++, Turbo C, Turbo Debugger, Borland International.
Epsilon, Lugaru Software Ltd.
FACET/TERM, Structured Software Solutions, Inc.

The programs and applications in this book are presented for instructional value. The programs have been carefully tested, but are not guaranteed for any particular purpose. The publisher does not offer any warranties and does not guarantee the accuracy, adequacy, or completeness of any information and is not responsible for any errors or omissions or the results obtained from use of such information.

ISBN 0-923667-21-0

To Lisa and Katelyn

Table of Contents

Foreward

While C is a small, syntactically simple language, even experienced programmers find that to become proficient in C, they must overcome an unusually steep learning curve.

This curve usually feels steepest at the two junctures labelled "pointers" and "file I/O."

In this book Leor Zolman addresses these obstacles (especially file I/O) through a series of large examples. In each example, he explains not only how the pieces work, but also why *these* particular pieces must be fitted together in *this* particular way to get the desired result.

His approach is to teach the components where their interdependence can be appreciated — in the context of practical applications.

Why Bother?

C is a subtle language design. The language remains small by relying on programmers to exploit non-obvious relationships between the various parts of the design. Instead of supplying a string type, C puts just the tiniest spin on the definition of a null, a pointer, and a relational expression. The result is a set of features that support a string convention — an officially unofficial (and remarkably efficient) programmer supplied string type.

Taken by themselves, C pointers and the various elements of C file I/O aren't particularly complex — and aren't particularly powerful. The power and elegance are accessible only to those who understand the subtle (and usually unexplained) connections between the various pieces.

Of course, if you don't understand how the string convention and its supporting design elements support one another, string intensive applications will be awkward at best. Similarly, if you don't know the assumptions underlying the structure of the file I/O package, attempting to write even the simplest file-handling program will degenerate into an exercise in futility.

Thus, unlike most other languages, you can't really master C by learning the individual components. Instead you must somehow absorb the whole.

Making the Connections

This book addresses the whole. Leor doesn't belabor the syntax and he doesn't agonize over searching for the Holy Grail of "object oriented programming." He explains instead how the language elements interact with one another, with the environment and with the design to accomplish pedestrian, but essential, tasks with the elegance and power for which C is famous.

The result is an eminently practical book that works nicely as a "second step" C text. If you've learned the syntax, but you're still struggling to "make sense" of C, read this book — and save yourself a lot of frustration.

Robert Ward

Introduction

To a fledgeling C programmer, the language must appear incredibly cryptic and idiomatic. At first glance, C program listings appear strange because they are composed of almost every printable character in the ASCII character set. It's as if someone created a language specifically so that none those under-used symbols would feel left out.

Soon the C student discovers pointers, and confusion reigns. The language allows coding styles with levels upon levels of pointers, indirection and abstraction. In fact, C's proponents seem to *encourage* such coding calisthentics in much of the popular literature.

Finally, after accepting C's seemingly gratuitous complexity, the bewildered neophyte will find there is no support at all in the language proper for such fundamental operations as string handling or file input/output! "You mean I must use library functions for all that!?"

With sufficient repetition it all becomes second-nature, but that is small consolation to the beginning C programmer. The ground between the novice stage and fluency can only be traversed through the experience of writing C programs and discovering through practice the true power and sensible philosophy behind C's features, and even its omissions.

Starting to C

Three factors will greatly ease the process of learning a new programming language, especially one like C:

- A well-written introductory text to cover the language fundamentals
- Access to an experienced programmer who is willing to answer questions
- Examples, more examples and then some other examples.

There are plenty of excellent introductory C texts available, geared to all different levels of previous programming experience. Some automated ones even lead you by the hand through programming exercises, and monitor your progress along the way. Choose your first C textbook carefully. There's no substitute for examining a copy of each candidate text and getting the one that has the most comfortable style for you.

When first struggling to learn C in 1978, I was lucky enough to be surrounded by C programmers I could badger with questions. And boy, did I ever badger them! If you don't have a source of direct support, such as a co-worker or cooperative C compiler vendor, then you might try looking up a computer club (e.g., The Boston Computer Society). Such organizations often have volunteer members available to answer technical questions in different areas of computing. Also, many of the subscription dial-up services, such as BIX and CompuServe, have forums for the exchange of questions and answers on C and other topics.

Illustrated C fills the third need above: the call for well-documented, substantive tutorial examples. The beginning books often teach C one piece at a time, with code fragments or "minimalist" programs to illustrate each point. Such code fragments and simple programs are fine for illustrating C's basic mechanics, but it may not always be clear how the building blocks fit together to form real-world applications. My series of "Illustrated C" columns in **The C Users Journal** is based on the idea of combining practical, useful C programs with substantial tutorial annotation. This approach has succeeded in filling the void between **CUJ** articles discussing elementary language features and those presenting very specialized applications.

What This Book Contains

This book is the first collection of my "Illustrated C" columns, comprising material that has appeared (or will appear) in **The C Users Journal** between February, 1990 and August, 1992. Various sections of code and text have been updated, edited and corrected as necessary to reflect both reader feedback received since the date of initial magazine publication and the conversion from magazine to book format.

The title of each chapter contains two parts: the purpose of the application being illustrated, and the aspect of C software design that figures most prominently in that application. You can find a particular topic of interest by either criterion.

Chapter 4, on Indexed File I/O (the Rolo program), was written especially for this collection and appears nowhere else.

Portability

One of the themes that has gained momentum in the "Illustrated C" column's first two years of publication is portability. While some of the programs in the earlier columns were written exclusively for use under DOS, later ones were designed for easy portability between the DOS and SCO XENIX environments.

In preparing the code disk for this book, it came to my attention that some of the earlier code was dependent on ANSI language features. This made conversion of these programs to pre-ANSI (or "K&R") C compilers tedious. Because compilers supporting only the K&R dialect are still common on various Unix-family platforms, I performed the conversions myself where applicable, and included the "retro-modified" versions of those programs in subdirectories named "K-R". The line numbers for the modified versions are no longer in sync with the printed versions of the listings, because the modifications included heavy work on function headers and prototypes. Even if you need to compile the modified versions, use only the printed listings for reference when reading through the associated chapter text.

All programs have been compiled with Borland C++ (in C mode) under DOS, and with the SCO XENIX 2.3.2 C compiler under XENIX. I've tried to write the code in as portable a style as possible, but minor modifications may be necessary for compilation of these programs on other platforms. Except for the DOS-specific applications (such as login and the directory navigation tools), all code has been successfully compiled and run under both the DOS and XENIX environments.

How to Use This Book

There are several ways you can use these programs. Most simply, you could read the book and let the text provide you with a guided tour of the anatomy of these C applications. If you have purchased the companion code disk with the book, you can first run the programs to get a feel for what they do, then work through some of the exercises at the end of each chapter, modifying the original source code. If you do not have a code disk and wish to purchase one, you can use the mail-in card at the back of the book to order the disk.

If you have more time available and really want to "get your hands dirty," I recommend you try to design the C programs on your own, given only the functional description in the text. Whether your attempts come to full fruition or not, you'll gain immense value from the effort. Then, compare your approach with my own published one. Each different approach you invent or examine will help expand your C expertise, because there is rarely "one right way" to write a program.

Finally, the programs themselves are provided in both source and executable format. They may be used as utilities and tools in their own right, or expanded to serve specific needs I haven't even imagined. For example, one **CUJ** reader wrote that he'd taken the personal journal program (intended for keeping a diary) and adapted it to aid in tracking C source code development history. There are no licenses associated with this code, so feel free to use it as you please.

Chapter 1

Directory Navigation: Manipulating the DOS Environment

As an MS-DOS user with a large amount of hard disk space to manage, I frequently find myself *cd*-ing all over a system in pursuit of source files and data. Unfortunately, the standard MS-DOS command processor, ***COMMAND.COM***, has a limited repertoire of commands to support such directory navigation. For instance, to change directly to an arbitrary logical drive and directory path, the user must enter the drive selector and path specification as two separate commands. Switching from the root directory of drive C: to the *\work* directory on drive D: requires the command sequence:

```
C:\>d:                (select drive D:)
D:\>cd work           (change to the desired directory)
D:\WORK>...
```

(All examples assume the PROMPT environment variable has been set to the value *pg* to show the current directory as part of the system prompt.)

If the user attempts to select a different drive and a path with one command, it will seem as though nothing has happened:

```
C:\>cd d:\work
C:\>...
```

The system has changed the selected path associated with the specified drive (*d:* in this case), but the specified drive is not selected to be current. The system maintains a current working directory for each logical drive. If the user were then to select that other drive, i.e.,

```
C:\>d:
D:\WORK>...
```

the selected path would then become the current directory.

Another missing feature in the standard command environment is a simple directory name aliasing mechanism that allows quick switching to commonly used directories, even if the path name happens to be lengthy. MS-DOS does provide a simple facility, the *subst* command, to relate an arbitrary path to a new drive designator. With *subst*, however, the alias names can only be a single letter. *CONFIG.SYS* typically requires modification to allow additional drive letter assignments, and there are other idiosyncracies that make *subst* awkward to use. I prefer the ability to assign arbitrary mnemonics to arbitrary paths, and to have those mnemonics recognized when they appear in *cd* commands.

I also appreciate having a clean mechanism for instantly switching to the previous directory, even if I've forgotten its location.

The Answer

To address these needs, I wrote an extended *cd* command that supports a combined drive/path specification, and a companion command that returns the user to the previous directory (taking the directory specification from information recorded in an environment variable by the extended *cd* command). The *cd* replacement stores the old full path name in an environment variable before switching to a new specified path. The companion command reads this environment variable and returns to the original directory upon request.

Modifying the Master Environment

Because the extended *cd* must modify its parent's environment, it uses the functions for modifying the master environment (written by Scott Robert Ladd), that appeared in the July 1989 issue of **The C Users Journal**. The code is reproduced in Listing 1.6. On the **Illustrated C** companion code disk the file is *env.c*. Listing 1.5 shows the header file, *env.h*, that contains the prototypes for the master environment library.

Whenever a DOS program is invoked, whether by a user command or by a direct system call from another program, the contents of the calling program's environment are cloned and a copy is handed to the subordinate program. The Standard Library functions provided for manipulating environment variables can only alter a program's local copies of those variables, and not the original values from which they were cloned. Thus, even after a C program makes changes to the values of environment variables, the variables revert to their original values after the C program terminates.

env.c is a short library of functions allowing a C program to access and alter the values of DOS master environment variables so changes remain after the C program terminates. Three functions constitute the library:

*char *m_getenv(char *name)*
returns value of the named master environment variable, or NULL if undefined;

*int m_putenv(char *name, char *text)*
assigns a value to a master environment variable, returns *0* on success;

*int m_delenv(char *name)*
deletes the named master environment variable, returns *0* on success.

The variable names provided to these functions may be specified in either lower or upper case; the functions convert their name parameters to all upper case characters before the names are used.

The *cde* and *ret* Commands

cde (mnemonic for *CD Extended*) works similarly to MS-DOS's *cd* command, with the following extensions:

1) when both a drive designator and a path name are specified, the specified drive is immediately selected with the path
2) when the argument is identified as the name of an existing MS-DOS environment variable, the value of the named variable is taken as the path name to be selected.

In support of the "return to previous directory" feature, I implemented a directory stack mechanism. This stack is maintained via environment variables, and the user may select the naming convention for those variables by customizing the *#define* statements in *cderet.h* (Listing 1.1).

One master environment variable (I call it *CHAINS*) specifies the maximum size of the directory stack. When *cde* is first invoked, it checks to see if the *CHAINS* variable has been previously defined in the environment. If it has, then its current value is used. If not, *cde* initializes *CHAINS* to a default value (specified by the *DEFAULT_CHAINS* definition in the header file). Thus, the user has the option of setting the value of *CHAINS* explicitly (using the standard DOS command *set*), or allowing *cde* to handle the initialization of *CHAINS* automatically (see Listing 1.2, lines 80-84).

A stack of size *CHAINS* is represented by a set of environment variables sharing a common base name (I use *CHAIN*), with position numbers appended. Thus, with *CHAINS* equal to *3*, after several *cde* commands have been issued the environment variables *CHAIN1*, *CHAIN2*, and *CHAIN3* will have been created to store the appropriate path names in the environment.

Every time *cde* is used to change directories, it pushes the old current working directory on the stack by reassigning all the relevant environment variables. *CHAIN1* is always the top of the stack, *CHAINn* (where *n = CHAINS*) is the base. Because no disk activity is involved, this process is fast.

The *ret* command (Listing 1.3) returns to the previous directory (either specified by *CHAIN1* or undefined), then pops the stack by reassigning all the active environment variables in reverse order.

As long as *CHAINS* is greater than *1*, then the directory stack behaves as described above and successive uses of *ret* unravel the stack.

When *CHAINS* is set to *1*, *ret* considers this a special case. After returning to the directory specified by *CHAIN1*, *CHAIN1* is reset to the name of the directory that was current at the time of the *ret* call. Thus, repeated usage of *ret* when *CHAINS* is equal to *1* effects a toggle between two directories. Depending on the way your system is organized, this toggling mechanism may be more useful to you than the directory stack mechanism.

Icing

The directory aliasing feature is activated by setting an environment variable to the full path name desired and using that environment variable's name as the parameter to *cde*. For example,

```
C:\>set WORK=d:\project\subproj\new\testing
C:\>cde work
D:\PROJECT\SUBPROJ\NEW\TESTING>...
```

As a special case, for convenience, issuing the *cde* command with no arguments causes *cde* to look for a special environment variable (I call it *HOME*), and switch to the directory it specifies. If you spend much of your time headquartered at one directory this is an easy way to go back to it from anywhere in the system, despite the state of the directory stack. When this special form of *cde* is used, the current directory will, as usual, be recorded in the environment (supporting the use of *ret* from the *HOME* directory).

When setting environment variables, be careful not to type spaces between the end of the variable name and the = sign. DOS includes spaces as part of the variable name, and things wouldn't work. The *cde* program ignores spaces after the = sign (and before the pathname text) without any problem. It's safest to be consistent and avoid the use of spaces altogether.

Implementation

Both *cde* and *ret* have two phases of operation. The first phase performs the required drive/directory selection. The second phase updates the related environment variables. If the first phase fails, then the programs exit immediately. There's no need to update environment variables if the current directory wasn't changed.

To obtain the name of the target directory in phase one, *ret* simply accesses the *CHAIN1* environment variable. If the variable does not exist, then *cde* has never been run and an appropriate message is displayed. If *CHAIN1* exists it specifies the target path. *cde* gets its target path name from the command line. If the name happens to be the name of an active environment variable, then the value of the variable with that name is used to obtain the target path.

The directory selection process is identical for both commands and takes two steps: the selection of the logical drive and the selection of the desired directory. The drive is selected first; if that fails, we quit and no harm has been done. Once the new drive has been selected, the new path is selected. If that fails, we have to go back and reinstate the original drive. If it succeeds we're done with phase one.

Phase two for *ret* is straightforward. If *CHAINS* is equal to *1*, then the *CHAIN1* environment variable is set to the original current directory name (before phase one) in order to support the toggling feature. For other values of *CHAINS*, the directory stack is popped by looping to reassign each *CHAINn* variable to the value of its next higher counterpart.

cde's phase two begins by making sure the *CHAINS* environment variable, used to specify the stack size, is present and initialized. If it exists, its value is assigned to the program variable *chaincnt*. If *CHAINS* does not exist, then it is initialized to the default value (specified by the symbolic string constant *DEFAULT_CHAINS*).

Finally, the directory stack is pushed by copying each *CHAINn* variable (for *n* = *1* to *CHAINS-1*) to its next higher counterpart. *CHAIN1* is a special case; it is assigned to the name of the directory that was current before phase one was completed.

Configuration

The following symbolic constants may be changed to suit your preferences:

CHAINS_VAR	the master directory chain size control variable
CHAIN_BASE	the base name of directory stack variables
DEFAULT_CHAINS	the default value for *CHAINS_VAR* (in quotes)
HOME_NAME	the name of the environment variable identifying the home directory

the *cde.exe* and *ret.exe* commands should be placed in a directory that is somewhere in your system search path. (I use *c:\bin* for all my personal utilities.)

System Dependent Functions

The two compiler dependent areas in this application, direct console I/O and DOS logical drive selection, have been isolated in a separate utility library named *util.c* (Listing 1.4). The only support function required by the functions in *util.c* is the *bdos()* function typically supplied with most popular compiler libraries.

If you need to write the *bdos()* function yourself, the prototype is shown at the top of the *util.c* source file. It takes an interrupt (*int 21h*) function number, a *DX* register value, and an *AL* register value as parameters (although the *AL* parameter is not needed for this application). The *bdos()* function can easily be written in terms of any of the more general operating system interface functions (*int86()*, *intdos()*, etc.,) you may have available.

To keep the commands' *.exe* file sizes as small as possible, all messages are displayed on the console using direct console I/O calls (through *bdos()* facilities) so as not to drag complete file I/O library support code into the executable files. The *util.c* functions *cputs()* and *putch()* are similar to their namesakes in the Microsoft library. They are provided here for the benefit of users of compiler packages not including these functions. The *setdrive()* function I provide is cleaner than Microsoft's *_dos_setdrive()*.

The library functions *chdir()* and *getcwd()* are used by the commands and should be available in your compiler's standard library.

The commands to compile and link *cde.c* and *ret.c* using Microsoft C or Borland C++ are shown at the top of the source file listings. When compiled with optimization, both *cde.exe* and *ret.exe* weigh in at just over 6K, so their load-and-run time is negligible.

Caveat

The following line in *CONFIG.SYS* will insure plenty of environment space for the *CHAIN* variables:

```
shell = c:\command.com /p /e:2500
```

Summary

The *cde* and *ret* commands provide a clean, quick and convenient mechanism for alleviating some of MS-DOS's command processor limitations. There are plenty of full-blown command processor replacements, shells and special purpose TSRs offering other ways to get around on your DOS system. Few (if any) of these can offer 100% compatibility with all other packages and TSRs, zero bytes of system RAM overhead (unless you count the few extra bytes of environment space required), and *cde/ret*'s ease of use.

LISTING 1.1 cderet.h

```
/*
 * cderet.h: Prototypes and definitions for the cde/ret
 *           Directory Navigation utilities.
 */


#define MAX_DIRNAME_SIZE 100 /* longest conceivable directory name size  */
#define MAX_EVARNAME_SIZE 20 /* max length of env. var. names created    */
#define DEFAULT_CHAINS "1"   /* initial default dir. stack size          */
#define CHAINS_VAR "CHAINS"  /* name of env. var. controlling stack size */
#define CHAIN_BASE "CHAIN"   /* base name of env. vars holding dir names */
#define HOME_NAME "HOME"     /* Name of 'home dir' environment variable  */

/*
 *  Prototypes for utility functions in cderet.c:
 */

void    error(char *msg);
int     cputs(char *txt);
int     putch(char c);
int     setdrive(int drive_no);
int     getdrive();
void    change_dir(char *newpath);
```

LISTING 1.2 cde.c

```
/*
 *  cde.c: Extended "cd" command for MS-DOS.
 *  Written by Leor Zolman, 9/20/89
 *
 *  Features:
 *      1)  Allows changing to another drive and dirctory in one step
 *      2)  Supports directory aliasing through environment variables
 *      3)  With no arguments, optionally switches to 'home' directory
 *          (if the HOME environment variable is currently defined)
 *      3)  Manages a "previous directory" stack through environment
 *          variables. The number of entries in the stack is dynamically
 *          configured through a special controlling environment variable.
 *      4)  For special case of stack size = 1, toggling back and forth
 *          between two directories is supported
 *
 *   Usage:
 *      cde [d:][path]      (changes to given drive/directory)
 *      cde <env-var-name>  (indirect dir change on environment variable)
 *      cde                 (changes to HOME directory, if defined, or
 *                           returns current working directory otherwise)
 *
 *  Compile/Link:
 *      cl /Ox cde.c util.c env.c
 * or   bcc cde.c util.c env.c
 *
 *  Uses the Master Environment library from CUJ 7/89.
 *
 */

#include    <stdio.h>
#include    <dos.h>
#include    <string.h>
#include    <stdlib.h>
#include    "cderet.h"
#include    "env.h"

main(int argc, char **argv)
{
    char    *pathp;
    char    cwdbuf[MAX_DIRNAME_SIZE];     /* buffer for current dir name  */

    int     chaincnt;                     /* size of dir stack            */
    char    chaincnt_txt[10], *chaincntp;
    char    chnevar1[MAX_EVARNAME_SIZE], /* env var names built here     */
            chnevar2[MAX_EVARNAME_SIZE];
    char    chndname_save[MAX_DIRNAME_SIZE], *chndname;
    char    itoabuf[10];                  /* used by itoa() function      */
    int     i;

                             /* Get current dir. name and current drive: */
    getcwd(cwdbuf, MAX_DIRNAME_SIZE);

    if (argc == 1)                        /* if no args given,            */
        if (pathp = m_getenv(HOME_NAME)) /* if HOME directory defined,   */
```

LISTING 1.2 cde.c *continued*

```
        {
            change_dir(pathp);            /* then try to change to it.     */
            strcpy(chnevar1, CHAIN_BASE);/* set top-stack env var          */
            strcat(chnevar1, "1");
            if (m_putenv(chnevar1, cwdbuf)) /* to old dir                  */
                error("Error setting environment variable");
            return 0;
        }
        else
        {                               /* just print current working dir   */
            cputs(cwdbuf);
            putch('\n');
            return 0;
        }

    if (argc != 2)
        error("Usage: cde [d:][newpath] or <environment-var-name>\n");

    pathp = argv[1];                     /* skip whitespace in pathname  */

    if (chndname = m_getenv(pathp))      /* if env-var-name given,       */
        pathp = chndname;                /* use its value as new path    */

    change_dir(pathp);

                    /* Read or initialize master chain length variable: */
    if ((chaincntp = m_getenv(CHAINS_VAR)) == NULL)
        if (m_putenv(CHAINS_VAR,
                    strcpy(chaincntp = chaincnt_txt, DEFAULT_CHAINS)))
            error("Error creating environment variable");

                            /* Update the environment directory chain:  */
    chaincnt = atoi(chaincntp);
    for (i = chaincnt; i > 0; i-)
    {                       /* construct name of previous dirname variable: */
        if (i != 1)
        {
            strcpy(chnevar2, CHAIN_BASE);
            strcat(chnevar2, itoa(i-1, itoabuf, 10));
        }

        if (chndname = ((i != 1) ? m_getenv(chnevar2) : cwdbuf))
        {                               /* copy value of prev. to current   */
            strcpy(chndname_save, chndname);      /* m_putenv() bashes it */
            strcpy(chnevar1, CHAIN_BASE);
            strcat(chnevar1, itoa(i, itoabuf, 10));
            if (m_putenv(chnevar1, chndname_save))
                error("Error setting environment variable");
        }
    }
    return 0;
}
```

LISTING 1.3 ret.c

```
/*
 *  ret.c: Return to previous working directory
 *  Written by Leor Zolman, 9/89
 *
 *      (companion to CDE.C)
 *  Uses the Master Environment package from CUJ 7/89
 *
 *  Usage:
 *    ret                   (returns to previous directory)
 *
 *  Compile/Link:
 *      cl /Ox ret.c util.c env.c
 *  or  bcc ret.c util.c env.c
 */

#include    <stdio.h>
#include    <string.h>
#include    <stdlib.h>
#include    <dos.h>
#include    "cderet.h"
#include    "env.h"

main(int argc)
{
    char *pathp;
    char cwdbuf[MAX_DIRNAME_SIZE];

    int     chaincnt;
    char    chnevar1[MAX_EVARNAME_SIZE], /* env var names built here     */
            chnevar2[MAX_EVARNAME_SIZE];
    char    chndname_save[MAX_DIRNAME_SIZE], *chndname;
    char    itoabuf[10];                 /* used by itoa() function      */
    int i;

                              /* Get current dir. name and current drive: */
    getcwd(cwdbuf, MAX_DIRNAME_SIZE);

    if (argc != 1)
        error("Usage: ret     (returns to last dir cde'd from)");

    if ((pathp = m_getenv(CHAINS_VAR)) == NULL)
        error("cde hasn't been run yet");
    else
        chaincnt = atoi(pathp);

                                   /* See if CDE has created any entries: */
    strcpy(chnevar1, CHAIN_BASE);
    strcat(chnevar1, "1");
    if (!(pathp = m_getenv(chnevar1)))   /* if so, pathp points to last  */
        error("No previous directory");  /*   dir, else no previous dir  */

    change_dir(pathp);                /* change to previous directory:    */

                              /* Update the environment directory chain: */
```

LISTING 1.3 ret.c *continued*

```
    if (chaincnt == 1)                  /* special case: record old dir */
    {
        if (m_putenv(chnevar1, cwdbuf))
            error("Error setting environment variable");
        return 0;
    }

    for (i = 1; ; i++)
    {                           /* get name of current dirname variable */
        strcpy(chnevar1, CHAIN_BASE);
        strcat(chnevar1, itoa(i, itoabuf, 10));

        strcpy(chnevar2, CHAIN_BASE);
        strcat(chnevar2, itoa(i + 1, itoabuf, 10));

        if (!(chndname = m_getenv(chnevar2)))
            break;                          /* found end of saved chain */

                                /* copy value of next higher to current */
        strcpy(chndname_save, chndname);        /* m_putenv() bashes it */
        strcpy(chnevar1, CHAIN_BASE);
        strcat(chnevar1, itoa(i, itoabuf, 10));
        if (m_putenv(chnevar1, chndname_save))
            error("Error setting environment variable");
    }
    return 0;
}
```

LISTING 1.4 util.c

```
/*
 * util.c:  Utility functions for cde/ret package
 *
 *      These functions rely on the "bdos" library function
 *      from your compiler's library. Prototype:
 *
 *      int bdos(int dosfn, unsigned dosdx, unsigned dosal);
 */

#include    <stdio.h>
#include    <dos.h>
#include    <ctype.h>
#include    "cderet.h"

/*
 *  Print error msg and abort:
 */

void error(char *msg)
{
    cputs("cde: ");
    cputs(msg);
    putch('\n');
    exit(1);
}

/*
 *  Change to specified drive/path, terminate program on error:
 */

void change_dir(char *new_path)
{
    int old_drive;

    old_drive = getdrive();

    while (*new_path && isspace(*new_path))  /* skip whitespace           */
        new_path++;

    if (new_path[1] == ':')                  /* if drive designator       */
    {                                        /* given, then set drive     */
        if (setdrive(tolower(*new_path) - 'a'))
            error("Can't select given drive\n");
        new_path += 2;
    }

    if (*new_path && chdir(new_path))    /* If path given, set new path. */
    {
        setdrive(old_drive);             /* If error, restore drive      */
        error("Can't change to given path");
    }
}
```

LISTING 1.4 util.c *continued*

```
/*
 *  DOS functions, written in terms of the "bdos" function:
 */

int cputs(char *txt)                      /* display msg, console I/O only */
{
    char c;

    while (c = *txt++)
    {
        if (c == '\n')
            putch('\r');
        putch(c);
    }
    return 0;
}

int putch(char c)                            /* display a char on console */
{
    return bdos(2, c, 0);
}

int setdrive(int drive_no)                   /* set logical drive. Return */
{                                             /* non-zero on error.       */
    int after;

    bdos(0x0E, drive_no, 0);
    after = bdos(0x19, 0, 0);
    if ((after & 0xff) == drive_no)        /* low 8 bits are new drive no. */
        return 0;                                       /* set correctly */
    else
        return -1;                                             /* error. */
}

int getdrive()                             /* return current logical drive */
{
    return bdos(0x19, 0, 0);
}

```

LISTING 1.5 env.h

```
/*
    env.h: Prototypes for Master Environment Control routines
*/

char *m_getenv(char *name);
int m_putenv(char *name, char *text);
int m_delenv(char *name);
```

LISTING 1.6 env.c

```
/*
    env.c: Environment modification routines
        From CUG, July/89, p. 60

    Usages:
        char *m_getenv(char *name);
            Returns value of named env variable, or NULL if undefined

        int m_putenv(char *name, char *text);
            Assigns a value to an env variable. Returns 0 if OK.

        int m_delenv(char *name);
            Deletes the given env variable. Returns 0 if OK.
*/

#include <dos.h>
#include <stddef.h>
#include <string.h>

#ifndef __TURBOC__
#define MK_FP(seg, off) \
        ((void far *) (((long) (seg) << 16L) | (long) (off)))
#endif

typedef struct {
    char reserved1[22];
    unsigned par_seg;
    char reserved2[20];
    unsigned env_seg;
} PSP;

#pragma pack(1)

typedef struct {
    char status;
    unsigned owner_PSP;
    unsigned len;
} MCB;

#pragma pack()

char far * env_ptr;
static unsigned env_len;
static int initialized = 0;
static char s[256];
static void m_findenv(void);

#define NUL '\x00'

char *m_getenv(char *name);
int m_putenv(char *name, char *text);
int m_delenv(char *name);
static void m_findenv();

```

LISTING 1.6 env.c *continued*

```
char *m_getenv(char *name)
{
    char far * e;
    char * n;
    int i;

    if (!initialized)
        m_findenv();

    e = env_ptr;

    while (*e)
    {
        n = strupr(name);

        while ((*e == *n) && (*e != '=') && (*e != NUL) && (*n != NUL))
        {
            ++e;
            ++n;
        }

        if ((*n == NUL) && (*e == '='))
        {
            ++e;

            for (i = 0; (i < 256) && (*e != NUL); i++)
            {
                s[i] = *e;
                ++e;
            }

            if (i < 256)
                s[i] = NUL;

            return s;
        }

        while (*e != NUL)
            e++;

        e++;
    }

    return NULL;
}

int m_putenv(char *name, char *text)
{
    char far *e;
    unsigned l = 0;
    char *sptr;

    if (!initialized)
        m_findenv();
```

LISTING 1.6 env.c *continued*

```

    e = env_ptr;

    if ((strlen(strupr(name)) + 2 + strlen(text)) > 256)
        return 1;

    strcpy(s, name);
    strupr(s);
    strcat(s, "=");
    strcat(s, text);

    m_delenv(name);

    e = env_ptr;
    l = 0;

    while (!((*e == NUL) && (*(e + 1) == NUL)))
    {
        e++;
        l++;
    }

    l = env_len - l - 3;

    if (l < strlen(s))
        return 1;

    sptr = s;

    e++;

    while (*sptr != NUL)
        *e++ = *sptr++;

    *e = NUL;
    *(e + 1) = NUL;

    return 0;
}

int m_delenv(char *name)
{
    char far *e1;
    char far *e2;
    char *n;
    int searching = 1;

    if (!initialized)
        m_findenv();

    e1 = env_ptr;

    while ((*e1 != NUL) && (searching))
    {
```

LISTING 1.6 env.c *continued*

```
        n = strupr(name);
        e2 = e1;

        while ((*e1 == *n) && (*e1 != '=') && (*e1 != NUL) && (*n != NUL))
        {
            e1++;
            n++;
        }

        if ((!*n) && (*e1 == '='))
            searching = 0;

        while (*e1 != NUL)
            e1++;

        e1++;
    }

    if ((*e1 == NUL) && searching)
        return 1;

    if (*e1)
        while (!((*e1 == NUL) && (*(e1 + 1) == NUL)))
        {
            *e2 = *e1;
            e2++;
            e1++;
        }

    *e2 = NUL;
    *(e2 + 1) = NUL;

    return 0;
}

static void m_findenv()
{
    union REGS regs;
    struct SREGS sregs;
    int far * SEGptr;
    MCB far * CONFIGmcb;
    MCB far * SHELLmcb;
    MCB far * ENVmcb;
    PSP far * SHELLpsp;

    regs.h.ah = 0x52;
    intdosx(&regs, &regs, &sregs);

    SEGptr = MK_FP(sregs.es, regs.x.bx - 2);
    CONFIGmcb = MK_FP(*SEGptr, 0);
    SHELLpsp = MK_FP(FP_SEG(CONFIGmcb) + CONFIGmcb ->len + 2, 0);

    if (SHELLpsp->env_seg == 0)
    {
```

LISTING 1.6 env.c *continued*

```
        SHELLmcb = MK_FP(FP_SEG(CONFIGmcb) + CONFIGmcb->len + 1, 0);
        env_ptr = MK_FP(FP_SEG(SHELLmcb) + SHELLmcb->len + 2, 0);
    }
    else
    {
        env_ptr = MK_FP(SHELLpsp->env_seg, 0);
    }

    ENVmcb = MK_FP(FP_SEG(env_ptr) - 1, 0);
    env_len = ENVmcb->len * 16;
    initialized = 1;
}
```

Chapter 2

A DOS Login Program: Supporting Multiple Users

Generic DOS is a single user, single process operating system. Only one person can directly use a particular client (as opposed to a network server) DOS system interactively at a time; that user may run only one program at a time.

If more than one person uses a DOS system, users will quickly discover that there are no built-in file management mechanisms for associating individual files with particular users. The users must keep track of their files (if they understand the DOS directory structure), or all the software applications must manage file ownership, perhaps by prompting users for their identity and then associating users with their own uniquely named directories, or maintaining ownership data in special system files.

Logging In

In contrast, systems designed to support multiple users (whether simultaneously via multiprocessing or not), such as the UNIX family of operating systems, maintain file ownership information for every program and data file on the system. These systems always require a user to log in at the beginning of any session. When logging in, a user must provide a public id with an optional, secret password before the system can be used. The id is typically an alphanumeric string derived from the user's name (although some systems, such as CompuServe, use a numeric format). The password is a text string known only to the user and protected by the system.

Once a user has given an acceptable login id and password, the system sets some globally accessible variables (so that other software on the system can identify the user), and executes an initial command sequence designed exclusively for that user. (On UNIX systems, the login program generally starts up one of several available command processors, and that command processor becomes responsible for executing customized start-up commands.)

I wrote the program presented in this chapter to make some rudimentary multiuser (although not multiprocessing) system features available under DOS. The program name is *login*, after the UNIX facility from which it has been patterned. As with the UNIX version, a password file containing information about each legal user must be present somewhere on the system. Password files typically contain one physical ASCII line of information for each user, including at least the user's id and optional password. My version supports only these two fields, while the UNIX version contains other fields for controlling features not supported by DOS. This DOS login program offers at least two useful features, even on a single user (at a time) system: security and simplified user interface.

login is a start toward preventing unauthorized use of a machine, although there probably aren't any 100 % reliable security measures for DOS. (My friend Jay Sage of ZCPR3 fame claims that the ZCPR3 system, an eight bit derivative of CP/M, is a more secure operating system than DOS can ever become.)

Probably the more practical benefit of *login* is the ability to simplify the user interface for those who are DOS illiterate. The user doesn't need to know about directories and command prompts. The user just needs to remember a personal login id, password, and how to use the applications the customized start-up sequence launches.

What the User Sees

From the user's point of view, my login, as well as UNIX's, behaves in the following manner. When invoked, *login* prints the string

```
login:
```

and waits for the user to enter a login id. When the user presses return, *login* checks to see if the user entered a valid id. If the login id is correct, and the password file contains no password associated with that user, then the login is approved. (Obviously, security can't be an issue under such a configuration.) If the login id requires a password, or even if the login id was invalid, *login* first displays

```
password:
```

then turns off keyboard echoing and waits for the user to enter a password. By prompting for a password even when the login id was invalid, *login* doesn't yield information concerning valid login ids. After the user enters a password and presses the ENTER key, *login* checks that the password is correct for the given user id. If so, then the login is approved. If it isn't, or if the user id was unrecognized, *login* says

```
login incorrect.
```

and repeats the whole process with

```
login:
```

This pattern continues until a login is approved. You can exit the program only by logging in correctly or rebooting the machine. If the machine has a bootable floppy drive, you can bypass *login* by inserting a floppy boot disk (that didn't have *login* as part of the start-up in *AUTOEXEC.BAT*) and rebooting — so much for bullet proof security. By configuring the floppy as *B:* on some systems, or if used on systems without any floppies, even most DOS literate users would be compelled to play the login game.

Starting Up the User

Once the user enters the correct login sequence, *login* performs two more tasks to get the session underway.

First, *login* writes the user's id string into the special file *CURRENT_USER* in the *STARTUP_DIR* directory (these names are all *#define*d constants you may modify in the source code). Applications can read the file and determine the current user.

Second, *login* looks for a start-up file named *USER.BAT* where *USER* is the user's login id, in the *STARTUP_DIR* directory. If found, the file is passed to the system command processor (named by the *COMSPEC* environment variable) for execution. This start-up file would be the place to put the name of the command(s) you want executed when that user logs in. The commands might include individual applications, menu systems, or any other kinds of programs.

For another blow to the security issue, many major applications have commands that allow shell escapes to DOS, giving the user complete access to all files on the system. There is usually no way to selectively disable such mechanisms.

How It Works

For console I/O, *login* contains several functions that talk directly to the low level console interface routines available via DOS's *BDOS* to disable the interrupt keys Control-C / Control-Break.

zgetch() reads a character from the keyboard, mapping carriage returns to newline characters for convenience. *zgets()* reads an entire line from the keyboard into a character buffer provided as a parameter, using *zgetch()* to read characters. The parameter *echo* to *zgets()* controls whether the keystrokes are echoed back to the screen as they are typed. The format of the line collected up by *zgets()* is the same as for the standard *gets()* function, i.e., null terminated with no newline character at the end.

zputs() writes a line of text to the screen. The library function *putch()* is used to write each character, and newlines are expanded to CR-LF sequences.

The main program begins by reading in all information from the password file into the array of structures named *users*. As each line reads in from the file using *fscanf()*, the *name* and *passwd* elements of *users* are assigned the first and second strings on the line, respectively. If at least one string is not found on a line, the program assumes the end-of-file has been reached (see Listing 2.1, line 68). After each line has been loaded successfully, the loop counter variable *nusers* is incremented.

If debugging is enabled, lines 70-74 display all the password information as it is read from the file. To enable debugging, insert the line

```
#define DEBUG 1
```

at the top of the source file.

Once all password information has been loaded (and lines 76-77 have verified that at least one valid user name is present), the password file is closed and the main loop is started. At this point, the variable `nusers` tells how many records were found in the password file.

Lines 83-84 prompt for a user id and read in a line of text from the console into the character buffer named *`linbuf`*, with keystroke echo enabled. Lines 86-88 loop through the list and compare the strings to see if the entered string matches any of the known user names. A match forces an immediate break out of the loop, leaving the counter variable *i* equal to the index into `users` of the matching user id (between *0* and `nusers` *– 1*). If no matching id was found, *i* ends up with the value of `nusers`.

Lines 91-92 handle the case in which no password is required by skipping over the password checking code. These statements skip the password checking code if and only if the following two conditions are met:

a valid user id was entered (*i* `!= nusers`), and

the password for that user is a null string (*!*users[i].passwd*).

If not, password checking springs into action. The password prompt displays and a line of text is read from the keyboard again, but this time with the echo turned off (line 95). Another two conditions must be met for the entered password to be accepted as valid:

the user id supplied above must be recognized (*i* `!= nusers`), and

the entered string must match the password from the password file.

Unless both conditions are met, the *`login incorrect`* message displays and the main loop repeats.

Upon Success

We reach line 102 after a correct login sequence. *login* prints a few blank lines for the sake of aesthetics, then lines 104-111 attempt to create the *CURRENT_USER* file and write out to it the name of the user who just logged in.

Finally, lines 113-127 construct the name of the appropriate batch file to run for the user, and try to execute the file if it exists. The name is created by starting with the name of the master start-up directory, appending the user id, and then appending the *.BAT* extension onto the end. Line 116 opens the file to see if it exists; if it does, the file is closed and the filename is passed to the system command processor for execution in line 125.

Logging Out

When a user finishes with a session, the *login* program must be started again. There are two approaches to making this happen.

The first is to have every user explicitly invoke the *login* program when they finish their session. To make it easier to remember, you could make a copy of *login.exe* and call it *bye.exe*; then the user would have to type the command *bye* when finishing with the computer. This method is simple but not secure.

Mr. Thomas Nelson, a reader of **The C Users Journal**, suggested a better approach. (He also illustrated the use of *execlp()* instead of *system()* for executing the individual start-up batch files. The original version of *login.c* as published in **The C Users Journal** had used *system()*.) Mr. Nelson pointed out that a loop can be created in the system start-up file, *AUTOEXEC.BAT*, that automatically invokes the *login* command and then loops back on itself. To allow a super-user (system administrator) to gain full access to the system, the super-user's start-up batch file could contain only the single command *command*, to invoke a system command processor.

Listing 2.2 illustrates this scheme with a twist. First, create a file in the root directory of your boot drive (typically C:) named *LOGIN.ON*. Each time through the loop in *AUTOEXEC.BAT*, a test is made to see if a file named *C:\LOGIN.ON* exists. Because this magic file exists, the login sequence is repeated. If the file ever disappears after a login session, then the loop is terminated.

For regular *login* operation, the file *C:\LOGIN.ON* must exist in the system root directory. The super-user can disable the *login* mechanism by logging in (starting up a command processor, if the start-up file is configured as described above), renaming the *C:\LOGIN.ON* file to something else, like *LOGIN.OFF*, and exiting the command processor (by issuing the *exit* command). This will cause the *AUTOEXEC.BAT* loop to terminate, and all memory will be available for whatever high powered stuff the super-user may want to do.

When ready to put the system back into regular *login* mode, the super-user can rename *LOGIN.OFF* back to *LOGIN.ON*, and reboot the system to start up the *AUTOEXEC.BAT* loop again. Or, to keep from having to reboot the system, the super-user can run a batch file containing the login loop (like the sequence shown in Listing 2.2) and nothing else.

This program is only a starting point. To use the facility most effectively, you must still be able to read information from the *CURRENT_USER* file into your applications. Whether used to its capacity or not, secured or otherwise, there is still some value in being able to customize each user's initial environment to suit personal needs in the most user friendly way.

Exercises

1. As written, *login* writes a file (specified by *CURRENT_USER*) containing the name of the active user. Another way to identify the current user to the system is to set an environment variable, say *CURUSER*, to the user's id. This method would be faster to execute but you would then need the appropriate tools to access the environment information from the application programs. Using the Master Environment Package (*env.c*, provided on the code disk), modify *login* to set an environment variable instead of (or in addition to) writing a file to disk.

2. Many compiler packages provide their own custom library functions for reading from the keyboard and writing to the console in raw mode (to prevent Control-C or Control-Break from working), while still supporting the standard line editing characters. For example, the Turbo/Borland C libraries include the functions *cgets()* and *getpass()*. If your compiler's library includes functions such as these, then adapt *login.c* to use them instead of *zgetch()*, *zputs()* and *zgets()*.

LISTING 2.1 login management program for DOS

```
/*
 *  login management program for DOS
 *
 *  Written by Leor Zolman, 5/1/89
 *
 *  Usage (typically in autoexec.bat):
 *      login
 *
 *  Control file (PASSWD_FILE) format:
 *
 *  -----------------
 *      name [password]
 *      name [password]
 *      .
 *      .
 *      .
 *  -----------------
 *
 *  The directory STARTUP_DIR should contain a batch
 *  file for each user, named name.BAT. Upon successful
 *  login, the batch file named for the user will be
 *  be executed.
 *  The file named by CURRENT_USER (c:\etc\startup\user.id
 *  as configured below) will be written containing the
 *  user id after a successful login.
 */

#include <stdio.h>
#include <conio.h>
#include <stdlib.h>
                            /* name of startup batch directory, current */
                            /* id file, and password control files:     */
#define STARTUP_DIR     "c:\\etc\\startup\\"
#define CURRENT_USER    STARTUP_DIR"user.id"
#define PASSWD_FILE     STARTUP_DIR"passwd.dat"


#define MAXUSERS 100               /* Max number of different users    */
#define MAXLINE 100                /* For login line input buffer      */

#define ECHO 1                             /* Parameters to zgets()    */
#define NOECHO 0

char *zgets(char *buffer, int echo);       /* prototypes               */
int zputs(char *str);

struct {                                   /* name/password structure  */
    char name[15];
    char passwd[15];
} users[MAXUSERS];

void main()
{
    int i;
```

LISTING 2.1 login management program for DOS *continued*

```
    FILE *fp;
    int nusers;
    char linbuf[MAXLINE];
    char *comspec;
                                /* open password file             */
    if ((fp = fopen(PASSWD_FILE, "r")) == NULL)
        exit(cprintf("Can't open %s\a\r\n", PASSWD_FILE));

                                /* read in user name/password data */
    for (nusers = 0; nusers < MAXUSERS; nusers++)
    {                           /* default to null password:      */
        *users[nusers].passwd = '\0';
        if (fscanf(fp, "%s %s", users[nusers].name,
            users[nusers].passwd) < 1) /* scan a line             */
                break;              /* break if empty             */
#if DEBUG
        else                        /* for debugging, show data   */
            cprintf("read user name: \"%s\", password: \"%s\"\r\n",
                users[nusers].name, users[nusers].passwd);
#endif
    }
    if (!nusers)
        exit(zputs("No valid entries in log file.\a\n"));

    fclose(fp);                     /* close password file        */

    while (1)                       /* mail loop                  */
    {
        zputs("login: ");           /* initial prompt             */
        zgets(linbuf, ECHO);        /* get user id w/echo         */

        for (i = 0; i < nusers; i++)  /* look it up               */
            if (!strcmp(users[i].name, linbuf))
                break;

                                    /* found id. need password?   */
        if (i != nusers && !*users[i].passwd)
                break;              /* if not, don't prompt       */

        zputs("\npassword: ");      /* prompt for password        */
        zgets(linbuf, NOECHO);      /* read w/o echo              */
        if (i != nusers && !strcmp(linbuf, users[i].passwd))
            break;                  /* if correct, exit the loop  */

        zputs("\nlogin incorrect.\n");
    }

    zputs("\n\n");                  /* success!                   */
                                    /* write id file              */
    if ((fp = fopen(CURRENT_USER, "w")) == NULL)
        cprintf("Couldn't create %s\a\r\n", CURRENT_USER);
    else
    {
        if (fputs(users[i].name, fp) == EOF)
```

LISTING 2.1 login management program for DOS *continued*

```
            cprintf("Couldn't write to %s\r\n", CURRENT_USER);
        fclose(fp);
    }

    strcpy(linbuf, STARTUP_DIR);        /* construct startup batch     */
    strcat(linbuf, users[i].name);      /*     filename                */
    strcat(linbuf, ".bat");
    if ((fp = fopen(linbuf, "r")) == NULL)/* is one there?             */
        cprintf("Couldn't find %s\a\r\n", linbuf);
    else
    {
        fclose(fp);                     /* yes. close it up.           */

        if ((comspec = getenv("COMSPEC")) == NULL)
            exit(cprintf("No COMSPEC in environment\r\n"));
                                        /* attempt to run it           */
        if (execlp(comspec, comspec, "/C", linbuf, NULL) == -1)
            cprintf("Couldn't execute user file %s\a\r\n", linbuf);
    }
}


/*
 * function zgets():
 *      Read a string from the console with optional echo,
 *      and all Ctrl-C / Ctrl-Break checks disabled:
 */

char *zgets(char *str, int echo)
{
    char c, *save = str;                /* save address of buffer      */

    zputs("        \b\b\b\b\b\b\b\b");  /* clear line                  */

    while ((c = zgetch()) != '\n')      /* read a char                 */
    {
        *str++ = c;
        if (echo)                       /* echo if required            */
            putch(c);
    }
    *str = '\0';                        /* terminate string            */
    return save;
}


/*
 * function zgetch():
 *      Read a character from the keyboard, without echo,
 *      performing newline conversion:
 */

int zgetch()
{
    char c;
```

LISTING 2.1 login management program for DOS *continued*

```

    c = bdos(7,0,0);                        /* Use a direct BDOS call   */
    return (c == '\r') ? '\n' : c;          /* Convert CR to newline    */
}


/*
 * function zputs():
 *      Print a string to the console, with newlines expanded:
 */

int zputs(char *str)
{
    char c;
    int i;

    while (c = *str++)
    {
        if (c == '\n')
        {
            for (i = 0; i < 30; i++)
                putch(' ');
            putch('\r');
        }
        putch(c);
    }
    return 0;
}
```

LISTING 2.2 AUTOEXEC.BAT

```
rem
rem Your AUTOEXEC.BAT file
rem
rem All your typicall AUTOEXEC.BAT stuff goes here
rem

:next
if not exist c:login.on goto :end
cls
login
goto :next
:end
```

Chapter 3

A Mini-Database System: Elementary File I/O

If you're a recent convert to C from any other high level language and you've tried to write programs that do any serious file input/output, then you've probably experienced frustration. The C standard library provides tools powerful enough to do anything you want, provided you know how to correctly combine those tools. For file I/O, almost the only operations supported in a trivial manner are reading and writing individual bytes, and reading and writing single lines of ASCII text.

For reading and writing any other data structure to or from the disk, some C sophistication is required. The task quickly moves beyond read and write to the general problem of finding the most appropriate way to represent this data for efficient reading and writing to disk.

In this tutorial I will develop a complete small scale mini-database system from scratch, to illustrate the process of designing file I/O-related C applications. The resulting program will be functional but simplistic; it could serve as a starting point for more elaborate data management systems.

This first section will consist of an operational description of the database, broken down into the following areas: data structures, functional description, and user interface (the menu system).

The next section will present the record creation, editing and management mechanism.

Finally, I will present several different approaches to storing the mini-database data on disk, discussing the relative merits of each approach. The first of these approaches will store all data to disk in a human readable text format, using statically allocated arrays in memory. On the **Illustrated C** companion code disk, the source files for this version of the program are in the directory FIO\STATONLY, and correspond to Listings 3.1-3.5.

The second approach will store all data to disk in binary format for rapid transfer. I'll also show two memory allocation systems for this binary approach: static array allocation (same as for the textual disk format), and dynamic array allocation (to optimize the use of system memory). On the code disk, the files for this generalized version of the program are located in FIO\STATDYN.

Note: only the header and main program files (*mdb.h* and *mdbmain.c*) are different in the two versions. The files corresponding to Listings 3.3 through 3.5 (*mdbutil.c*, *mdbedit.c* and *mdbftxt.c*) are identical in the two subdirectories. I've duplicated these common files so each subdirectory contains a complete set of files.

Section 1: Operational Description

Mini-Database Data Record Structure

This will not be a general purpose database system, but a program built to handle only one specific record format: a personnel record, as in Table 3.1.

The definition of the structure tag for this record, named *record*, is shown in the header file (Listing 3.1, lines 30-37).

The system will be able to handle only one active database at a time. Eventually we'll use dynamic memory allocation to obtain storage for the data records, so data memory is allocated only when necessary. For the first version of the system, however, the list of data record pointers will be kept in a statically allocated (i.e., fixed length) array. The definition of this array is shown on line 49 of the header file. The name of the array is *recs*, and its type is

```
array (of MAX_RECS elements) of
pointers to structures of type record
```

The programmer must explicitly size a fixed length array. In my code the size is *MAX_RECS*. Thus, the total amount of fixed memory needed for storing the records of the database is the value of *MAX_RECS* times the size of a single record pointer. Later, I'll show how to dynamically allocate the storage for the *recs* array itself. To facilitate this later modification, the symbol *RECS* is introduced (Listing 3.1, line 50) as an alias for *recs*.

Table 3.1

Name:	Type:	Value:
active	*char*	*1* if record is active, *0* if deleted
last	*char[25]*	Last name
first	*char[15]*	First name
id	*long*	ID number
age	*int*	Age
gender	*char*	***M*** or ***F***
salary	*float*	Annual salary

Personnel Record Format

Lines 42-46 (of Listing 3.1) illustrate a necessary complication when writing multiple source file programs: global data must be defined in one module and one module only. If the data is to be known in any other modules of the program, it must be declared in those other modules. Definitions reserve storage for the specified data, while declarations serve to inform the compiler about the nature of data defined elsewhere. A simple rule of thumb will usually distinguish between definitions and declarations appearing in header files. If the *extern* modifier is used, you're probably looking at a declaration; if not, you're probably looking at a definition.

Each data item should be defined only once among all the source modules of a program. At first it might seem sufficient to insert an *extern* keyword in front of all but one declaration, making that one the definition. Unfortunately, this is not easily done. Typical multiple module programs use lots of shared data. Do we really want to maintain separate lists of declarations/definitions in separate modules, some with and some without the *extern* keyword? Preferably not. We'd prefer to have each piece of data defined/declared in one place, a *.h* header file. If, however, the declarations must be written differently than the definitions, is there a way to combine them into a single header file? Yes. Lines 42-46 of Listing 3.1 define a symbolic constant named *EXTERN* to control whether the *extern* keyword is generated for the critical declarations. If the symbol *MAIN_MODULE* has been defined, then we are compiling the main module of the program and the symbolic constant *EXTERN* is assigned a null value (so the items of data in lines 49, 52 and 53 are defined). If not, the *EXTERN* symbol is assigned the value *extern* and lines 49, 52 and 53 are treated as declarations of external data. To force definitions to be created during compilation of the main module only, we *#define MAIN_MODULE* (see Listing 3.2, line 24) before the header file *mdb.h* is included. The other modules of the program do not contain this definition.

Over the years, variations among C compilers blurred the difference between definitions and declarations. Microsoft, perhaps to eliminate the need for conditional compilation games, decided to make its linker allow multiple definitions of identical data in more than one source file of a program (although multiple initializations are still flagged as errors). While relying on this feature can simplify development, it may render the programs nonportable. Turbo C 2.0, under which this database program was developed, makes you do it right, even if that requires a small amount of extra coding.

Other Global Data

The program maintains a minimal amount of global data to describe the currently open database's state. The variable *n_recs* tells how many records are currently held in memory. The variable *max_recs* contains the maximum number of records that can be represented. For the fixed length array version, *max_recs* is assigned the value of the symbolic constant *MAX_RECS* (Listing 3.2, line 72).

A Simple Menu System

A simple line oriented menu system serves as the user interface. The menu function *do_menu()* is shown in *mdbutil.c* (Listing 3.3, lines 21-40). The menu consists of a list of pointers to structures of type *menu_item* (Listing 3.1, lines 55-58), where each *menu_item* consists of an integer action code and a string description of the action. The *do_menu()* function numbers and lists out each description (up to but not including the first entry with a null *action_code*), asks the user to select one choice, and returns the *action_code* value associated with the selected item. The *action_code* values need not correspond to the choice numbers displayed by the function.

The Main Menu Options

The database operations are divided into two menus. The first menu (Listing 3.2, lines 37-48) contains the options for controlling database selection, disk I/O and program termination. The second menu, in the *mdbedit.c* module (Listing 3.4) controls all the options associated with editing the data records of the currently active database.

The main menu controls the top level system functions. A variable, *db_active*, tells whether a database is currently open and, thus, whether certain operations are appropriate. For example, we don't allow the user to open a new database if one is currently open. The main menu options are as follows:

CREATE

Initialize a new database. This option asks the user to pick a name for the new database and checks to make sure another file does not already exist by that name. This will be the name of the file used to store the database on disk. If the name is acceptable, then the variables *max_recs*, *n_recs* and *db_active* are initialized.

EDIT

Calls the *edit_db()* function to edit the records of the database.

OPEN

Loads a previously stored database from disk (via the *read_db()* function), then immediately starts an editing session on that database by calling *edit_db()*. *read_db()* allocates the appropriate amount of memory for the database records, assigns the pointers to elements in the *RECS* array, and returns the number of records loaded. We announce the number of records before calling *edit_db()*.

BAKUP

This menu entry is included to encourage backup facilities in your applications. The backup function shown here, *backup_db()*, is just a no-op.

CLOSE

Terminates operations on the current database, writes it to disk and frees all associated storage.

SAVE

Writes the database to disk, preventing loss of any work, so far, in case of a subsequent system crash. Does not close the database.

ABANDON

Closes the database without saving it to disk, and frees up all storage.

QUIT

Exits the program.

Utility Functions

Listing 3.3 shows the source module *mdbutil.c*, containing utility functions used throughout the program. In addition to the *do_menu()* function (already described), this module includes *error()*, *alloc_rec()* and *free_up()*.

The *error()* function is a general purpose fatal error handler. It prints a message and exits.

The *alloc_rec()* function is basic to the operation of the program. *alloc_rec()* is called to obtain enough memory from the system to store a single database data record. The *malloc()* standard library function is used to obtain the block of storage. *alloc_rec* returns either *NULL*, signaling that the system lacks more storage to spare, or the valid memory pointer returned by *malloc()*.

The *free_up()* function returns all storage (originally obtained through calls to *alloc_rec*) back to the system. In this program, storage is always freed up for the entire database when the current database file is closed or abandoned. To free that storage, the program walks through all the records of the database and calls the *free()* function for each pointer.

Section 2: Editing and Record Management

The Editing Module

So far we've seen the global data structures and main program. The ultimate goal of this tutorial is to illustrate the design interdependencies between data structures and disk I/O techniques. There is still one major component of the system to fit into place before beginning with the actual file I/O code: the data entry and editing module.

The source code for the editing module is in *mdbedit.c* (Listing 3.4). Most of the module is taken up by the function *edit_db()*, primarily consisting of a large switch statement handling all the editing procedures. *edit_db()* is called from two places in the main program: to edit an existing database (via the *EDIT* main menu command), and to edit a newly created database (after the *CREATE* command has been issued).

edit_db() maintains an internal state variable, *cur_rec*, identifying the currently selected record. Upon entry to *edit_db()*, *cur_rec* is set to *0* (the index of the first record of the file). For coding convenience, the variable *rp* (a pointer to structures of type *record*) holds a pointer to the *cur_rec*'th element of the *RECS* array; this allows any expression of the form

```
RECS[cur_rec]->member
```

to be written more efficiently as

```
rp->member
```

provided, of course, *rp* is updated to reflect any changes made to the value of *cur_rec*.

The global variable *n_recs* (declared externally in header file *mdb.h*) is also vital to the record editing process: whenever a record is added to or deleted from the database, the value of *n_recs* is adjusted accordingly. *n_recs* always reflects the total number of records, both active and inactive, currently stored in the database.

Record Management

To simplify the task of inserting and deleting records, I've selected a simple scheme for record management. Each record is either active or inactive, as reflected by the value of the *active* flag associated with the record. When a new record is created, its *active* flag is set to *TRUE*. To delete a record, the *DELETE* command sets the record's *active* flag to *FALSE*. The rest of a deactivated record's data remains completely intact until the *FIX* command is used at some later point to release the storage of all inactive records.

The commands for perusing data records sequentially, *NEXT* and *PREVIOUS*, both ignore inactive records. The *LIST* command, however, lists all records in the database, both active and inactive. To access an inactive record, the *SELECT* command may be used to address the record directly via the record number shown by the *LIST* command. Once an inactive record has been *SELECT*ed, the *UNDELETE* command may be used to make the record active again, if desired.

Inactive records remain only until the next time the *FIX* command is invoked. Each time *FIX* is run, the storage for all deleted records is freed and the record pointers are compacted and sorted.

The User Interface And Main Editing Loop

A menu structure, similar to the one used in the main menu, controls the option menu for the *edit_db()* function. The record editing options I chose to implement under this menu are rudimentary to any data retrieval system and are limited to line oriented operation for simplicity.

Upon entry to *edit_db()*, *cur_rec* is initialized to the first record of the database and an infinite loop is begun. For each iteration of the loop, *rp* is set to point to the new current record's data, and the values of all fields in the current record are displayed on the console output. If there are currently no records in the database (determined by checking *n_recs* for a value of *0*), then the current record display sequence is suppressed.

Next, the menu is displayed and the user selects from the list of editing options. Those options are:

LIST_RECS

This option displays a short form listing of all records in the database. For each record, the record number (equal to the record pointer's index number in the *RECS* array) and name fields are always listed. If the value of the structure member *active* for the current record is *FALSE* (shows that the record is inactive), then the message *(deleted)* is also displayed. Records are displayed in their physical order in the *RECS* array. This will correspond to the order of entry until the first time the *FIX* option is invoked (see below).

NEXT, PREVIOUS

These two options select the next or previous active record (in physical sequence) to be the current record by adjusting the value of *cur_rec*, as required. Before adjusting *cur_rec*, we check that we're not sending its value out of bounds by iterating the variable *i* forward or backward through the records. If an active record is encountered, then *cur_rec* is set accordingly. If, however, the end-of-file (or beginning-of-file) is reached, then a message to that effect is displayed and *cur_rec* remains unchanged.

NEW

Creates a new record. If we have reached maximum record capacity, then an error message is displayed and the option is aborted. The *alloc_rec()* function returns a pointer to storage for the new record. If the return value is *NULL*, then memory could not be allocated and the option is aborted.

Once storage is acquired, *cur_rec* is set to the old value of *n_recs* (the record count) and *n_recs* is incremented to reflect the new number of records (Listing 3.4, line 128). After this operation, *cur_rec* is the subscript of the slot in *RECS* that will hold the new record pointer. Next, *rp* is copied into the new slot (line 129) and the element *active* is made *TRUE* (line 130). In lines 132 though 137, all data elements of the new record are initialized to empty values and control falls through to the next case, *MODIFY*.

MODIFY

This section is a quick, simple editing sequence for the data elements of the current record. For each element in sequence, the following is performed:

1. the record description and current value are displayed
2. a line of input text is read from the console
3. if the line is empty (if the ENTER key was pressed immediately), then the original value of the element is left intact
4. if the line is not empty, the value of the element is overwritten with the value of the input (converted to the appropriate data type).

In a serious application, additional input validations would occur at this point. For example, to limit the *gender* field to the values *M* or *F*, exclusively, you could change the *if* sequence in lines 157-158 to:

```
while (strlen(gets(buf)) > 0 /* if not empty line */
{
    char c = toupper(*buf);
    if (!(c == 'M' || c == 'F'))  /* if not legal */
    {
        printf("Please enter 'M' or 'F': ");
        continue; /* ask again */
    }
    rp->gender = c; /* assign the value */
    break; /* exit the loop */
}
```

DELETE

Deleting a record is simply a matter of setting the *active* flag to *0*. If the flag is already *0*, we display a message to that effect. If not, we make the user confirm the deletion by typing a 'y'.

UNDELETE

This option restores a deleted record by setting its *active* flag back to *1*. If the record was active in the first place, a message is issued.

SELECT

Used with the *LIST* option, this option can directly select any record in the database. *SELECT* asks for a record number and checks to make sure the value is within bounds. If the record number is valid, it is assigned to *cur_rec*. Because we wish to allow both active and inactive records to be selected, there are no further validity checks necessary.

FIX

The *FIX* option serves a dual purpose. *FIX* purges all inactive (deleted) records from the database and sorts the remaining records. The *fix_db()* function does the work, and here lies the only really tricky code in this module.

To purge deleted records, a single pass is made over the database records using two indices. The first index, the loop variable *i*, iterates over the entire array of record pointers (that is, all *n_recs* records). The second index, *new_n_recs*, is incremented only for active records. When an inactive record is encountered, *new_n_recs* is not incremented, and the pointer to the inactive record's data is passed to the *free()* function to deallocate the storage.

At the start of each iteration through the loop, record *i* is copied into position *new_n_recs* (line 225), and then *new_n_recs* is adjusted as described. The result is that the memory used by all inactive records is de-allocated. The positions in the *RECS* array formerly occupied by inactive record pointers are filled in with active pointers.

After the purge loop completes, a single call to the *qsort()* library function sorts the remaining records. *qsort()* is a wonderfully versatile function, but the interface can be a bit confusing. Here, we wish to sort the pointers in the *RECS* array by the *last* field. We first set up the call to *qsort()* and then set up a comparison function that *qsort()* uses to determine the relationship between two pointers.

qsort() takes four parameters: a pointer to an array of data items to be sorted, the number of items in the array, the size of each item, and a pointer to a user supplied function that *qsort()* will call directly. The user supplied function takes two pointers to data array elements as parameters. It compares the two data items specified by the pointers, and returns (to *qsort()*) one of several predefined values indicating the relative ordering of those two data items.

Because we are sorting the pointers in the *RECS* array, we pass *RECS* as the first parameter. The number of items in the array is *new_n_recs* (as a result of the purge loop just completed). Because we are sorting an array of pointers, we pass the expression

```
sizeof(struct record *)
```

as the data item size. By using the *sizeof* operator instead of a hardwired constant value, such as *2* for this parameter, we insure portability of this code between different memory models or processor families. For the final parameter, we supply the name of the comparison function, *compar()*.

The comparison function, as described above, must be designed to accept parameters that are pointers to the data type being sorted. Because the data we are sorting have type "pointer to structure", the parameters to the comparison function must be of type "pointer to pointer to structure." For a return value, the comparison function must return *0* if the data items are equivalent (using whatever arbitrary ordering rules we wish to apply), a negative value if the first item is less than the second (by those same rules), or a positive value if the first item is greater than the second. The function header (line 244) reflects these specifications.

If you find yourself totally confused by the use of pointers to pointers, remember that the comparison function called by *qsort()* must always be supplied with pointers to the data type being sorted. If that data type is a pointer to begin with, then sorting an array of such pointers necessarily involves the use of pointers to those pointers. At that level of abstraction, we are no longer concerned with the data within a database record, but with an array of addresses to all those database records. Instead of dealing with "data" and "pointers to the data," we're now dealing with "pointers" and "pointers to the pointers." I hope this explanation didn't make things worse.

A prototype for the *compar()* function is specified in line 217, so the identifier *compar* is recognized when *fix_db()* calls *qsort()* in line 233. The types, however, defined for *compar()*'s parameters in this prototype conflict with the ANSI standard library header *stdlib.h*'s declaration for the *qsort()* function. In the standard header, *qsort()*'s fourth parameter is declared as being a pointer to a function that takes two parameters of type *const void* *. Our *compar()* function, however, takes parameters that are actually of type *struct record* **.

To keep ANSI compilers from crying uncle when our comparison function's address is passed to *qsort()*, I've created a special *typedef* named *FARG* (see line 44). In the *qsort()* call (line 233), I cast the address of the *compar()* function to type *FARG*. This seems to make the compiler happy.

The body of the *compar()* function compares the element *last* (a string representing the last name of the person described in the record) from both records using the *strcmp()* standard library function. *strcmp()* is ideally suited for use with *qsort()* because its return value is defined exactly as specified for the *qsort()* comparison function. The tricky part of *compar()* is remembering to de-reference the "structure pointer pointer" parameters to use them as simple "structure pointers" (line 246). Parentheses are needed around the indirection subexpression of each parameter to *strcmp()*. Without the parentheses, the selection operator (->) would take precedence over the indirection operator (*) and draw a compiler error.

As For The File I/O . . .

The Mini-Database System is now complete except for the *read_db()* and *write_db()* functions. Before reading on, you may wish to try out the system as presented so far (inserting a pair of dummy functions in lieu of the real *read_db()* and *write_db()*). Play around with entering, deleting and editing records to get a feel for the system's operation.

Next, I'll show some different approaches to the implementation of *read_db()* and *write_db()*. As a challenging exercise, see if you can come up with a scheme for implementing these functions yourself. Would you save the data on disk in the form of ASCII text or binary data? Which standard library functions would you employ in each case? What would be the advantages of ASCII over binary, or vice versa?

For a smaller scale exercise, see if you can develop a replacement for the *do_menu()* function that has a more elegant user interface. For example, you might include the ability to specify commands by a highlighted letter within the text of the command, as well as by a sequential number. Part of the menu specification would then have to include information about which letter to highlight — perhaps by including a magic character in the menu item text that flags the subsequent character as special. Or, you may choose to adapt a windowing menu routine from some general C library function package.

Section 3: Text Based File I/O

File I/O: Text Or Binary?

The fundamental design of the *read_db()* and *write_db()* functions depend on whether we store the data as human readable ASCII text or as a straight (raw) binary image. If efficiency is a major concern, then binary mode is the right choice. The data will take up less space on disk, and require the minimum amount of format translation during input and output operations. To make the routines easier to debug, however, the ASCII format is often more appropriate. Storing the data in human readable form allows convenient visual inspections (using *type* or any text editor) after the data has been written to disk.

Other considerations need attention when deciding upon a disk format. Will there ever be a need for the data to be read in by other applications, such as spreadsheets or full-blown database management systems? If so, the text format is probably the better choice.

Depending on which of these two approaches is chosen, a different set of standard library functions will be required. For the ASCII approach, the line oriented formatted I/O functions *fprintf()* and *fscanf()* will do all the work. The binary approach will rely on the byte oriented functions *fread()* and *fwrite()*.

The Interface

Both versions of *read_db()* and *write_db()* interface with their calling routine (the *main* function) via the same set of external data:

1) *RECS*: the array of pointers to data records. The actual array name is *recs*, with *RECS* being a defined synonym for *recs*. This synonym will ease a future transition to dynamic array allocation.
2) *n_recs*: the number of records currently stored in *RECS*.

The only additional piece of information specified by the caller is the file name to be used for the operation.

write_db() does not return any value; either the data is written correctly, or the error is diagnosed within *write_db()* and the program aborts through a call to the *error()* function. See the Exercises section at the end of this chapter for more on *write_db()* error recovery.

read_db() returns the number of records loaded.

The *read_db()* Function

Listing 3.5 shows the *read_db()* and *write_db()* functions written to work with ASCII data files.

read_db() begins by defining several control variables, along with a set of temporary variables for containing record field values in transition from disk to memory array storage.

The control variables are:

1) *fp*: the file pointer for buffered input
2) *rec_no*: the number of records read in so far
3) *rp*: a temporary record buffer pointer
4) *nitems*: the number of items read in each line of input

read_db() starts out by setting the *max_recs* variable to the maximum number of records the system can handle (line 35). Because the *recs* array is defined statically to contain *MAX_RECS* elements, the value of *max_recs* will never change in this version. We'll make better use of *max_recs* later when adding dynamic array allocation to the system.

To open the input file, the *fopen()* library function is called with a mode of *"r"* to specify text mode. *NULL* (*0*) is returned if the file cannot be opened.

The text format chosen for the data consists of a single line of ASCII text (terminated by newlines) per record, with whitespace (one space character) between each field of a record and no other whitespace permitted.

The main read loop (lines 43-74) begins with a call to the *fscanf()* function. The format specification contains one format conversion specifier of the appropriate type for each field of the record, and the remaining parameters are the locally defined temporary variables. Because the parameters to the *scanf()* family of input functions must all be pointers, the *&* operator must be used on the scalar parameters to generate pointers to those objects. The character array parameters (*last* and *first*) do not need the *&* operator applied to them, because an array name used alone is equivalent to a pointer to its first element.

fscanf returns a value telling how many items were actually matched from the input, and we assign that value to the variable *nitems*. If the value was *EOF*, then a normal end-of-file has been reached. We fall out of the loop, close the file, and return with the total number of records loaded (*rec_no*, initialized to *0* at the top of the function).

If *nitems* ends with any value other than *7*, then something unexpected was encountered in the input. A warning message is printed and the reading loop is terminated.

Having avoided all the possible error conditions from the *fscanf()* call, we are ready to deal with a valid record of new data. The first step is to get some memory to store the data; the *alloc_rec()* function (Listing 3.3, lines 57-73) does this for us. *alloc_rec()* returns either a valid pointer to the needed block of memory, or *NULL* if the memory could not be allocated. This return value is assigned to the *rp* variable.

Using the *rp* pointer, each field value is copied into the memory block obtained from *alloc_rec*. The address of this memory block is then installed in the *RECS* array and the record counter *rec_no* is incremented (line 73) for the next loop iteration.

The *write_db()* function is set up much like *read_db()*. Because the *fprintf()* function takes values, not pointers, for its list of parameters to write, there is no need for *&* operators (using them would cause incorrect results).

The return value from *fprintf()* is checked only for a single negative error flag, according to *fprintf()*'s definition.

An interesting feature in *write_db()* is the use of a temporary file for writing the output text. This practice insures against losing both the results from the current session and the previously stored database data file in the event of catastrophic failure during the output writing process. Only if the temporary file is written without incident, is the previous version of the file erased and the temporary file renamed. To be safe, a check is performed on the return value of the *rename()* call (line 122-128) in case the new filename is not accepted. Here, the user is given the opportunity to enter other names until the *rename()* call succeeds.

Section 4: Using Binary File I/O

The ASCII routines just presented used the text line oriented library functions *fprintf()* and *fscanf()* to perform their data transfers. While ASCII data files are easily examined and debugged, they are generally less efficient than binary files. An application that manipulates ASCII data must perform format conversions on the data objects: from binary to ASCII on output to disk, and vice versa when the data is read back from disk. The performance penalty isn't really noticeable for small sets of data (such as after entering a few records into the Mini-Database). For larger amounts of data, however, the time needed to perform these conversions can be prohibitive, especially when a larger percentage of the data is numeric.

The Mini-Database system uses a set of disk routines for reading and writing the data files in raw, binary format. Instead of formatting the data into ASCII text, these binary routines simply dump the data from memory into disk files and back, with no translation. The effective results, at least as far as a user of the Mini-Database may notice, will be the same as if the data were being translated to ASCII and back to binary. To make any sense of the data files outside of the application, however, you would probably need a low level debugging tool and some knowledge of the specifics of the target machine's data type characteristics.

The Modular Approach

The ASCII based versions of read_db() and *write_db()* were placed in a source file by themselves. The rest of the Mini-Database System code makes no assumptions about how *read_db()* and *write_db()* perform their tasks. We can, therefore, simply substitute a new source file containing the binary versions for the source file containing the ASCII based versions of these functions. You won't even have to recompile the other modules; just compile the one new source module, and then link it in with the other existing object modules to get a complete, new executable module.

Variations On A Theme

The Mini-Database (as presented up to now) has used a fixed length array named *recs* to store the pointers to data records in memory. The maximum number of records that the system can handle has been fixed by the value of the *MAX_RECS* symbolic constant, defined in the header file. This arrangement is efficient (because memory for the data records themselves is still obtained dynamically). We could, however, improve the system by allowing the memory used by the *recs* array to be allocated at runtime, based upon anticipated requirements.

When using a binary format for representing the data on disk, we can tell exactly how much runtime memory will be required to hold an existing Mini-Database file saved in binary format. This is done by finding the length of the saved binary file. (Note that this would not be true for files saved in ASCII text format).

How can we arrange to allocate only the amount of memory we'll really need for the array of record pointers, and no more? The answer lies in the effective use of C's powerful data typing mechanisms. The technique is dynamic array allocation.

Building And Using A Dynamic Array

Simple arrays in C are defined using notation such as

```
type-name identifier[size-constant];
```

The array dimension expression *size-constant* may be omitted in certain special instances, such as when the array is a formal parameter in a function definition (or in a prototype). Take, for example, a prototype for the common C library function *strlen()*:

```
int strlen(char str[]);
```

The dimension isn't necessary because in such cases the identifier *str* is acting purely as a pointer. There is no memory allocated except a single pointer's worth. That pointer becomes a place-holder for an existing, previously allocated array whose address is passed to the function.

We can set up a dynamic array that works somewhat like the formal array parameter described above, but explicitly rather than implicitly. Listings 3.6 and 3.7 show new versions of the header file and main program file for the Mini-Database System, enhanced to provide the option for a dynamically allocated *recs* array. (The original versions, limited to a statically allocated array, are shown in Listings 3.1 and 3.2). Note: with the *DYN_ARRAY* symbol defined to *FALSE*, the program compiles as in the original version, with *recs* defined as a simple array of pointers (Listing 3.6, line 57). With *DYN_ARRAY* set to *TRUE*, *recs* is defined as a pointer to an array of pointers to structures (line 53).

Notice the empty square brackets. Because we now have a data type that is primarily a pointer, not an array, the compiler doesn't really care how many elements the array being pointed to may contain at runtime. As programmers, we care very much because we are going to be managing the memory for this virtual array explicitly. We will obtain memory for the dynamic array via *malloc()*, and assign the address of the memory to the *recs* variable. Once *recs* is initialized, the expression *(*recs)* will be valid when used as the base array expression in array subscripting operations.

Now the reason for the symbolic constant *RECS* (lines 54 and 58) begins to emerge. Wherever the simple array name *recs* was used in the original (static array) version of the program, we now must substitute the more complex expression *(*recs)* to support dynamic array allocation. Rather than using awkward conditional blocks (e.g., *#if...#else*) every time an array operation appears, I've chosen to use *RECS* as the generalized expression for the array base, greatly reducing the number of places where code must be changed to support the dynamic arrays. In the few places where alternate coding was unavoidable, I've used conditional compilation based on the value of the *DYN_ARRAY* symbol.

Binary I/O Without Dynamic Allocation

First, I'll explain how the binary file I/O functions work where *DYN_ARRAY* is *FALSE*, i.e., *RECS* is defined as the simple static array name *recs*.

To write the currently active database to disk, the *write_db()* function (Listing 3.8, lines 73-114) is called with the filename as the only formal parameter. To safeguard against wiping out previously stored versions of the data file in the event of a write error, a temporary filename is used to write the file. If the write operation completes without error, then the temporary file is renamed with the supplied filename parameter.

The first interesting difference between the binary and text based versions of the function is the way the *fopen()* library call is invoked. Instead of using a mode of *"w"*, the binary version uses *"wb"*. This mode prevents system dependent automatic newline conversions. With a mode of *"w"*, newlines (represented in memory by a single ASCII linefeed [*0x0a*] character) are expanded into CR-LF pairs on certain systems (like MS-DOS) before being written to disk. With the *"wb"* mode, this conversion is never performed; therefore, *"wb"* is the mode that must be used to write binary data.

To perform the disk writes, we call upon the standard library function *fwrite()* within a *for* loop that iterates through the records pointed to by *RECS*. The *fwrite()* function has been designed to accept its data parameters in logical records of convenient size for the programmer, not solely in terms of individual bytes. Such organization easily supports the writing of fixed length records with effective error checking, and all in a very portable manner.

Our data is organized by records, each of which is a structure of type *record* being pointed to by an entry in the *RECS* array. Listing 3.8, lines 95 and 96 show the *fwrite()* call for a single record. The first parameter is a pointer to the data, the second is the size of each logical record, the third is the number of such logical records to be written, and the final parameter is the file pointer.

Notice how the *sizeof* operator is used to obtain the size of the data record. This C idiom is far preferable to absolute byte counts embedded as numeric constants. Using *sizeof* renders the code immune to variations in data representation between different kinds of computers. There is no additional runtime overhead incurred because *sizeof* expressions are always evaluated at compile time.

fwrite() returns the number of logical records successfully written. The error checking is easy. If the return value does not match the value of the third parameter, there must have been a fatal error. Then, we diagnose the error, clean up, and return. If the return value agrees, the write loop continues.

After all records have been written without incident, the old version of the disk file is removed (line 105) and we begin a *while* loop. This loop is another safeguard for the file renaming process. If, for any reason, the temporary file cannot be renamed to the filename supplied, then the user is given the opportunity to enter another filename. This process continues until the *rename()* function succeeds.

This safety feature wasn't in my first draft, but during the testing process, I once created a new database and accidentally gave it an illegal filename. Because no filename checking was performed until *write_db()* was called, the program wouldn't let me save my data, and I had to start over. Safety checks like this *while* loop help reduce the chance of losing data, making a program more user friendly.

Reading a saved database file into memory with *read_db()* follows a similar pattern. Again, the letter *b* is appended to the mode string (yielding *"rb"*) to turn off text conversions on input. The *fread()* standard library function is analogous to *fwrite()*, with one minor variation. We must be able to distinguish between error conditions and a normal end-of-file condition. If the *ferror()* function returns a logical *TRUE* (nonzero) value after a call to *fread()*, then we know some kind of error has occurred. If not, any return value less than the value of the third parameter indicates an end-of-file condition, with the number of records read equal to the return value. Lines 56–60 of Listing 3.8 perform the checks for error and end-of-file conditions. If both tests are passed, then lines 62–63 allocate memory for the record (checking for an out-of-memory condition), and the data is copied over from the temporary holding buffer *recbuf* using structure assignment (line 65).

Going Dynamic

Setting *DYN_ARRAY* to *TRUE* configures the system to use dynamic array allocation. A new symbolic constant, *MAX_TO_ADD* and the previously discussed changes to the definitions of *recs* and *RECS* are added to the header file (Listing 3.6, lines 52-54).

MAX_TO_ADD controls the allocation of memory for database records beyond the existing memory requirements. When *MAX_TO_ADD* is 100, only 100 or fewer new records can be added to any database file within a single session (between opening and closing the file). If the *MAX_TO_ADD* limit is reached, the user must close the file and reopen it before adding additional records. We cannot dynamically extend the *RECS* array once it has been initially allocated, because the memory must be contiguous. (Remember, we're dealing with memory for the array of pointers to the data records, not the memory for data records. The data record memory can be allocated in record sized chunks as necessary.)

Within the *CREATE* option of the main menu, the dynamic array mechanism requires some special setup (Listing 3.7, lines 74-81). The size for *RECS* is calculated as the product of the data record pointer size multiplied by *MAX_TO_ADD* (because the database will be initially empty). The required memory is obtained via *malloc()*, and the array pointer *recs* is initialized with the address of the allocated memory block. This is one of only two locations in the program code where the variable *recs* is operated on directly (the second comes up shortly). In all other references, *recs* appears only in conjunction with the indirection operator as specified in the definition of *RECS* (Listing 3.6, line 54).

The other section of code that must change to support the dynamic array is in the *read_db()* function. Before a saved database file is loaded into memory, we must know its size so the appropriate amount of memory can be allocated. The file size is obtained by calling the *fseek()* and *ftell()* standard library functions. After a data file is opened for binary input, we seek to the end of the file using *fseek()* (Listing 3.8, line 37). Then we call *ftell()* to get the byte position of the end-of-file marker. That byte position value is divided by the logical data record size to yield the number of records stored in the file, *MAX_TO_ADD* is added, and (finally!) that resulting value is scaled by the size of a record pointer to determine the appropriate quantity of memory to allocate (line 40). After all that, we must call *fseek()* one more time to reposition the file pointer at the beginning of the file, in preparation for reading the data.

Note: there may be a library function included with your particular C implementation that simply returns the size of a file, eliminating the need to use *fseek()* and *ftell()* as shown. Not all compiler vendors provide such a function. Use the technique shown here for maximum portability; this method is efficient because file seeks are typically performed via fast, random access system calls.

Exercises

1. When reading in a database stored in the ASCII format, the *%s* format conversions used to read in the first and last name fields effectively prevent those fields from being able to contain space characters. What if a two part first or last name needs to be represented, or a middle name? A way to extend the system to allow strings with embedded spaces would be useful. This can be accomplished by changing the text format to require a delimiter character between each field item. A special form of format conversion may be used in place of *%s* to read such variable length string fields. If the delimiter character chosen were the vertical bar, for example, then a *scanf()* call to read a single line containing a variable length string (terminated by a vertical bar character) followed by an integer would look like:

```
scanf("%[^|]|%d\n", string, &i);
```

The sub-sequence *%[^|]* tells *scanf()* to match all characters up to, but not including, the first | character encountered. The final | in the format sequence says to then skip the | character in the input stream.

Modify *mdbftxt.c* to allow spaces within the first name and last name fields, using this technique.

2. As written, if an error occurs during the main loop of a *write_db()* call it is possible to lose all data modified in the current session. Modify the program to recover gracefully from a file output error so the user has a chance to try again on, perhaps, a different drive. Note that *write_db()* is currently called from both the *SAVE* and *QUIT* main menu options.

3. As the program is now structured, all data for an open database file must be present in memory simultaneously. How might the system be enhanced

to allow the handling of databases too large for available memory? This is not a trivial proposition. For a first attempt, think about keeping only the current record in memory and don't worry about how to sort the database.

4. When you have that much designed, create an indexing scheme based on an in-memory index array that represents the ordering of the records in the data file. When the file is stored, the array occupies the first block of file data (preceded by some parameters indicating the length of the index array, by necessity, and perhaps also the length of the data portion of the file for convenience). As individual records are added and deleted, the index array can be updated to reflect logical ordering. After you have designed (and perhaps implemented) such an indexing scheme, compare your approach with the method used in the next chapter.

In addition, the package could be generalized by allowing the index array to be kept in its own data file and to grow larger than the existing main memory capacity. At that point, you'd have a basic framework similar to the scheme used by many full-blown relational database systems. I'd recommend using one of those commercial systems rather than designing one yourself, unless you're ready for a major challenge.

LISTING 3.1 MDB.H (Static Only)

```
/*
 *  MDB.H      (Static-Array-Only version of mdb.h)
 *
 *  Program:    Mini-Database
 *  Written by: Leor Zolman
 *  Module:     Program Header File
 */

#define TRUE    1
#define FALSE   0

/*
 * Prototypes:
 */

int do_menu(struct menu_item *mnu, char *title);
void write_db(char *filename);
int read_db(char *filename);
void edit_db(char *db_name);
void backup_db(void);

void error(char *msg);
struct record *alloc_rec(void);
void free_up(void);

/*
 * Data Definitions:
 */

struct record {                          /* Database record definition   */
    char    active;                      /* TRUE if Active, else FALSE   */
    char    last[25], first[15];                     /* Name             */
    long    id;                                      /* ID Number        */
    int     age;                                     /* Age              */
    char    gender;                                  /* M or F           */
    float   salary;                                  /* Annual Salary    */
};

#define MAX_RECS    1000                  /* Maximum number of records    */


#ifdef MAIN_MODULE                       /* Make sure data is only       */
#define EXTERN                           /* DEFINED in the main module,  */
#else                                    /* and declared as EXTERNAL in  */
#define EXTERN  extern                   /* the other modules.           */
#endif


EXTERN  struct  record *recs[MAX_RECS];                /* Array of ptr */
#define RECS    recs                       /* to struct of type record */

EXTERN  int n_recs;                      /* # of records in current db   */
EXTERN  int max_recs;                    /* Max # of recs allowed        */

```

LISTING 3.1 MDB.H (Static Only) *continued*

```
struct menu_item {                            /* Menu definition record   */
    int action_code;                          /* Menu item code           */
    char *descrip;                            /* Menu item text           */
};
```

LISTING 3.2 MDBMAIN.C (Static Only)

```
/*
 *  MDBMAIN.C       (Static-Array-only version)
 *
 *  Program:    Mini-Database
 *  Written by: Leor Zolman
 *  Module:     Main Program Module
 *
 *  Program Description:
 *      This system is an "introductory showcase" of
 *      C programming techniques for File I/O-related
 *      applications. Areas of focus include:
 *          Static and Dynamic Array Allocation
 *          Text-based and Binary-based Disk Data Storage
 *          Elementary user-interface and error-handling
 *
 *  Compile & Link (Turbo C):
 *      tcc mdbmain.c mdbedit.c mdbutil.c mdbftxt.c
 *
 */

#include <stdio.h>
#include <stdlib.h>

#define MAIN_MODULE 1                       /* force data definitions   */
#include "mdb.h"


#define CREATE  1                           /* Main menu action codes   */
#define OPEN    2
#define EDIT    3
#define SAVE    4
#define BAKUP   5
#define CLOSE   6
#define ABANDON 7
#define QUIT    8

static struct menu_item main_menu[] =
{
    {CREATE, "Create New Database"},
    {OPEN, "Select Existing Database to Work With"},
    {EDIT, "Edit Database Records"},
    {SAVE, "Write Database to Disk"},
    {BAKUP, "Backup Database to Floppies"},
    {CLOSE, "Close the Database"},
    {ABANDON, "Abandon Changes to the Current Database"},
    {QUIT, "Quit"},
    {NULL}                                          /* End of list  */
};


main()
{
    char db_name[150];
    int db_active = FALSE;                      /* No Database open */
```

LISTING 3.2 MDBMAIN.C (Static Only) *continued*

```
    FILE *fp;

    while (1)
    {
        switch(do_menu(main_menu, "Main Menu"))
        {
          case CREATE:
            if (db_active)
                goto still_open;
            printf("Name for new Database? ");
            gets(db_name);
            if ((fp = fopen(db_name,"r")) != NULL)
            {
                printf("That filename already exists.\n");
                fclose(fp);
                break;
            }
            max_recs = MAX_RECS;

            db_active = TRUE;
            n_recs = 0;
            printf("New database created. Entering EDIT mode:\n");
                                /* After creating, fall through to EDIT */

          case EDIT:
            if (!db_active)
                goto inactive;
            edit_db(db_name);                   /* Edit recs in memory */
            break;

          case OPEN:
            if (db_active)
            {
   still_open: printf("Current Database still open.\n");
                break;
            }
            printf("Database Name? ");
            gets(db_name);
            if ((n_recs = read_db(db_name)) != NULL)
            {
                printf("\nLoaded %d Record(s).\n", n_recs);
                db_active = TRUE;
                edit_db(db_name);
            }

            break;

          case BAKUP:
            if (!db_active)
                goto inactive;
            backup_db();                        /* Perform backup       */
            break;
```

LISTING 3.2 MDBMAIN.C (Static Only) *continued*

```

          case CLOSE:
            if (!db_active)
                goto inactive;
            write_db(db_name);                             /* write to disk    */
            free_up();
            db_active = FALSE;
            break;

          case SAVE:
            if (!db_active)
                goto inactive;
            write_db(db_name);                             /* write to disk    */
            break;

          case ABANDON:
            if (!db_active)
            {
      inactive: printf("Please select a Database first!\n");
                break;
            }
            free_up();
            db_active = FALSE;
            break;

          case QUIT:
            if (db_active)
            {
                write_db(db_name);                         /* write to disk    */
                free_up();
            }
            exit(0);
        }
    }
}

/*
 * Function:        backup_db
 * Purpose:         Backup current Database to floppies
 * Parameters:      None
 * Return Value:    None
 */

void backup_db()                                               /* Backup module */
{}
```

LISTING 3.3 MDBUTIL.C

```
/*
 *  MDBUTIL.C
 *
 *  Program:    Mini-Database
 *  Written by: Leor Zolman
 *  Module:     Utility functions
 */

#include <stdio.h>
#include <stdlib.h>
#include "mdb.h"


/*
 * Function:        do_menu
 * Purpose:         Simple line-oriented menu handler
 * Parameters:      None
 * Return Value:    None
 */

int do_menu(struct menu_item *mnu, char *title)
{
    int i, j;
    char buf[150];

    printf("\n%s -- Options:\n", title);
    for (i = 0; mnu[i].action_code != NULL; i++)
        printf("%2d) %s\n", i+1, mnu[i].descrip);

    while (1)
    {
        printf("\nYour choice? ");
        j = atoi(gets(buf));
        if (j >= 1 && j <= i)
            break;
        printf("Please select from options 1-%d: ", i+1);
    }

    return mnu[j - 1].action_code;
}


/*
 * Function:        error
 * Purpose:         Report error and terminate program
 * Parameters:      Message to display
 * Return Value:    None
 */

void error(char *msg)
{
    printf("Fatal Condition: %s\n", msg);
    exit(-1);
}
```

LISTING 3.3 MDBUTIL.C *continued*

```


/*
 * Function:       alloc_rec
 * Purpose:        Allocate memory for a Database record,
 *                      checking for an allocation error
 * Parameters:     None
 * Return Value:   Pointer to memory, or NULL on error
 */

struct record *alloc_rec(void)
{
    struct record *temp;

    if ((temp = malloc(sizeof(struct record))) == NULL)
        return NULL;
    else
        return temp;
}


/*
 * Function:       free_up
 * Purpose:        De-allocate all recs in the Database
 * Parameters:     None
 * Return Value:   None
 */

void free_up()
{
    int i;

    for (i = 0; i < n_recs; i++)
        free(RECS[i]);
}
```

LISTING 3.4 MDBEDIT.C

```
/*
 *  MDBEDIT.C
 *
 *  Program:    Mini-Database
 *  Written by: Leor Zolman
 *  Module:     Edit the Current Database
 */

#include <stdio.h>
#include <stdlib.h>
#include <string.h>
#include <ctype.h>

#include "mdb.h"

static void fix_db(void);

#define LIST_RECS   1                          /* Edit menu action codes   */
#define NEXT        2
#define PREVIOUS    3
#define MODIFY      4
#define NEW         5
#define DELETE      6
#define UNDELETE    7
#define QUIT        8
#define SELECT      9
#define FIX         10

static struct menu_item edit_menu[] =
{
    {LIST_RECS, "List Records"},
    {NEXT, "Go to Next Record"},
    {PREVIOUS, "Go to Previous Record"},
    {MODIFY, "Modify Current Record"},
    {NEW, "Add New Record"},
    {DELETE, "Delete Current Record"},
    {UNDELETE, "Un-Delete Current Record"},
    {SELECT, "Select Record (by Record Number)"},
    {FIX, "Fix Up Database"},
    {QUIT, "Return to Main Menu"},
    {NULL}
};

typedef int (*FARG) (const void *p1, const void *p2);


/*
 * Function:        edit_db
 * Purpose:         Perform operations on current Database
 * Parameter:       Database Name
 * Return Value:    None
 */

void edit_db(char *db_name)                /* line-oriented edit module */
```

LISTING 3.4 MDBEDIT.C *continued*

```
{
    int cur_rec = 0;                          /* current record number */
    struct record *rp;                    /* pointer to current record */
    char buf[150];
    int i;

    while (1)
    {
        rp = RECS[cur_rec];
        printf("\nDatabase: %s\n", db_name);
        if (n_recs)
        {
            printf("Current Record is #%d", cur_rec);
            if (!rp->active)
                printf(" (Deleted)");
            printf(":\n");

            printf("Name:   %s %s\n", rp->first, rp->last);
            printf("ID#:    %ld\n", rp->id);
            printf("Age:    %d\n", rp->age);
            printf("Gender: %c\n", rp->gender);
            printf("Salary: $%.2f\n", rp->salary);
        }

        switch(do_menu(edit_menu, "Edit Menu"))
        {
            case LIST_RECS:
                for (i = 0; i < n_recs; i++)
                    printf("%4d: %s%s\n", i, RECS[i]->last,
                        RECS[i]->active ? "" : " (Deleted)");
                printf("Press RETURN to continue:");
                gets(buf);
                break;

            case NEXT:                     /* find next active record: */
                for (i = cur_rec + 1; i < n_recs; i++)
                    if (RECS[i]->active)            /* skip inactives */
                        break;
                if (i == n_recs)                     /* over the top? */
                {
                    printf("\aAt end of file.\n");
                    break;
                }
                cur_rec = i;
                break;

            case PREVIOUS:             /* find previous active record: */
                for (i = cur_rec - 1; i >= 0; i--)
                    if (RECS[i]->active)            /* skip inactives */
                        break;
                if (i < 0)                     /* "under the bottom"? */
                {
                    printf("\aAt beginning of file.\n");
                    break;
```

LISTING 3.4 MDBEDIT.C *continued*

```
            }
            cur_rec = i;
            break;

        case NEW:
            if (n_recs+1 > max_recs)
            {
                printf("Maximum # of records ");
                printf("(%d) reached.\n", max_recs);
                break;
            }

            if ((rp = alloc_rec()) == NULL)
            {
                printf("Out of memory. Try Fixing ");
                printf("Database first...\n");
                break;
            }

            cur_rec = n_recs++;          /* make new record current  */
            RECS[cur_rec] = rp;
            rp->active = TRUE;

            strcpy(rp->last,"");         /* initialize the record    */
            strcpy(rp->first,"");
            rp->id = 0;
            rp->age = 0;
            rp->gender = ' ';
            rp->salary = 0.;             /*  fall through to MODIFY  */

        case MODIFY:
            printf("Last Name [%s]: ", rp->last);
            if (strlen(gets(buf)) > 0)
                strcpy(rp->last, buf);

            printf("First Name [%s]: ", rp->first);
            if (strlen(gets(buf)) > 0)
                strcpy(rp->first, buf);

            printf("ID# [%ld]: ", rp->id);
            if (strlen(gets(buf)) > 0)
                rp->id = atol(buf);

            printf("Age [%d] ", rp->age);
            if (strlen(gets(buf)) > 0)
                rp->age = atoi(buf);

            printf("Gender [%c]: ", rp->gender);
            if (strlen(gets(buf)) > 0)
                rp->gender = toupper(*buf);

            printf("Salary [%.2f]: ", rp->salary);
            if (strlen(gets(buf)) > 0)
                rp->salary = (float) atof(buf);
```

LISTING 3.4 MDBEDIT.C *continued*

```
                break;

            case DELETE:
                if (!rp->active)
                {
                    printf("Record is already deleted.\n");
                    break;
                }
                printf("Press 'y' to delete record,\n");
                printf("anything else to abort: ");
                gets(buf);
                if (tolower(*buf) == 'y')
                    rp->active = FALSE;
                break;

            case UNDELETE:
                if (rp->active)
                {
                    printf("Record is not deleted.\n");
                    break;
                }
                rp->active = TRUE;
                printf("Record restored.\n");
                break;

            case SELECT:
                printf("Enter new record number: ");
                i = atoi(gets(buf));
                if (i < 0 || i > n_recs)
                {
                    printf("Record # out of range.\n");
                    break;
                }
                cur_rec = i;
                break;

            case FIX:
                fix_db();                       /* clean up database    */
                break;

            case QUIT:
                return;
        }
    }
}


/*
 * Function:        fix_db
 * Purpose:         Purge deleted records and sort the Database
 * Parameters:      None
 * Return Value:    None
 */

```

LISTING 3.4 MDBEDIT.C *continued*

```
static  int compar(struct record **p1, struct record **p2);

static void fix_db()                                /* File Fix module */
{
    int i, new_n_recs;

    for (i = 0, new_n_recs = 0; i < n_recs; i++)
    {
        RECS[new_n_recs] = RECS[i];
        if (RECS[i]->active)
            new_n_recs++;
        else
            free(RECS[i]);
    }

    n_recs = new_n_recs;
    qsort(RECS, new_n_recs, sizeof(struct record *), (FARG) compar);
}

/*
 * Function:        compar
 * Purpose:         Comparison function for qsort(),
 *                      sorting simply on last name
 * Parameters:      Two pointers to record pointers
 * Return Value:    As per strcmp()
 */

static int compar(struct record **p1, struct record **p2)
{
    return strcmp((*p1)->last, (*p2)->last);
}
```

LISTING 3.5 MDBFTXT.C

```
/*
 *  MDBFTXT.C
 *
 *  Program:    Mini-Database
 *  Written by: Leor Zolman
 *  Module:     File I/O, Text Representation Version
 */

#include <stdio.h>
#include <stdlib.h>
#include "mdb.h"


/*
 * Function:        read_db
 * Purpose:         Load an existing Database from disk
 * Parameters:      Name of Database to load
 * Return Value:    NULL on error, else # of records.
 */

int read_db(char *filename)
{
    FILE *fp;                               /* File pointer        */
    int rec_no = 0;                         /* # of records read   */
    struct record *rp;                      /* Single record ptr   */
    int nitems;

    int active;                             /* Temporary variables */
    char last[26], first[20];               /* to hold the         */
    long id;                                /* values of fields    */
    int age;                                /* during file input   */
    char gender;
    float salary;

    max_recs = MAX_RECS;

    if ((fp = fopen(filename, "r")) == NULL)
    {
        printf("Database not found.\n");
        return NULL;
    }

    while (1)
    {
                                /* Read one record (one line) of data: */
        nitems = fscanf(fp, "%d %s %s %ld %d %c %f\n",
            &active, last, first, &id, &age,
            &gender, &salary);
        if (nitems == EOF)                  /* stop reading on EOF  */
            break;
        if (nitems != 7)                    /* Check for bad record */
        {
            printf("Warning: Last record ignored ");
            printf("(matched only %d items!)\n", nitems);
```

LISTING 3.5 MDBFTXT.C *continued*

```
            break;
        }

                                      /* Allocate memory for one record: */
        if ((rp = alloc_rec()) == NULL)
        {
            printf("Out of memory loading Database.\n");
            return NULL;
        }
                                        /* rp points to the memory area */
        rp->active = active;            /* assign field values          */
        strcpy(rp->last, last);
        strcpy(rp->first, first);
        rp->id = id;
        rp->age = age;
        rp->gender = gender;
        rp->salary = salary;
                                        /* Save pointer to memory area  */
        RECS[rec_no++] = rp;            /* in RECS, and bump count      */
    }

    fclose(fp);                     /* Finished reading input file      */
    return rec_no;                  /* Return number of records read    */
}


/*
 * Function:        write_db
 * Purpose:         Write current Database to disk
 * Parameters:      Name of Database
 * Return Value:    None
 */

void write_db(char *filename)
{
    FILE *fp;
    int rec_no, result;
    struct record *rp;

                                      /* Write into temporary file first: */
    char *tempname = "TEMPFILE.$$$";

    if ((fp = fopen(tempname, "w")) == NULL)
    {
        printf("Can't open temporary file %s ", tempname);
        printf("for writing.\n");
        return;
    }

    printf("Writing Database %s To Disk...\n", filename);

                                /* Each loop iteration writes one record:   */
    for (rec_no = 0; rec_no < n_recs; rec_no++)
    {
```

LISTING 3.5 MDBFTXT.C *continued*

```
        rp = RECS[rec_no];                      /* set rp to next rec   */

                                                /* write rec. in ASCII  */
        result = fprintf(fp, "%d %s %s %ld %d %c %f\n",
            rp->active, rp->last, rp->first, rp->id,
            rp->age, rp->gender, rp->salary);

        if (result < 0)                         /* Check for error      */
            error("Error writing output database.\n");
    }

    fclose(fp);                             /* close temporary file     */
    remove(filename);                       /* remove old version       */
    while (rename(tempname, filename) == -1)
    {                                       /* if renaming didn't work..*/
        printf("Error renaming temp file: %s\n",
                        _strerror(NULL));
        printf("Please enter a new filename: ");
        gets(filename);                     /* try for a legal filename */
    }
    printf("Database written successfully.\n");
}
```

LISTING 3.6 MDB.H (Static/Dynamic)

```
/*
 *  MDB.H       (Generalized Static/Dynamic Array Version)
 *
 *  Program:    Mini-Database
 *  Written by: Leor Zolman
 *  Module:     Program Header File
 */

#define TRUE    1
#define FALSE   0

#define DYN_ARRAY TRUE        /* make this FALSE for static-array-only */

/*
 * Prototypes:
 */

int do_menu(struct menu_item *mnu, char *title);
void write_db(char *filename);
int read_db(char *filename);
void edit_db(char *db_name);
void backup_db(void);

void error(char *msg);
struct record *alloc_rec(void);
void free_up(void);

/*
 * Data Definitions:
 */

struct record {                         /* Database record definition   */
    char    active;                     /* TRUE if Active, else FALSE   */
    char    last[25], first[15];                /* Name                 */
    long    id;                                 /* ID Number            */
    int     age;                                /* Age                  */
    char    gender;                             /* M or F               */
    float   salary;                             /* Annual Salary        */
};

#define MAX_RECS    1000                /* Maximum number of records    */


#ifdef MAIN_MODULE                      /* Make sure data is only       */
#define EXTERN                          /* DEFINED in the main module,  */
#else                                   /* and declared as EXTERNAL in  */
#define EXTERN  extern                  /* the other modules.           */
#endif


#if DYN_ARRAY                           /* Dynamic array allocation:    */
#define MAX_TO_ADD  100                 /* Limit on # of new records    */
EXTERN  struct  record  *(*recs)[];             /* recs: ptr to ar- */
#define RECS    (*recs)                 /* ray of ptrs to struct record */
```

LISTING 3.6 MDB.H (Static/Dynamic) *continued*

```

#else                                        /* Static array allocation: */
EXTERN  struct  record *recs[MAX_RECS];               /* Array of ptr */
#define RECS    recs                         /* to struct of type record */
#endif

EXTERN  int n_recs;                      /* # of records in current db   */
EXTERN  int max_recs;                    /* Max # of recs allowed        */

struct menu_item {                           /* Menu definition record   */
    int action_code;                         /* Menu item code           */
    char *descrip;                           /* Menu item text           */
};
```

LISTING 3.7 MDBMAIN.C (Static/Dynamic)

```
/*
 *  MDBMAIN.C  (Generalized Static/Dynamic Array Version)
 *
 *  Program:    Mini-Database
 *  Written by: Leor Zolman
 *  Module:     Main Program Module
 *
 *  Program Description:
 *      This system is an "introductory showcase" of
 *      C programming techniques for File I/O-related
 *      applications. Areas of focus include:
 *          Static and Dynamic Array Allocation
 *          Text-based and Binary-based Disk Data Storage
 *          Elementary user-interface and error-handling
 *
 *  Compile & Link (Turbo C):
 *      tcc mdbmain.c mdbedit.c mdbutil.c
 *                            {mdbftxt.c or mdbfbin.c}
 */

#include <stdio.h>
#include <stdlib.h>

#define MAIN_MODULE 1                       /* force data definitions   */
#include "mdb.h"


#define CREATE  1                           /* Main menu action codes   */
#define OPEN    2
#define EDIT    3
#define SAVE    4
#define BAKUP   5
#define CLOSE   6
#define ABANDON 7
#define QUIT    8

static struct menu_item main_menu[] =
{
    {CREATE, "Create New Database"},
    {OPEN, "Select Existing Database to Work With"},
    {EDIT, "Edit Database Records"},
    {SAVE, "Write Database to Disk"},
    {BAKUP, "Backup Database to Floppies"},
    {CLOSE, "Close the Database"},
    {ABANDON, "Abandon Changes to the Current Database"},
    {QUIT, "Quit"},
    {NULL}                                          /* End of list  */
};

```

LISTING 3.7 MDBMAIN.C (Static/Dynamic) *continued*

```

main()
{
    char db_name[150];
    int db_active = FALSE;                      /* No Database open */
    FILE *fp;
#if DYN_ARRAY
    int array_size;
#endif
    while (1)
    {
        switch(do_menu(main_menu, "Main Menu"))
        {
          case CREATE:
            if (db_active)
                goto still_open;
            printf("Name for new Database? ");
            gets(db_name);
            if ((fp = fopen(db_name,"r")) != NULL)
            {
                printf("That filename already exists.\n");
                fclose(fp);
                break;
            }
#if DYN_ARRAY
            array_size = MAX_TO_ADD * sizeof(struct record);
            if ((recs = malloc(array_size)) == NULL)
            {                                  /* allocate the memory  */
                printf("Couldn't allocate recs array.\n");
                break;
            }
            max_recs = MAX_TO_ADD;
#else
            max_recs = MAX_RECS;
#endif

            db_active = TRUE;
            n_recs = 0;
            printf("Database created; entering EDIT mode:\n");
                            /* After creating, fall through to EDIT */

          case EDIT:
            if (!db_active)
                goto inactive;
            edit_db(db_name);           /* Edit records in memory   */
            break;

          case OPEN:
            if (db_active)
            {
    still_open: printf("Current Database still open.\n");
                break;
            }
            printf("Database Name? ");
```

LISTING 3.7 MDBMAIN.C (Static/Dynamic) *continued*

```
              gets(db_name);
              if ((n_recs = read_db(db_name)) != NULL)
              {
                  printf("\nLoaded %d Record(s).\n", n_recs);
                  db_active = TRUE;
                  edit_db(db_name);
              }

              break;

            case BAKUP:
              if (!db_active)
                  goto inactive;
              backup_db();                          /* Perform backup       */
              break;

            case CLOSE:
              if (!db_active)
                  goto inactive;
              write_db(db_name);                    /* write to disk    */
              free_up();
              db_active = FALSE;
              break;

            case SAVE:
              if (!db_active)
                  goto inactive;
              write_db(db_name);                    /* write to disk    */
              break;

            case ABANDON:
              if (!db_active)
              {
        inactive: printf("Please select a Database first!\n");
                  break;
              }
              free_up();
              db_active = FALSE;
              break;

            case QUIT:
              if (db_active)
              {
                 write_db(db_name);                 /* write to disk     */
                 free_up();
              }
              exit(0);
        }
    }
}

/*
 * Function:        backup_db
 * Purpose:         Backup current Database to floppies
```

LISTING 3.7 MDBMAIN.C (Static/Dynamic) *continued*

```
 * Parameters:      None
 * Return Value:    None
 */

void backup_db()                                    /* Backup module */
{}
```

LISTING 3.8 MDBFBIN.C

```
/*
 *  MDBFBIN.C
 *
 *  Program:    Mini-Database
 *  Written by: Leor Zolman
 *  Module:     File I/O, Binary Representation Version
 */

#include <stdio.h>
#include <stdlib.h>
#include "mdb.h"

/*
 * Function:        read_db
 * Purpose:         Load an existing Database from disk
 * Parameters:      Name of Database to load
 * Return Value:    NULL on error, else # of records.
 */

int read_db(char *filename)
{
    FILE *fp;
    int nrecs, result;
    struct record recbuf;

#if DYN_ARRAY
    int array_size;
#endif

    if ((fp = fopen(filename, "rb")) == NULL)
    {
        printf("Database not found.\n");
        return 0;
    }

#if DYN_ARRAY                   /* Allocating array space dynamically     */
    fseek(fp, 0L, 2);                     /*      skip to end of data     */
    nrecs = ftell(fp) / sizeof(struct record);        /* # of recs        */
    max_recs = nrecs + MAX_TO_ADD;          /* allow MAX_TO_ADD more      */
    array_size = max_recs * sizeof(struct record *);
                                                /* allocate the memory   */
    if ((recs = malloc(array_size)) == NULL)
    {
        printf("Couldn't allocate recs array; aborting.\n");
        return NULL;
    }
    fseek(fp, 0L, 0);                     /* reset to beginning of data   */
#else
    max_recs = MAX_RECS;
#endif

    for (nrecs = 0; ;nrecs++)
    {
        result = fread(&recbuf, sizeof(struct record), 1, fp);
```

LISTING 3.8 MDBFBIN.C *continued*

```

        if (result == 0)                                        /* EOF */
            break;

        if (ferror(fp))
            error("Error on file input. Aborting.\n");

        if ((RECS[nrecs] = alloc_rec()) == NULL)
            error("Out of memory. Aborting.\n");

        *RECS[nrecs] = recbuf;                          /* Copy the record  */
    }

    fclose(fp);
    return nrecs;
}


/*
 * Function:        write_db
 * Purpose:         Write current Database to disk
 * Parameters:      Name of Database
 * Return Value:    None
 */

void write_db(char *filename)
{
    FILE *fp;
    char *tempname = "TEMPFILE";
    int result, i;

    if ((fp = fopen(tempname, "wb")) == NULL)
    {
        printf("Can't open Database file for reading.\n");
        return;
    }

    printf("Writing Database %s To Disk...\n", filename);

    for (i = 0; i < n_recs; i++)
        if (fwrite(RECS[i], sizeof(struct record),
                                        1, fp) != 1)
        {
            printf("Error writing file. Aborting attempt.\n");
            fclose(fp);
            remove(tempname);
            return;
        }

    fclose(fp);
    remove(filename);
    while (rename(tempname, filename) == -1)
    {
        printf("Error renaming temp file: %s\n",
```

LISTING 3.8 MDBFBIN.C *continued*

```
                              _strerror(NULL));
        printf("Please enter a new filename: ");
        gets(filename);
    }
    printf("Database written successfully.\n");
}
```

Chapter 4

An Address Book Manager: Indexed File I/O

I wrote the Mini-Database System of the previous chapter as an illustration of C file I/O techniques. That tutorial focused solely on sequential read/write operations and their related memory management issues. It only scratched the surface of file I/O; the entire subject of random (nonsequential) data access was never addressed.

When the suggestion came for collecting my **Illustrated C** columns together in a book, we decided the book should contain more than previously published, or soon to be published, material. **The C Users Journal** has received more positive feedback about the Mini-Database series than about all my other columns. I, therefore, decided to take the theme of that tutorial the next logical step forward and create a variation, especially for this book, to illustrate random access file I/O techniques.

A Hybrid Implementation

The original Mini-Database System loaded an entire data file into memory at the beginning of a session, and performed its tasks with all the data residing in RAM. When finished, it wrote the data file out to disk in one big dump. This approach presents a severe limitation on the size of data files that the system can handle.

As mentioned, a database application truly immune to RAM based file size restrictions requires the availability of some heavy duty file management package such as ISAM (Indexed Sequential Access Method) to manage the storage and indexing of data records on disk. ISAM packages typically maintain both a data and an index file for each data table on disk, with neither file size subject to RAM imposed limitations.

For this new chapter, I sought a way to introduce the methodology of disk based, indexed data access without dragging in the complexities of a general purpose ISAM package. The result is *rolo*, an electronic address book system build upon a data structure perhaps best characterized as hybrid indexed. The data file consists of fixed length binary records for easy direct access. There is an index file associated with each data file, but the index file is in ASCII format rather than binary. When the user asks the *rolo* program to open a file, the index for that file is loaded entirely into memory. This is similar to the way the original mini-database loaded text based data files entirely into RAM.

The amount of RAM required to hold an index entry for a *rolo* card is significantly less than that required for the associated card itself (roughly 90% less, in the configuration I've chosen). There is still an upper limit on the total number of records, but that limit is a good deal higher than if all the data were required to fit in RAM. Because the data records reside on disk, the quantity of nonindexed data stored in each data record may be arbitrarily increased, without having any affect on the record quantity limitation.

Spicy Searching

The fields in a database requiring the most indexing are the ones needing the ability to be searched on. In deciding how the *rolo* system should be indexed, I asked myself the question, "What are the fields of an address book I most often need to search on?" I realized there were two fields on which I consider searching capability essential: last names and company names. My index record format, therefore, includes information from these two fields for each record in the database.

I don't always remember how to spell a name , so the searching algorithm should be able to accept a partial string and show all records including that string in the field I'm searching on. In addition, it would be helpful if inconsistent capitalization were forgiven. To support these searching features, I took my version of the standard library function *strstr()* and modified it for case independence. The new version is included in *rolo.c* as *strstr2()* (Listing 4.1 lines 1026-1055).

The idea behind an index is to allow quick searching and sorting of data records, even when those records might be physically unsorted on disk. The searching algorithm I chose to use performs a dumb sequential scan through all the memory resident index data. For search results to show up in sorted order, the index records themselves must be sorted in search field order before a search is initiated. *rolo*'s *SORT* command provides this service.

Portability

The *rolo* program complies with my current policy of keeping **Illustrated C**'s sample programs portable between DOS and UNIX. There aren't many system dependent features in the *rolo* program. At least one obscure portability issue, however, did surface when I first tried to port the program from DOS to XENIX. We'll take a closer look at this "gotcha" during discussion of the function *rolo_read()* near the end of the chapter.

Using *rolo*

The command to invoke *rolo* is

```
rolo [dbname]
```

If *dbname* is omitted, a default *rolo* file name (defined in line 26 of the program) is used. This can be your default address book, while other named files can contain specialized lists of some kind.

If the named (or default) *rolo* file does not exist, it is created and initialized to empty.

The *SEARCH* command has a two state global mode associated with it: searches may be performed either by last name or company name. When the *SEARCH* command is issued, the *search()* function receives control and prompts the user for a search pattern. The ENTER key may be pressed to select all records. The toggle mode key (+) may be used to toggle the search mode between last name and company name.

After a search pattern is entered, *rolo* displays a line containing the text of the two indexed fields and an index reference number for each matching record. After every screenful of these lines, the program pauses and waits for input. If the user presses the ENTER key, the display continues with the next set of matching entries. If the user types in one of the index numbers shown, then the data record corresponding to that index record loads from disk into RAM, becoming the active record. All data fields for the new active record then show, and control returns to the main menu.

The `NEXT` and `PREVIOUS` commands cycle through data records in indexed order, either by name or by company (depending on which field the index was most recently sorted).

The `GOTO` command may be used to directly access a `rolo` card by its record ID number. The record ID number, shown for each active record at the top of the full data display, corresponds to the record's physical position in the data file. The index values shown in the search process may vary after each `ADD`, `DELETE`, or `SORT` operation. The record ID numbers, however, remain constant throughout the lifetime of their associated data records.

The `ADD` command allows the input of a new data record from scratch, while the `EDIT` command allows selective editing of individual fields within an active, previously created data record. To keep the focus of this tutorial as much as possible on file I/O, all editing operations are performed in a simple line oriented manner with no full screen editing features. Several special keys allow the user some control over the input process: the period (.) key skips all remaining fields of a card, saving the data for all fields input up to that point. The ESC key discards all changes made during the current field editing session.

Admittedly, `rolo`'s field editing capabilities are primitive. Slick, full screen field editing, however, could be added to this application by using any of the many available general purpose screen handling packages.

The `DELETE` command marks a record as inactive and causes it to be ignored during search and viewing operations. The physical data is not deleted, however, until the next time that use of the `ADD` command happens to reclaim the deleted record's old physical space in the disk based data file.

Configuration

Lines 22-24 specify the configurable compile time options for the `rolo` program. The `MAX_CARDS` symbol specifies the size (maximum number of elements) of the array used for index data. The memory for index data is dynamically allocated. The actual maximum number of records `rolo` can work with at once will vary with the memory model used in compilation and the actual length of strings in the indexed data fields. *MAXLINE* and *MAXPATH* specify the internal buffer sizes for the text lines and pathnames, respectively, used in the program.

Data Representation

There are two major structure types in *rolo*: *struct rndx* for the index records and *struct rdata* for the data records. A third structure type, *menu_item*, is used for the main menu. The menu system is identical to the one from the Mini-Database, so I won't bother to rehash it here.

The index table is configured as an array of structures of type *rndx* named *rindex*. Each *rindex* entry contains three elements. First, a pointer *lname* points to a last name string or has the magic value *DELETED*. Second, a pointer *company* points to a company name string. The third element is a physical record index (ID) number *recno* stored as an integer (if you intend to store more than 32,767 records, you should change *recno*'s type to *long.*).

If a *rolo* card is deleted, the *lname* pointer of the index record for that card is set to the value *DELETED* (as defined in line 52). We can't simply set the *recno* value to some magic number to flag a deletion because the physical record numbers of deleted cards must be preserved even after those records are logically deleted. If the physical record numbers were not preserved there would be no way for *rolo* to reuse the old data space for new records; *rolo* wouldn't know where the old data space was located. By using the deleted record's index string pointer to mark the deletion, no significant information is lost. We don't need to waste space by creating a new field in the index file just to flag deleted cards.

Because of the way I've chosen to perform indexing, every active card in the *rolo* file will have two index numbers associated with it: a logical record number (also called the index number), and a physical record number (known as the record ID number).

The index number is the subscript of the card's index record in the *rindex* array. Most of the operations performed by *rolo* are concerned only with this logical index number. Whenever a sorting operation is performed on the index array, the logical index values typically change for some cards in the *rolo* file.

The record ID number is the physical position of a *rolo* card in the disk based data file. Once a card is created, its record ID number never changes. If a card is deleted, some future addition will recycle that physical record ID position. Only when all deleted slots have been filled, and not before, will the addition of a new card cause the data file to increase in size. The physical size of the data file never decreases.

A test performed often in the program shows whether a given index number represents a deleted record. To simplify the code around such operations, I've created a macro named *deleted* (line 55) to perform the desired test.

Line 57-68 define a data structure of type *struct rdata* to hold the full information stored on a *rolo* card. An instance of this structure type, named *rcurr*, is defined to hold the data for the currently selected *rolo* card. Remember that the contents of this structure type can easily be expanded to contain additional fields and/or longer versions of the given fields without reducing the maximum record capacity of the program.

Lines 70-73 define the menu structure used with the *do_menu()* function, a hold-over from the Mini-Database program.

Globals

Several global variables describe the status of the currently open *rolo* file:

1) *ncards* tells the number of cards present in the physical data file (including deleted ones)

2) *nactive* tells how many of those physical records are active (i.e., nondeleted)

3) *rcurrno* is the logical index number of the currently selected record

4) *mode* specifies the index field currently used for search operations: *'n'* for *lname* or *'c'* for *company*

5) *changed* is a Boolean flag that starts out as *FALSE*, and changes to *TRUE* if the user does anything is change the database. When the user quits out of *rolo*, *changed* controls whether the program bothers to write out the index file. If no changes of any kind were made (when the user only performed a lookup, for example) then the index file is not rewritten.

The other globals are used to hold file name information (lines 91-93) and to pass extra information back from function calls (lines 86 and 89).

Starting Up

rolo begins in *main()* by initializing global modes *mode* and *changed* (lines 152-153). Then it gets the data file name, using either the name given on the command line, or if none was given, the file name specified by the *DEFAULT_FILE* definition.

Lines 158-165 start-up the processing for a data file. If *rolo_read()* returns *TRUE*, that means the data file was opened without error, the index file has been loaded into memory, and *rcurrno* has been initialized to point to the first active record (if any). If *rolo_read()* returns *FALSE*, the file could not be opened. In that case, *rolo* asks if the user wants to create the file anew. If the response is yes, the *rolo_init()* function prepares for work on a new *rolo* file. If not, *rolo* throws its hands up and quits.

The Main Loop

Lines 167-323 comprise the main processing loop of the *rolo* program. At the start of this loop, the *get_card()* function loads the currently selected data record from disk, and the *show_card()* function displays it on the screen. If there are no active records in the *rolo* file, these steps are skipped.

get_card() (lines 483-508) takes two parameters, a logical index number *recno* and a pointer *curr* to the memory location where the data for that logical record is to be placed. *get_card()* begins by translating the logical index number into a physical record ID number (line 493), then seeking out to that physical position in the data file. Note that the exact seek position is computed as the product of the record ID number and the record size. The *fread()* block in lines 501-506 goes on to load the data into memory and check for errors.

The *show_card()* function (lines 511-558) displays some general information about the currently open *rolo* file: the filename, total number of physical records, and the number of active (nondeleted) records. Then it displays the data for a specific record, a pointer to which has been passed as the parameter *r*. To avoid big blank areas on the display, most fields are displayed only if they contain text.

After showing the current record, *rolo* displays the main menu and waits for the user to make a selection. Control then passes to the appropriate case of the big switch statement in lines 176-322. The details of each case follow.

SEARCH

When this option is selected, the *search()* function takes over to prompt for search parameters, display search results, and process possible card selection requests. If the user does not select a new logical record number, *search()* returns *FALSE* and the main loop repeats.

If the user does select a new logical record number, then lines 182-194 validate that record number. If it is in range and active (undeleted), it becomes the new currently selected record (line 196).

The *search()* function begins by prompting the user for a text string to be used for a search key (lines 373-388). The search key may contain any number of characters; any active card containing that string will be reported as a match. Case is ignored during the matching process. The user also may toggle the search field between last name and company name by pressing the + key; if the choice is to do so, the user will again be prompted for a search key. Lines 390-428 perform the searching operation. *search()* scans all index records, in the order they appear in the index table, for a matching index string. An index is considered matching if either the search key is null, or the *strstr2()* function returns a non-null value when called to compare the search key to an index string.

For each index record, the pointer *str* is set to point to the primary index string (last name or company name). The pointer *other* is set to point to the other index string. While the comparison operation is always performed on the primary index string pointed to by *str*, the other index string is also shown in parentheses for convenience when matching records are displayed.

The search loop pauses after every screenful of matching records, and the user is prompted to either press RETURN for the next screenful of matches or to enter an index number to select directly a record. When the search loop is finished scanning the index table and at least one matching record has been found since the last time the screen filled up, then the same prompting sequence is issued. To keep from duplicating the input processing code in two places, I've broken it out into a separate function named *ask_sel()*.

One final note about searching: for the results to appear in sorted order, the index file must have been sorted on the search index field (last name or company name) before the *SEARCH* command was issued. The search will still yield the same records if the index table isn't properly sorted, but they won't necessarily be in any meaningful order.

GOTO

This is a way to allow the user to directly select a *rolo* card by record ID number, leapfrogging the usual *SEARCH* procedure. Because the record ID numbers are not indexed, *rolo* must perform a sequential scan through the index table to find the entry with the requested ID number. Even so, the *rolo* file would have to get mighty large before such a search yields any perceptible delay.

NEXT, PREVIOUS

These two commands step through sequential active logical records in the index table. At the start of both commands, the current record number is saved in the variable *i*. If moving in the requested direction yields another active record before the beginning or end of file is found, then *rolo* updates the current record value (*rcurrno*) accordingly. If not, *rcurrno* remains unchanged.

DELETE

To delete a record, *rolo* frees the memory allocated for that record's index string pointers. *rolo* then assigns the magic value *DELETED* to the *lname* pointer, and decrements the global active record count (lines 261-266). Then, *rolo* starts at the beginning of the index table and searches for the first active record. When it finds one, that record becomes the currently active record.

SORT

Because index data is all stored in main memory, sorting the index table is easily accomplished through use of the *qsort()* function. The address of the comparison function passed to *qsort()* is determined by asking the user to select a sorting mode. If sorting by last name is selected, the *cmpname()* function is used. If not, *cmpco()* is passed as the comparison function for sorting by company name.

Within the comparison functions themselves, there are several subtle points worth mentioning. First, to satisfy an ANSI compliant C compiler, the definition of the comparison functions must jibe with the prototype for *qsort()* given in the *.h* header file. The *qsort()* prototype is explicit about the types of the parameters accepted by any comparison function: they must be of type *const void **. To prevent compiler errors, the *cmpname()* and *cmpco()* functions must accept the very same types for their parameters. The parameters getting passed here are actually pointers to structures. We need, therefore, to cast those pointers to their proper types in the comparison functions whenever they appear in expressions.

The other point, present only in the *cmpname()* function, relates to the special treatment of deleted records. The last name pointers for deleted records are not really being used as pointers. We don't want *cmpname()* to call *strcmp()* with such nonpointers as argument values. Therefore, deleted records must be detected before *strcmp()* is ever called. This is done by the code in lines 338-341.

After sorting, *rcurrno* is set to the first active record (if any).

ADD

The *add_card()* function guides the user through the process of creating a new card in the *rolo* file. The first two blocks of code in *add_card()* (lines 573-588) determine where the new card's index and data records will reside. The first loop scans the index table sequentially, looking for a deleted record. If one is found, the position is recorded for reuse by the new card.

If there are no deleted record positions to recycle, the second block (lines 581-588) attempts to position the new record at the end of the data file. If the number of records is already at the maximum specified by the *MAX_CARDS* symbol, an error message is shown and the ADD process aborts. If not, *ncards* is incremented and the new card takes its position at the end of both the data file and the index table.

When we reach line 590, *rcurrno* has been set to the logical index position for the new record, and *newphys* has been set to the corresponding new physical record ID number. Next, the fields are all cleared and a call to *edit_card()* lets the user enter information into all the fields of the new card. If the user decides to discard the new card, then the *abortf* flag will be set upon return from the *edit_card()* call, telling *add_card()* to abort the add operation. If *abortf* wasn't set, then lines 604-610 finally add the card to the database by calling *write_card()* and *add_index()*.

write_card() looks a lot like *get_card()* with the direction of data transfer reversed. There are two other differences between the functions, however: *get_card()* takes a logical record number as the first parameters, while *write_card()* takes a physical record ID number. In addition, *write_card()* contains a call to the Standard Library function *fflush()* to make sure the data is written to disk immediately.

add_index() takes four parameters: a logical index position *pos*, and the values for the three items to be placed in the index table entry for the given index position. If the given *lname* string has the special value "**DELETED**", then the *lname* pointer in the new index record is set to the magic value *DELETED*. This case occurs only when *add_index()* is called by *rolo_read()* during the process of reading in an index table file in from disk at the start of a session. The way *rolo* is written now, if the user enters the string "**DELETED**" for the last name field of a new card, that card will immediately disappear. Because the only way I can conceive of this happening is intentionally, there is no code to guard against it.

EDIT

Both the *ADD* and *EDIT* commands employ the same function, *edit_card()* (lines 687-755), to input field values into the current record. *edit_card()* and its related function *getstring()* behave slightly differently whether called from ADD or EDIT. The *new* parameter to *edit_card()* controls the variations. When *new* is equal to *1*, then *edit_card()* is being called by the *ADD* command. Here, the previous contents of the card fields (which are all blank at this point) are not displayed. When *new* is *0*, then the *EDIT* command is calling *edit_card()*, and the current value for each field is displayed in square brackets as part of the field input prompt.

The general purpose, variable length text field input function *getstring()* (lines 758-801) does the data entry for each field. *getstring()* prompts the user with a field description supplied as parameter *label*, shows the previous field contents if parameter *new* is *TRUE* (nonzero), and accepts text of up to *length* characters as the new value for the field. *getstring()* returns *TRUE* or

FALSE, depending on whether the user wishes to continue editing the remaining fields of the current card.

getstring() interprets several keys as having special meaning in the first position of a field input string. If *new* is *FALSE*, then an empty input line (ENTER key only) causes the current field contents to be left unchanged. If the first character of the input field is a period (.), then the current field remains unchanged and *getstring()* returns *TRUE* to signal *edit_card()* to skip the remaining fields. If the first character of the input field is ESC, then *getstring()* sets the global *abortf* flag as well as returning *TRUE*. With *abortf* set, all changes entered in the current *edit_card()* call will be discarded.

Upon return from *edit_card()*, the EDIT code checks to see if *abortf* has been set. If so, the remaining EDIT steps are skipped and control returns to the top of the main loop, where the original values for all fields in the current record are immediately restored from disk.

If *abortf* was not set, then lines 311-312 write the modified data record to disk, and line 314 calls *update_index()* to insert the new index strings into the index table. *update_index()* (lines 463-480) frees the memory allocated for the old values of the two index strings, then calls *add_index()* to install the two new index string values.

QUIT

If any changes were made to the *rolo* file, the *QUIT* routine calls *rolo_write()* to write the new index data out to disk. *rolo_write()* is discussed below.

Reading and Writing the *rolo* File

The final two functions I'll discuss in this chapter are *rolo_read()* and *rolo_write()*. *rolo_read()* is called at the start of the program to open a *rolo* file for processing. *rolo_write()* gets called when the user quits the program to update and close all *rolo* data files.

When opening an existing *rolo* file for processing, *rolo_read()* loads the entire index table into memory from the ASCII disk file where the index resides between sessions. Because the index data is stored in ASCII form, I use the standard functions *fprintf()* and *fscanf()*, respectively, to write out and read back the index data.

Each index record contains three fields: two indexes and a record ID number. This enables each of those records to be represented by a single line of text separated into three logical fields. Index fields are allowed to contain embedded spaces, so we can't use a simple *fscanf()* statement such as

```
fscanf(fp, "%s %s %d", &lname, &company, recno);
```

to read in a single record. The first whitespace on a line would terminate the conversion for the string *lname* and go on to assign the next set of text to *company*. If the last name were something like "von Braun," this would misdirect the input field assignments. Even if the last name didn't contain spaces, the company name probably would. Another way to read in the text is needed.

The Standard C Library's *scanf* family of functions contains a useful variable length string input feature that comes to the rescue. This feature allows the use of any arbitrary character to delimit string fields on input. I chose to use the vertical bar character (|) to delimit my three fields. The following *fscanf()* function call performs the input (see lines 834-835):

```
fscanf(fp, "%[^|]|%[^|]|%d\n", &lname, &company, &recno);
```

The format sequence *%[^|]* says to read all text up to, but not including, the first occurrence of the vertical bar character, and place that text at location *lname*. The next character in the format specification is a vertical bar, to match the vertical bar that terminated the just completed string scan. This entire sequence is then duplicated for the *company* field. The final format conversion is a simple decimal integer specification to read in the *recno* value. Finally, a trailing newline sequence in the format string matches the newline that terminates the input line.

This use of *fscanf()* does almost exactly what I need. There is one complication: empty fields are not handled correctly by the square bracket form of string format conversion. If the user enters a new card containing an empty company name or last name field, so there are no characters at all between two vertical bar delimiters written to the ASCII format index file, then *fscanf()* (at least the version supplied with the C compiler I'm mostly using these days, Borland C++) fails to scan the line as expected when *rolo* reopens the file.

To get past this problem, I convert each null index string into a string consisting of one space character for output to disk, then translate those strings back to the null string when the index records are reloaded into RAM. On input, this code is part of the *add_index()* function, lines 660-661 and 671-672. On output, the conversions are performed in the *rolo_write()* function, lines 912-913. Writing the index file to disk is a simple matter of looping through all the index records and dumping each one to the output file in ASCII format with an *fprintf()* call. This loop is lines 905-930 of *rolo_write()*. Note that deleted records are special cased: the last name field is written as "**DELETED**" and the company name is written as a space (lines 908-909). The physical record ID of deleted cards, however, is preserved as described above.

In addition to loading up and dumping the index data, *rolo_read()* and *rolo_write()* also take care of opening and closing the *rolo* data file. There's not much else the data file needs to have done to it, because all *rolo* ever does is read one record at a time at the top of the main processing loop and occasionally write a new or modified record to disk. Despite this simplicity, the most frustrating bug I encountered in this entire program involved the simple act of opening that data file.

The Bug

At the start of this chapter, I mentioned there was a "gotcha" in *rolo* relating to portability. Here is what happened. As I do with all my C programs, I originally developed *rolo* under DOS with Borland C (to take advantage of Borland's excellent debugging facilities). When I wrote the *fopen()* call that opened the data file (line 854), it appeared as follows:

```
if ((fpd = fopen(data_name, "rb+")) == NULL)
```

Notice the mode string: the first character *r* says I'm opening the file for reading, the next character *b*, says the file is being opened in binary mode (as opposed to ASCII), and the final character + says I'm going to perform both read and write operations on the file.

When I tried to run *rolo* under XENIX with the *fopen()* line written as above, the program didn't work. My data was not being written out to disk. I put *printf()* statements everywhere to try to find a bug, but couldn't find anything wrong. All the data seemed set correctly, but I kept getting mysterious system errors when the program tried to write anything out to the data file.

Finally it hit me. The distinction between binary and text files is only an issue on DOS systems, because of the different ways that UNIX and DOS store ASCII files on disk. Under DOS, lines are terminated with two characters each: a carriage return and a linefeed. Under UNIX, a single linefeed character (also called a "newline") terminates ASCII text lines. Because the Standard C library functions evolved under UNIX, they are all geared toward the single newline ASCII line termination philosophy. To maintain source compatibility between UNIX and DOS systems, the DOS versions of all the library functions perform their translation of the DOS ASCII line termination sequence into the UNIX style sequence, but only for text files. Such automatic conversion during operations on binary files would be disastrous. This is because a binary file could easily contain random data that could be mistaken for a line termination sequence and incorrectly translated. To distinguish between ASCII and binary files, the *b* modifier was created for the mode string in *fopen()* calls. Under DOS, the mode strings *rb+* and *r+b* are completely equivalent, specifying that a binary file is being opened for reading and writing.

Because UNIX systems never need to perform translation on newline sequences, their *fopen()* library function lacks use for the *b* mode modifier. Rather than generate an error, however, *fopen()* simply ignores any extraneous characters it finds in a mode string passed to it. Thus, in my original *fopen()* call, the mode of *rb+* was being treated as a simple *r* so that writing to the file was not supported.

The solution was simply to flip the order of the characters in the mode string. Now, as *r+b*, the XENIX *fopen()* sees the *r+*, which is all it needs, and ignores the *b*. Under DOS, all three characters are still meaningful as before. If there's a moral to this story, I'm not sure what it is. All I can say is: Caveat C Programmer!

LISTING 4.1 rolo.c

```
/*****************************************************************
 * rolo.c:
 *  Electronic Rolo-file program
 *  Written by Leor Zolman, 9/91
 *
 * Usage:
 *  rolo [dbname]
 *
 * Compile:
 *  (Borland C++):  bcc -A rolo.c
 *  (Unix C):       cc rolo.c -o rolo
 *****************************************************************/

#include <stdio.h>
#include <stdlib.h>
#include <string.h>
#include <ctype.h>


/************** Configurable Options: *******************/

#define MAX_CARDS       1000                /* max # of cards in a file */
#define MAXLINE         200                 /* longest text line        */
#define MAX_PATH        50                  /* longest full pathname    */

#define DEFAULT_FILE    "c:/etc/rolo/names"    /* DOS-format filename   */
                                            /* alter as needed for Unix */

#if !__STDC__                               /* If not Standard C,       */
#   define const                            /* disable "const" keyword  */
#endif


/*************** End of Configurable Options ************/

#define TRUE    1
#define YES     1
#define FALSE   0
#define NO      0
#define OK      0
#define ESC     0x1b


/************************ Data Structures: *******************/

struct rndx {                       /* Index data structure           */
    char *lname;                    /* ptr to last name, or DELETE    */
    char *company;                  /* company name pointer           */
    int recno;                      /* physical record # in data file */
} rindex[MAX_CARDS];

#define DELETED ((void *) -1)         /* magic lname value on deletion */

           /* macro: true when given logical record has been deleted   */
```

LISTING 4.1 rolo.c *continued*

```
#define deleted(recno) (rindex[recno].lname == DELETED)

struct rdata {                     /* Card data structure            */
    char fname[20], mname[10], lname[30];
    char title[20];
    char company[40];
    char addr1[40];
    char addr2[40];
    char city[25], state[15];
    char zip[10];
    char hphone[20], wphone[20];
    char fax[20], modem[20];
    char memo1[78], memo2[78];
} rcurr;

struct menu_item {                         /* Menu definition record   */
    int action_code;                       /* Menu item code           */
    char *descrip;                         /* Menu item text           */
};

                                           /* for casting function     */
                                           /* pointer in qsort() calls */
typedef int (*FARG) (const void *, const void *);


/*************************** Globals: ********************/

int ncards;                                /* Total number of cards    */
int nactive;                     /* Total number of non-deleted cards  */
int rcurrno;                               /* current index table entry*/
FILE *fpd;                                 /* fp for data file         */
int abortf;                                /* flags set by edit_card() */
int mode;                                  /* search mode, 'n' or 'c'  */

int sel_rec;                               /* selected record number   */

char data_name[MAX_PATH];                  /* name of data file        */
char index_name[MAX_PATH];                 /* name of index file       */
char *roloname;                            /* base name of Rolo file   */

int changed;                               /* true if any changes made */


/****************  Main menu definition: ****************/

#define SEARCH  1
#define NEXT    2
#define PREV    3
#define ADD     4
#define EDIT    5
#define DELETE  6
#define QUIT    7
#define SORT    8
#define GOTO    9
```

LISTING 4.1 rolo.c *continued*

```

static struct menu_item main_menu[] =
{
     {SEARCH, "List cards (all or by pattern)"},
     {NEXT, "Next card"},
     {PREV, "Previous card"},
     {GOTO, "Select card directly (by record number)"},
     {ADD, "Add a new card"},
     {EDIT, "Edit the current card"},
     {DELETE, "Delete the current card"},
     {SORT, "Sort the index by Name or by Company"},
     {QUIT, "Quit"},
     {NULL}                                           /* End of list  */
};


/********************* Prototypes **************************/

int get_card(int, struct rdata *);
void show_card(struct rdata *);
int add_index(int, int, char *, char *);
void add_card(void);
void edit_card(struct rdata *, int);
int getstring(char *, char *, int, int);
int rolo_read(char *);
int rolo_init(void);
int rolo_write(void);
int do_menu(struct menu_item *, char *);
void message(char *);
int cmpname(struct rndx *, struct rndx *);
int cmpco(struct rndx *, struct rndx *);
void update_index(int, char *, char *);
void pause(void);
int search(void);
char *strstr2(char *, char *);

int main(argc, argv)
int argc;
char **argv;
{
     int i;
     char scratch[MAXLINE];

     mode = 'n';                       /* search by name, by default    */
     changed = FALSE;                  /* no changes yet                */

     roloname = (argc == 1) ? DEFAULT_FILE : argv[1];

                             /* if named file doesn't exist, try to create:  */
     if (!rolo_read(roloname))
     {
         printf("Can't open Rolo file '%s'; ", roloname);
         if (ask("Create new one") == NO)
             exit(0);
```

LISTING 4.1 rolo.c *continued*

```
        if (!rolo_init())
            exit(1);
    }

    while (1)
    {
        if (nactive)
        {
            if (!get_card(rcurrno, &rcurr))
                break;
            show_card(&rcurr);
        }

        switch(do_menu(main_menu, "Main Rolo Menu"))
        {
            case SEARCH:
                if (!search())
                    break;

                if (sel_rec < 0 || sel_rec > ncards - 1)
                {
                    fprintf(stderr, "Choose between 0 and %d only.\n",
                        ncards - 1);
                    pause();
                    break;
                }

                if (deleted(sel_rec))
                {
                    message("That record has been deleted.\n");
                    break;
                }

                rcurrno = sel_rec;
                break;

            case GOTO:
                printf("Select which record ID? ");
                sel_rec = atoi(gets(scratch));

                for (i = 0; i < nactive; i++)
                    if (rindex[i].recno == sel_rec)
                        break;

                if (i == nactive)
                {
                    message("No such ID found.\n");
                    break;
                }

                if (deleted(i))
                {
                    message("That record has been deleted.\n");
                    break;
```

LISTING 4.1 rolo.c *continued*

```
            }

            rcurrno = i;
            break;

        case NEXT:
            i = rcurrno;
            while (1)
            {
                if (rcurrno >= ncards - 1)
                {
                    fprintf(stderr, "At end of Deck");
                    break;
                }
                if (!deleted(++rcurrno))
                {
                    i = rcurrno;
                    break;
                }
            }
            rcurrno = i;
            break;

        case PREV:
            i = rcurrno;
            while (1)
            {
                if (rcurrno == 0)
                {
                    fprintf(stderr, "At start of Deck");
                    break;
                }
                if (!deleted(--rcurrno))
                {
                    i = rcurrno;
                    break;
                }
            }
            rcurrno = i;
            break;

        case DELETE:
            if (ask("Are you SURE you want to delete this card"))
            {
                if (rindex[rcurrno].lname)
                    free(rindex[rcurrno].lname);
                if (rindex[rcurrno].company)
                    free(rindex[rcurrno].company);
                rindex[rcurrno].lname = DELETED;
                nactive--;
                changed = TRUE;

```

LISTING 4.1 rolo.c *continued*

```
                    for (i = 0; i < ncards; i++)
                        if (!deleted(i))
                        {
                            rcurrno = i;
                            break;
                        }
                }
                else
                    message("Leaving this card intact.\n");
                break;

            case SORT:
                do
                {
                    printf("Sort by Name or by Company [n/c]? ");
                    gets(scratch);
                    mode = tolower(*scratch);
                } while (mode != 'n' && mode != 'c');

                printf("Sorting. . . ");
                qsort((void *) rindex, ncards, sizeof (struct rndx),
                        (FARG) ((mode == 'n') ? cmpname : cmpco));
                printf("Finished sorting.");

                rcurrno = 0;
                if (nactive)            /* scan for first active record */
                    while (deleted(rcurrno))
                        rcurrno++;

                changed = TRUE;
                break;

            case ADD:
                add_card();
                if (!abortf) changed = TRUE;
                break;

            case EDIT:
                edit_card(&rcurr, 0);                /* edit all fields */
                if (abortf)
                    break;

                if (!write_card(rindex[rcurrno].recno, &rcurr))
                    break;

                update_index(rcurrno, rcurr.lname, rcurr.company);
                changed = TRUE;
                break;

            case QUIT:
                if (changed)
                    rolo_write();
                exit(0);
        }
```

LISTING 4.1 rolo.c *continued*

```
    }
    return OK;
}


/*
 * cmpname(), cmpco():
 * Comparison functions for sorting index data by name or company
 */

int cmpname(r1, r2)
struct rndx *r1, *r2;
{
                            /* if either record deleted, just skip it */

    if (r1 -> lname == DELETED)
        return 1;
    else if (r2 -> lname == DELETED)
        return -1;
    else
        return strcmp(r1 -> lname, r2 -> lname);
}


int cmpco(r1, r2)
struct rndx *r1, *r2;
{
    return strcmp(r1 -> company, r2 -> company);
}


/*
 * search():
 *  Perform search operation. Return TRUE if user selects a
 *  record index number, else FALSE. If a record is selected,
 *  its index number is stored in sel_rec.
 */

int search()
{
    int nfound;
    char search_text[MAXLINE], *str, *other;
    int i;

    if (!nactive)
    {
        printf("There are no active cards in the file.\n\n");
        return FALSE;
    }

    while (1)                               /* Get the search pattern */
    {
        printf("\nEnter %s name pattern to search for, ",
            (mode == 'n') ? "Last" : "Company");
```

LISTING 4.1 rolo.c *continued*

```
        printf("Return to list all,\n");
        printf("'+' to change mode (currently: by %s) ?",
            mode == 'n' ? "Name" : "Company");
        gets(search_text);

        if (!strcmp(search_text, "+"))              /* '+' toggles mode */
        {
            mode = (mode == 'n') ? 'c' : 'n';
            continue;
        }
        break;                     /* if not '+', then we've got a pattern */
    }

    nfound = 0;                            /* used to control pagination   */

    printf("\n");
    for (i = 0; i < ncards; i++)
    {
        if (deleted(i))                    /* don't consider deleted ones  */
            continue;
        if (mode == 'n')                   /* if mode is 'n', search on    */
        {                                  /* the last name field only     */
            str = rindex[i].lname;
            other = rindex[i].company;
        }
        else                               /* if mode is 'c', search on    */
        {                                  /* the company field only       */
            str = rindex[i].company;
            other = rindex[i].lname;
        }

                                   /* now show all cards that contain the  */
                                   /* search pattern in the desired field  */
        if (!*search_text || strstr2(str, search_text))
        {
            printf("%4d) %-30s ",  i, str);
            if (*other)
                printf("(%s) ", other);
            printf("\n");

            if (++nfound == 20 || i == ncards - 1)          /* paginate */
            {
                nfound = 0;
                if (i != ncards - 1)
                    printf("\nRETURN for more, or # to select: ");
                else
                    printf("\nRETURN for Main Menu, or # to select: ");
                if (ask_sel())
                    return TRUE;
            }
        }
    }
    printf("\n");
    if (nfound)               /* if we haven't paused since the last card */
```

LISTING 4.1 rolo.c *continued*

```
    {
        printf("\nRETURN for Main Menu, or # to select: ");
        return ask_sel();
    }
    return FALSE;
}
/*
 * ask_sel():
 *  Utility function used by search().
 *  Accept response to prompt after a screenful of matching cards
 *  is displayed. Response is an optional index number and the
 *  RETURN key.
 */
int ask_sel()
{
    char scratch[MAXLINE];
    gets(scratch);
    printf("\n");
    if (*scratch)
    {
        sel_rec = atoi(scratch);
        return TRUE;
    }
    else
        return FALSE;
}
/*
 * update_index():
 *  Update an index table entry
 */
void update_index(recno, lname, company)
int recno;
char *lname, *company;
{
    struct rndx *ip = &rindex[recno];
    if (ip->lname)
        free(ip->lname);
    if (ip->company)
        free(ip->company);
    add_index(recno, ip -> recno, lname, company);
}
/*
 * get_card:
```

LISTING 4.1 rolo.c *continued*

```
 *  Retrieve logical record no. recno from disk:
 *  Return TRUE on success, FALSE on failure.
 */

int get_card(recno, curr)
int recno;
struct rdata *curr;
{
    long phys_recno = rindex[recno].recno;

    if (fseek(fpd, phys_recno * sizeof (struct rdata), 0))
    {
        fprintf(stderr, "Seek error\n");
        return FALSE;
    }

    if (fread((void *) curr, (size_t) sizeof (struct rdata),
                1, fpd) != 1)
    {
        fprintf(stderr, "Error reading from data file\n");
        return FALSE;
    }
    return TRUE;
}


/*
 * show_card():
 *  Display contents of a card:
 */

void show_card(r)
struct rdata *r;
{

    printf("\nRolo File: %s --  Deck size: %d (%d used)\n",
        roloname, ncards, nactive);
    printf("--------------------------------------------------\n");
    printf("                Record ID: #%d\n\n", rindex[rcurrno].recno);

    printf("Name:       %s ", r -> fname);
    if (* r -> mname)
        printf("%s ", r -> mname);
    printf("%s", r -> lname);
    if (* r -> title)
        printf(", %s", r -> title);
    printf("\n");

    if (* r -> company)
        printf("Company:    %s\n", r -> company);

    if (* r -> addr1)
        printf("            %s\n", r -> addr1);
```

LISTING 4.1 rolo.c *continued*

```
    if (* r -> addr2)
        printf("            %s\n", r -> addr2);

    if (* r -> city || * r -> state || * r -> zip)
        printf("            %s, %s %s\n", r -> city,
                r -> state, r -> zip);

    if (* r -> hphone || * r -> wphone)
        printf("Home Phone: %s           Work Phone: %s\n",
                r -> hphone, r -> wphone);

    if (*r -> fax || *r -> modem)
        printf("Fax Phone:  %s           Modem Phone: %s\n",
                r -> fax, r -> modem);

    if (*r -> memo1)
        printf("%s\n", r -> memo1);
    if (*r -> memo2)
        printf("%s\n", r -> memo2);
    printf("---------------------------------------------------\n");
}


/*
 * add_card():
 *  Add a card to the database. First look for a deleted slot, and
 *  use it if found. Otherwise, add record to end of data file.
 */

void add_card()
{
    struct rdata rec;
    int i;
    int newphys;

    for (i = 0; i < ncards; i++)              /* scan for deleted slot */
        if (deleted(i))
        {
            rcurrno = i;                        /* if found, use it */
            newphys = rindex[i].recno;
            break;
        }

    if (i == ncards)                           /* if no empty slots,   */
        if (ncards == MAX_CARDS)
        {                                       /* fail if max'ed out   */
            message("The Rolo is full");
            return;
        }
        else                                    /* use next slot        */
            newphys = rcurrno = ncards++;

    *rec.fname = *rec.mname = *rec.lname =             /* clear fields */
        *rec.title = *rec.company =
```

LISTING 4.1 rolo.c *continued*

```
            *rec.addr1 = *rec.addr2 =
            *rec.city = *rec.state = *rec.zip =
            *rec.hphone = *rec.wphone =
            *rec.fax = *rec.modem =
            *rec.memo1 = *rec.memo2 = '\0';

        edit_card(&rec, 1);                 /* edit all fields, new record  */
        if (abortf)                         /* if ESC typed, ignore changes */
            return;

                    /*************** Add Data Record: **********************/

        if (!write_card(newphys, &rec))
            return;

                    /**************** Add index entry: *********************/

        if (add_index(rcurrno, newphys, rec.lname, rec.company))
        nactive++;
}


/*
 * write_card:
 * Write a card to physical position pos, taking data from
 *      structure rec.
 * Return TRUE on success, FALSE on failure.
 */

int write_card(pos, rec)
int pos;
struct rdata *rec;
{
    if (fseek(fpd, ((long) sizeof (struct rdata)) * pos, 0))
    {
        fprintf(stderr, "Seek error\n");
        return FALSE;
    }

    if (fwrite((void *) rec, sizeof(struct rdata), 1, fpd) != 1)
    {
        fprintf(stderr, "Error writing data record\n");
        return FALSE;
    }
    fflush(fpd);
    return TRUE;
}


/*
 * add_index():
 *  Allocate memory for and install an entry into the index
 *  table. The index table position is "pos" and the data
 *  file record number corresponding to that index entry
```

LISTING 4.1 rolo.c *continued*

```
 *  is "recno".
 *  Special case: an lname string of "**DELETED**" forces the
 *      lname pointer to the value DELETED.
 *  Return TRUE on success, FALSE on failure.
 */

int add_index(pos, recno, lname, company)
int pos, recno;
char *lname, *company;
{
    if (!strcmp(lname, "**DELETED**"))
        rindex[pos].lname = DELETED;
    else
    {
        if (!strcmp(lname, " "))
            *lname = '\0';
        if ((rindex[pos].lname =          /* get memory for last name */
            (char *) malloc(strlen(lname) + 1)) == NULL)
        {
            fprintf(stderr, "Out of memory\n");
            return FALSE;
        }
        else
            strcpy(rindex[pos].lname, lname);     /* install last name */

        if (!strcmp(company, " "))
            *company = '\0';
        if ((rindex[pos].company =          /* get memory for company */
            (char *) malloc(strlen(company) + 1)) == NULL)
        {
            fprintf(stderr, "Out of memory\n");
            return FALSE;
        }
        else
            strcpy(rindex[pos].company, company);   /* install company */
    }
    rindex[pos].recno = recno;          /* install data record number */
    return TRUE;
}


/*
 * edit_card()
 *  Edit contents of an existing card
 */

void edit_card(temp, new)
struct rdata *temp;
int new;
{
    char buf[80];

    abortf = FALSE;

```

LISTING 4.1 rolo.c *continued*

```
    printf("Please enter values for each field.\n");
    if (!new)
        printf("The previous value will be shown in brackets.\n");
    printf("To clear a field, enter: <space> <RETURN>.\n");
    printf("A '.' alone skips editing the remaining fields ");
    printf("(saving changes.)\n");
    printf("The ESC key alone discards all changes.\n\n");

    if (getstring("First name", temp->fname, 20, new))
        return;

    if (getstring("Middle name", temp -> mname, 10, new))
        return;

    if (getstring("Last name", temp -> lname, 30, new))
        return;

    if (getstring("Title", temp -> title, 20, new))
        return;

    if (getstring("Company name", temp -> company, 40, new))
        return;

    if (getstring("Address (line 1 of 2)", temp -> addr1, 40, new))
        return;

    if (getstring("Address (line 2 of 2)", temp -> addr2, 40, new))
        return;

    if (getstring("City", temp -> city, 25, new))
        return;

    if (getstring("State/Province", temp -> state, 15, new))
        return;

    if (getstring("Zip/Mail code", temp -> zip, 10, new))
        return;

    if (getstring("Home Phone", temp -> hphone, 20, new))
        return;

    if (getstring("Work Phone", temp -> wphone, 20, new))
        return;

    if (getstring("Fax Number", temp -> fax, 20, new))
        return;

    if (getstring("Modem Number", temp -> modem, 20, new))
        return;

    if (getstring("Memo (line 1 of 2)", temp -> memo1, 78, new))
        return;

    if (getstring("Memo (line 2 of 2)", temp -> memo2, 78, new))
```

LISTING 4.1 rolo.c *continued*

```
        return;
}


/*
 * getstring():
 *  Enter an ASCII field value 'field', prompting with 'label',
 *  maximum length 'length'. If 'new' is true, then this is the
 *  first time the field is being edited (no prior value).
 *  Return TRUE if the user enters ESC or the '.' as the field
 *  value (with abortf set accordingly), else FALSE.
 */

int getstring(label, field, length, new)
char *label, *field;
int length, new;
{
    char buf[MAXLINE];
    int i;

    printf(label);
    if (!new)
        printf("[%s]", field);
    printf(": ");
    if (length + strlen(label) + strlen(field) > 79)
        putchar('\n');

    fgets(buf, length, stdin);

    if (!new && *buf == '\n')          /* If old, Return means no change */
        return FALSE;

    for (i = strlen(buf) - 1; i >= 0; i--)         /* delete all        */
        if (isspace(buf[i]))                       /* trailing spaces   */
            buf[i] = '\0';
        else
            break;

    for (i = 0; buf[i]; i++)
        if (buf[i] == ESC)
            return abortf = TRUE;

    if (*buf == '.')
        return TRUE;

    strcpy(field, buf);
    return FALSE;
}


/*
 * rolo_read():
 *  Open an existing Rolo data/index file pair,
 *  reading the index file into memory.
```

LISTING 4.1 rolo.c *continued*

```
 *
 *  Return TRUE on success, FALSE on failure.
 */

int rolo_read(name)
char *name;
{
    char lname[30];
    char company[40];
    int recno;
    int i, n;
    char lbuf[MAXLINE];
    char *vert, *vert2;
    FILE *fp;

    strcpy(data_name, name);
    strcat(data_name, ".ROL");
    strcpy(index_name, name);
    strcat(index_name, ".RDX");

    if ((fp = fopen(index_name, "r")) == NULL)
        return FALSE;

    nactive = 0;
    for (i = 0; i < MAX_CARDS; i++)
    {
        n = fscanf(fp, "%[^|]|%[^|]|%d\n",
                &lname, &company, &recno);
        if (n != 3)
        {
            if (n > 0)
            {
                fprintf(stderr, "Bad format in %s, line %d\n",
                    index_name, i+1);
                exit(-1);
            }
            break;
        }
        if (!add_index(i, recno, lname, company))
                exit(1);
        if (!deleted(i) && !nactive++)          /* set rcurrno to first */
                rcurrno = i;                    /* active rec. index #  */
    }

    ncards = i;

    if ((fpd = fopen(data_name, "r+b")) == NULL)
    {
        fprintf(stderr, "Cannot open data file %s\n",
            data_name);
        return FALSE;
    }

```

LISTING 4.1 rolo.c *continued*

```
    return TRUE;
}


/*
 * rolo_init():
 *  Initialize a new Rolo database
 *  Return TRUE if successful.
 */

int rolo_init()
{
    ncards = nactive = 0;
    if ((fpd = fopen(data_name, "w+b")) == NULL)
    {
        fprintf(stderr, "Cannot create data file %s\n",
            data_name);
        return FALSE;
    }
    changed = TRUE;                     /* force output to be written */
    return TRUE;
}


/*
 * rolo_write():
 *  Save the current Rolo database to disk.
 *  Return TRUE on success.
 */

int rolo_write()
{
    int i, n;
    FILE *fp;

    printf("Writing Index file to disk. . . ");

    if ((fp = fopen(index_name, "w")) == NULL)
    {
        fprintf(stderr, "Can't create new index file %s\n",
            index_name);
        return FALSE;
    }

    for (i = 0; i < ncards; i++)
    {
        if (deleted(i))
            n = fprintf(fp, "%s|%s|%d\n", "**DELETED**",
                    " ", rindex[i].recno);
        else
            n = fprintf(fp, "%s|%s|%d\n",
                *rindex[i].lname ? rindex[i].lname : " ",
                *rindex[i].company ? rindex[i].company : " ",
                rindex[i].recno);
```

LISTING 4.1 rolo.c *continued*

```

        if (n == EOF)
        {
            fprintf(stderr, "Error writing index file %s, line %d\n",
                index_name, i + 1);
            return FALSE;
        }

        if (!deleted(i))
        {
            if (rindex[i].lname)
                free(rindex[i].lname);
            if (rindex[i].company)
                free(rindex[i].company);
        }
    }

    if (fclose(fp))
    {
        fprintf(stderr, "Error closing %s\n", index_name);
        return FALSE;
    }

    printf("Index written.\n");

    if (fclose(fpd))
    {
        fprintf(stderr, "Error closing %s\n", data_name);
        return FALSE;
    }

    return OK;
}


/*
 * do_menu():
 * Simple line-oriented menu handler
 * Takes Menu structure pointer, menu title string.
 * Returns the action code associated with selected menu entry.
 */

int do_menu(mnu, title)
struct menu_item *mnu;
char *title;
{
    int i, j;
    char buf[150];

    printf("%s -- Options:\n", title);
    for (i = 0; mnu[i].action_code != NULL; i++)
        printf("%2d) %s\n", i+1, mnu[i].descrip);

    while (1)
```

LISTING 4.1 rolo.c *continued*

```
    {
        printf("Your choice? ");
        j = atoi(gets(buf));
        if (j >= 1 && j <= i)
            break;
        printf("Please select from options 1-%d: ", i);
    }

    return mnu[j - 1].action_code;
}


/*
 * message():
 *  Display a message and wait for a keystroke before continuing.
 */

void message(txt)
char *txt;
{
    fprintf(stderr, txt);
    pause();
}


/*
 * ask():
 *  Ask a yes/no question.
 *  Return TRUE if response was "yes", else FALSE.
 */

int ask(text)
char *text;
{
    char buf[MAXLINE];

    while (1)
    {
        printf("%s [y/n]? ", text);
        gets(buf);

        if (toupper(*buf) == 'Y')
            return YES;
        if (toupper(*buf) == 'N')
            return NO;

        printf("Please answer 'y' or 'n'...\n\n");
    }
}

void pause()
{
    char scratch[MAXLINE];
    printf("Press return to continue: ");
```

LISTING 4.1 rolo.c *continued*

```
    gets(scratch);
}

/*
 * strstr2():
 * Search for first occurence of substring s2 in s1
 * case is IGNORED.
 * Return pointer to substring in s1, or NULL if none
 */

char *strstr2(s1, s2)
char *s1, *s2;
{
    int i, j, nposs;
    int len1 = strlen(s1);
    int len2 = strlen(s2);
    char *p1;

    if (len1 < len2)
        return NULL;

    nposs = len1 - len2;

    for (i = 0; i <= nposs; i++)
    {
        for (j = 0, p1 = &s1[i]; j < len2;  j++)
            if (tolower(*p1++) != tolower(s2[j]))
                break;
        if (j == len2)
            return &s1[i];
    }
    return NULL;
}
```

Chapter 5

A Personal Journal Program: Text File Management

Once upon a time I kept a regular written journal. Although I did have a personal computer (a CP/M machine), it didn't feel personal enough for automated journal keeping. I chose the venerable spiral bound notebook as my medium.

Recently, I felt a stirring of the old journal keeping urge. This time, taking advantage of my SuperSport 286 laptop seemed preferable to writing all the entries in longhand, and a program to maintain a personal journal would provide an excellent opportunity to illustrate some handy C techniques.

My journal program must meet two primary requirements. First, it should be simple to use (no new user interface to learn). Second, it should maintain journal entries in a structured, easy to access manner for subsequent perusal and/or compression into archive files.

I wrote the initial version exclusively for DOS. Then, my wife Lisa expressed interest in using the program herself, but not on the laptop. She wanted to use our main machine with the big VGA monitor. That system is now running SCO XENIX twenty four hours a day, and I've never really gotten VP/ix, the XENIX based DOS emulator, to work satisfactorily. I decided to recode the program with conditional `#define`s to work under both DOS and XENIX.

To avoid confusion, I'll begin by describing the program from the DOS point of view, then explain differences at the end of the chapter for compiling under XENIX.

The User Design

To keep the usage simple, I named the program *j* and designed it to take only one optional parameter to support multiple users and/or subject classifications. All journal text is in a master journal directory, defined by the *JOURN_DIR* symbol in the program, or in a subdirectory of *JOURN_DIR*.

To initiate a new journal entry, type the command

```
j
```

or

```
j subdir
```

If you omit the *subdir* parameter, the journal entry will be stored directly in *JOURN_DIR*.

If *subdir* is specified, then *j* tests for the existence of a subdirectory under *JOURN_DIR* with the specified name, and creates it if not already present (subject to the user's approval). The new journal entry will be placed into that subdirectory.

Next, *j* creates a temporary three line ASCII file consisting of a leading blank line, a line containing the current date and time, and a trailing blank line. Then *j* invokes your favorite text editor on that temporary file, allowing you to compose the text of your journal entry.

The symbolic constant *ED_INVOKE* specifies how to invoke the text editor of choice via a call to the standard library function *system()*. I use Lugaru's Epsilon, renamed as *e*, and have therefore included some code specific to the DOS version of Epsilon (controlled by the symbolic constants *EPSILON* and *DOS*).

When you have finished editing your journal entry, *j* checks to see if you have saved your changes by comparing the size of the temporary file before and after the editing session. If the size has not changed, *j* assumes you have intentionally scrapped your work, and terminates with a message to that effect. If not saving your work was unintentional, there's nothing *j* can do about it at that point.

If *j* finds changes, it appends the new entry onto the end of the file containing the cumulative text of the current month's entries. All these monthly files are kept in either the journal directory or its specified subdirectory. *j* creates new monthly files as necessary whenever it makes the first entry of a new month.

A Debugging Trick

When writing the *j* program, I knew it would be necessary to use the `system()` library function for invoking the desired text editor. The process of building an appropriate command string to pass to the `system()` function might require some debugging. Rather than insert statements for printing and pausing before each system call, I chose to create a generalized conditional macro definition to perform system calls, with optional built-in support for debugging the system call text strings.

Lines 46-48 of Listing 5.1 show the `DBSYS` parameterized macro definition used when the `DEBUG` constant is defined as `TRUE` (nonzero). The macro, taking advantage of the comma operator, expands into a four part compound expression. The first subexpression is a call to `printf` displaying the value of the system call command string supplied as the parameter. The second asks the user to press ENTER, the third waits for the user to press ENTER; the last subexpression actually submits the command string to the `system()` function for DOS to execute.

Once satisfied with the construction of *j*'s system calls, I was able to turn off all debugging of system calls by changing the value of `DEBUG` to `0` (in line 27). In this case, the definition of `DBSYS` turns into a straight call to `system()`, as defined in line 50.

Epsilon Specifics

The shell escape command in the DOS version of Epsilon maximizes available RAM for the subordinate shell by shuffling both Epsilon itself and all text being edited out of main RAM and into either expanded memory or onto the hard disk. The annoying side effect of this feature is that Epsilon refuses to start-up again if invoked from the subordinate shell. Epsilon tests for a previous invocation of itself by looking in the environment for a line reading

```
EPSRUNS=Y
```

If it finds such a line, Epsilon complains and quits. Rather than let Epsilon discover this condition, *j* checks for it on start-up and terminates immediately if the environment line is found. Lines 78-83 accomplish this by iterating through the environment list (supplied by the DOS C runtime initialization code via the *envp* parameter to the *main()* function) in search of the magic entry.

j uses a another, less troublesome feature of Epsilon to good advantage; the option to start an editing session on a specific line of the existing text file by specifying the *+n* option on the command line. When compiled under DOS, *j* invokes Epsilon with the *+3* option, to place the cursor on line 3, in the generalized editor invocation string *ED_INVOKE* defined in line 34. If you are using an editor that does not support such a feature, or supports it differently, then modify the value of the *ED_INVOKE* string to suit your editor's needs.

Testing For Subdirectories

After checking for an active Epsilon session, *j* checks for existence of both the master directory (line 95) and any named subdirectory (lines 97-102) by calling the *testdir()* function. *testdir()* calls the *stat()* function to get information about the supplied pathname parameter. If the pathname exists and is a directory, no problem. If it exists and is not a directory, the program prints a message and terminates.

If the supplied pathname does not exist at all (the *stat()* call returned *0*), then lines 172-178 ask if the user wants to create a directory with the given name. If the response is negative, the program terminates. If not, the program creates the directory.

Creating The Journal Entry

j creates a temporary file (lines 107-110) to hold the text of the new journal entry. The program uses the *time()*, *localtime()*, and *asctime()* functions to obtain a time/date string that is written into the temporary file in line 114. It calls *fstat()* to obtain the size in bytes of the resulting text file. Note that *fflush()* must be called before *fstat()* to guarantee that the information returned by *fstat()* reflects the results of the most recent buffered output operations.

After closing the temporary file, *j* creates the command string for invoking the text editor in line 121. With all preparations made, *j* now invokes the text editor on the temporary file.

Upon return from a successful editor invocation, the program reopens the temporary file (line 126), and calls *fstat()* again to obtain the file's new size. If the size has not changed, the program terminates. If the size has changed, the program constructs the name of the current month's cumulative text file and executes a system command to concatenate the temporary file onto the end of the cumulative file, using the *cat* command (line 146). *cat* is ideally suited to this application and much easier than doing all the file I/O via function calls. The *cat* command is standard on UNIX compatible systems. For those who haven't written or obtained a version for DOS, mine is in Listing 5.2.

The XENIX Version

The main difference between running *j* under DOS and under XENIX is in the location of the master journal directory. Under DOS, this directory is in a fixed location on the hard disk. Under XENIX, the location is always relative to the invoking user's home directory path, typically specified by the shell variable *$HOME*. To obtain the value of *$HOME*, the XENIX version of *j* uses the *getenv()* function. Because all file I/O is performed in directories under the user's home directory, any number of users may invoke *j* simultaneously. No one user, however, should start more than a single *j* session at a time.

The character used to delimit directories in pathnames is / for UNIX compatibles and \ for DOS. To generalize the code, the symbolic constant *DIR_DELIM* is set to a string containing the appropriate character. I use a string constant, instead of a character constant, to support functions such as *strcat()* and *sprintf()*.

Finally, I used old style function headers and type-only prototypes to keep the XENIX C compiler happy. For some reason, the XENIX C compiler accepts prototypes of the form

```
int foo(char *, char *);
```

while choking on

```
int foo(char *str1, char *str2);
```

Exercises

1. As written, the text editor invocation string *ED_INVOKE* is hardwired into the program. People using the program may prefer to use different editors. Add support for individualized editor specifications. Here are some ideas.

Under UNIX compatible systems, you might have each user's *.profile* or *.login* file define an environment variable to serve as a customized *ED_INVOKE* string. *j* can then access the value of that string using the *getenv()* function.

Under DOS, you can do something similar with shell variables — in conjunction with my *login* program presented in Chapter 2, for example. Or, you might make the *subdir* parameter mandatory and hard code different *ED_INVOKE* strings for different specific values of *subdir*.

2. As mentioned above, the XENIX version makes the assumption that no single user has more than one *j* session active at any one time. To get around this limitation, the name of the temporary file used for the editing session could be constructed with help from the *tmpnam()* system call. Modify the code to have *j* place the temporary file in the system */tmp* directory, using a unique filename obtained via *tmpnam()*.

3. After publication of this program in **The C Users Journal**, a reader wrote in to say he had put *j* into use as a software maintenance logging tool. There are probably lots of applications other than simple journal keeping that *j* might easily be adapted to perform. A useful feature in a UNIX environment might be sharing journal files among several programmers working on projects, with automatic insertion of the login name of each user making an entry. For an exercise, modify *j* to work in such a manner (or, create a command line option that enables *j* to be used both ways).

LISTING 5.1 j.c

```
/*************************************************************
 *  j.c:    Personal Journal Management Program
 *          Written by Leor Zolman, 1/91
 *  Usage:
 *      j [<subdir>]
 *
 *  What it does:
 *      Creates a journal entry and appends it to the
 *      appropriate  monthly incremental journal file
 *      in the JOURN_DIR (DOS) or $HOME/journ (Xenix)
 *      directory.
 *      If the <subdir> argument is given, then the
 *      <subdir> subdirectory (of JOURN_DIR or
 *      $HOME/journ) is used instead.
 *
 *  Compile:
 *      Turbo C[++]:
 *          tcc j.c
 *      Xenix C:
 *          cc j.c
 *************************************************************/

#include <stdio.h>
#include <time.h>

#define DOS     0                       /* 1 for DOS, 0 for Xenix/Unix  */
#define DEBUG   0                       /* 1 to debug system() calls    */
#define EPSILON 0                       /* using Epsilon editor         */

#if DOS
    #include <sys\stat.h>
    #define DIR_DELIM   "\\"                    /* pathlist delimiter   */
    #define JOURN_DIR   "c:\\etc\\journ"        /* master dir           */
    #define ED_INVOKE   "e %s +3"               /* editor invokation    */
#else
    #include <sys/types.h>                      /* stat.h needs this    */
    #include <sys/stat.h>
    #include <errno.h>
    char *getenv();
    #define DIR_DELIM   "/"
    #define JOURN_DIR   "journ"
    #define ED_INVOKE   "/usr/bin/e %s"
#endif

#if DEBUG                                /* expand DBSYS() to show text */
    #define DBSYS(string)   \
        (printf("\nAbout to make sys call: %s\n", string),\
        printf("press enter..."), getchar(), system(string))
#else
    #define DBSYS(string)   system(string)              /* no debugging */
#endif

#define JTMP        "journ.tmp"                         /* temp file    */

```

LISTING 5.1 j.c *continued*

```
int testdir(char *);
void abortf(char *, char *);

main(argc, argv, envp)
int argc;
char **argv, **envp;
{
    char j_dir[80];                 /* Directory where entry will go    */
    char j_tmp[80];                 /* temporary file name buffer       */
    time_t timer;                   /* For creating ASCII date string   */
    struct tm *tblock;

    long nfsize, ofsize;            /* For saving file sizes            */
    struct stat statbuf;            /* open file statistics buffer      */

    char fname[50];                 /* for constructing file names      */
    char cmd[100];                  /* system command text              */
    FILE *fp;
    int i;

    printf("Electronic Journal Management System v1.0\n\n");

#if EPSILON && DOS                  /* If Epsilon running, abort        */
    for (; *envp; envp++)
    {
        strcpy(j_dir, *envp);
        if (!strcmp(j_dir, "EPSRUNS=Y"))
            abortf("Epsilon is active. Please exit first.");
    }
#endif

#if DOS
    strcpy(j_dir, JOURN_DIR);                   /* construct directory name */
#else
    sprintf(j_dir, "%s/%s", getenv("HOME"), JOURN_DIR);
    #if DEBUG
        printf("j_dir set to: %s\n", j_dir);
    #endif
#endif

    testdir(j_dir);                     /* check for/create master dir  */

    if (argc == 2)                      /* subdir specified?            */
    {
        strcat(j_dir, DIR_DELIM);               /* yes, append name     */
        strcat(j_dir,argv[1]);              /* to master directory name */
        testdir(j_dir);                 /* test for/create subdirectory */
    }

    printf("\nStarting up your text editor ");
    printf("on a new journal entry...\n");

    sprintf(j_tmp, "%s%s%s", j_dir, DIR_DELIM, JTMP);

```

LISTING 5.1 j.c *continued*

```
    if ((fp = fopen(j_tmp, "w")) == NULL)
        abortf("Can't create %s\n", j_tmp);

    timer = time(NULL);                 /* get ASCII time/date string   */
    tblock = localtime(&timer);
    fprintf(fp, "\n\t\t\t\t\t\t%s", asctime(tblock));

    fflush(fp);                                 /* so fstat works       */
    fstat(fileno(fp), &statbuf);                /* get file stats       */
    ofsize = statbuf.st_size;                   /* save file length     */
    fclose(fp);

    sprintf(cmd, ED_INVOKE, j_tmp);             /* construct sys call   */
    if (DBSYS(cmd))                             /* edit the temp file   */
        abortf("Error invoking editor.", NULL);
    printf("\n");

    if ((fp = fopen(j_tmp, "r")) == NULL)       /* can't happen...      */
        abortf("Error: %s has disappeared! Aborting.\n", j_tmp);

                                /* Check if the temp file was modified: */
    fstat(fileno(fp), &statbuf);            /* stat the updated file    */
    nfsize = statbuf.st_size;               /* get new file size        */
    fclose(fp);
    if (nfsize == ofsize)                   /* size unchanged?          */
    {
        unlink(j_tmp);
        abortf("You didn't make any changes. Ignored.\n", NULL);
    }

    printf("\n");
                                    /* construct name of journal file   */
    sprintf(fname, "%s%s%02d-%02d.txt", j_dir, DIR_DELIM,
        tblock->tm_year % 100, tblock->tm_mon + 1);

                                    /* update journal file              */
    sprintf(cmd, "cat %s >> %s", j_tmp, fname);
    DBSYS(cmd);
    unlink(j_tmp);
    printf("\nEntry appended onto journal file %s\n", fname);
    exit(0);
}

/*
 * Test for existence of the named directory, and create
 * if necessary (pending user's approval):
 */

int testdir(dirname)
char *dirname;
{
    char cmd[100];                  /* system command text              */
    char str[80];
    struct stat statbuf;            /* open file statistics buffer      */
```

LISTING 5.1 j.c *continued*

```

    if (stat(dirname, &statbuf) != 0)             /* if doesn't exist */
        ;                            /* then prompt for creation        */
    else if (statbuf.st_mode & S_IFDIR)
        return;                      /* if directory, no problem        */
    else                             /* exists, but not a directory...  */
        abortf("%s exists, but isn't a directory!\n", dirname);

                                     /* does user want to create it?    */
    printf("Create new directory '%s' (y/n)? ", dirname);
    if (tolower(*gets(str)) == 'n')
        abortf("Program over.\n", NULL);

    sprintf(cmd, "mkdir %s", dirname);
    if (DBSYS(cmd))
        abortf("Error creating directory.\n", NULL);
}

void abortf(fmt, arg)
char *fmt, *arg;
{
    printf(fmt, arg);
    exit(1);
}
```

LISTING 5.2 cat.c

```
/*
 *  cat.c: concatenate files.
 *      written by Leor Zolman
 *
 *  usage:
 *      cat [list of files]
 *  Sends the contents of all specified files (or the standard
 *  input, if no filenames are specified) to the standard output.
 *
 *  This version is intended for DOS systems only, since all *nix
 *  systems should already have it as standard equipment.
 */

#include <stdio.h>

main(int argc, char **argv)
{
    int i, c;
    FILE *fp;

    if (argc == 1)              /* if no filenames supplied, read input */
    {                                       /* from standard input only */
        while ((i = getchar()) != EOF)
            putchar(i);
    }
    else
    {
        for (i = 1; i < argc; i++)
        {
            if ((fp = fopen(argv[i], "r")) == NULL)
            {
                fprintf(stderr, "%s: can't open %s\n",
                            argv[0], argv[i]);
                exit(1);
            }
            while ((c = getc(fp)) != EOF)
                putchar(c);
        }
    }
    return 0;
}
```

Chapter 6

Processing Code Listings for Publication Part I: Controlling Structured Space

If you page through most programming magazines, you may notice how the material is organized into columns. While advertising material and editorial narrative tend to make effective use of their allotted number of columns, long program listings are usually a different story.

The trouble is inherent to the nature of structured programming. Liberal use of indentation is standard practice for maintaining readability. Once you've indented enough tab stops to the right, however, there may not be much space remaining for code. This is especially so if the listing needs to fit in a space narrower than one full page.

Then there is the messy issue of comments. Unless you take advantage of the C++ // comment delimiter, it costs at least six columns of overhead to delimit a complete comment on a single line of code ("/* " and " */", shown with a space character at each end to keep the comment text from bumping-up to each delimiter).

There are two traditional solutions to excessive code girth problems. First, code listings can be set in a very small point size, or photographically reduced. Second, authors can rewrite listings to reduce maximum line length. The first approach tends to result in printed listings that are difficult to read and scan. In this and the next chapter, I'll present a pair of C programs that together provide an effective automated solution to the second approach.

Those Pesky Tabs

Most program editing today is probably performed using intelligent text editors, such as EMACS/Epsilon, Brief, and others. One feature common to such editors is the ability to specify a custom hard tab value. When you insert a tab character, the cursor moves over to the next column of the display that is a multiple of *n*, where you have specified *n* as a global setting. The usual default for this tab setting is 8. With this default in 80 columns, it doesn't take many nested loops to cause C programs to begin storming the right margin. To make matters worse, the space normally available for code listings is usually 65 or fewer character columns.

The varying interpretation of hard tabs is a confusing factor in processing code listings. While an author may have written code with a tab setting of 4 to conserve horizontal space, the program used by a magazine publisher to print out listings for publication may assume that a hard tab setting of 8 was used in the preparation of the text. The result is an incorrectly formatted listing.

To deal with this possible conflict, an author may choose to use only 8 column hard tabs in listings to be published, leading to the line length problem. The author also can provide listings with all tabs converted to spaces. While this eliminates the possibility of misalignment, it also makes editing of the listing more difficult and time consuming.

Line Numbers

I include line numbers in listings appearing with my articles because reference to specific lines of code is easier. The line numbers, however, take several valuable columns of space. The number of columns reserved for line numbers can be limited to the minimum necessary by knowing how many lines a listing contains. Line number generation is easy. A field with sequential line numbers is prepended onto each line of output.

The *plist* Utility

The two programs described in this and the next chapter descended from a trivial program I wrote years ago to attach line numbers to a text file. That original program eventually became *plist.c* as described in this chapter. The three main jobs that *plist* tackles are:

1) generation of line numbers (with arbitrary field width)

2) translation of tabs into spaces, with automatic translation from one hard tab setting to another

3) alignment of single line code comments along an arbitrary specified right margin, with automatic preservation of vertical comment alignment (via adjustment for the hard tab translation performed by job 2).

Tab translation is the process with the greatest potential for reducing code width. It works by detabbing the original code (converting tabs to spaces), using a hard tab value that might be different from the one originally in effect when the code was written. Setting aside the issue of comment alignment for the time being, tabs mostly appear at the beginning of code lines. Changing the hard tab value does not have any effect on the structure of the code when tabs are used only at the beginning of each line of code and/or at the end (after the last significant token) of each line. All indentations will still be correct, relative to all others; only the physical scale of the indentations will change.

Dealing with comments is tricky. A listing without comments that has tab translation performed ends-up being just a "squashed" version of the original listing. When comments are present, however, all bets are off. The author of a C program will often meticulously format comments to reflect a personal aesthetic standard. Typically, tabs are used to align comments in consecutive lines of code neatly beneath each other whenever possible. (OK, not everyone does it, but the code is more pleasant to read when the comments are neatly aligned.)

Once such explicitly formatted code is put through tab translation, the number of tabs required in various places to reach a common column is altered, and neatly aligned comments turn into a random mess. More on this later.

The final job *plist* performs is to align inline comments along the right margin. An arbitrary right margin column number may be specified. Because a major goal is to reduce the overall listing width, the right margin value should be the smallest that allows the existing comments to fit in the available space, without overlapping program code. *plist* will add or remove white space as necessary between code and comments to align comments on the right. Any lines containing comments that would not fit in the available space are flagged with an error message.

What about aligning the left end of comment lines? If the author painstakingly created perfectly aligned comments, this structure should be preserved, even following tab translation. The algorithm I use in *plist* to achieve this preservation requires that comments be aligned in the original listings to remain aligned through the process. *plist* will not produce perfectly aligned comments from raggedly aligned input (except occasionally, for odd sequences of lines by random luck).

plist does the trick by keeping track of both original and translated column numbers while processing a line of text. When an inline comment is encountered, tabs are converted to spaces as specified by the original hard tab setting, not the translated one. Thus, the exact length of comments is preserved despite their horizontal placement in the output file, and comments that were originally aligned remain that way in the processed listing. Note: all this happens only when the *-c#* option is used to enable right-hand alignment for comments, and the *-tm,n* option is used to specify both the original (*n*) and new (*m*) hard tab settings.

Command Line Options And Compilation

Line numbering is activated with the *-n[#]* option. By default, line numbers are generated using a field width of *NUM_WIDTH* columns. This default may be overridden by giving an explicit field width value of *#*. A colon and single space character always separate the line number from the start of text lines.

To line up comments along the right margin, use the *-c#* option, where *#* is the desired column width of the output text. This value must include provision for columns occupied by line numbers (if *-n* is used).

The *-t* option controls tab-to-space conversion. Both the original and new hard tab settings default to the value *TAB_SETTING*. The *-t* option may be used to specify both the old and new hard tab setting (separated by a comma, new first), or only the new tab setting. If comment alignment is not required, then the old tab setting may be omitted.

plist takes its input from each file named on the command line and writes the processed listing to the standard output by default. If the *-o* option is used, then the output for each file processed is written to a new file having the same base name as the input file and the extension *.lst*.

In the continuing spirit of portability, both *plist.c* and *maxl.c* are written so as to compile without modification under either DOS or XENIX. Because I could not find the *strstr()* function or any equivalent function in the XENIX library, I wrote one myself and include it for the convenience of XENIX users (Listing 6.1, lines 292-325). To cause this version of *strstr()* to be compiled, set the *NEEDSTR* symbol definition to 1 (line 30).

Figure 6.1

```
/*
        This is a sample test file for the plist program.
*/

main()                                          /* this is a comment    */
{
        int i, j, k;
        printf("Hello\n");                      /* this is another one  */
        for (i = 0; i < 8; i++)                 /* here's a third       */
                for (j = 0; j < 8; j++)         /* and a fourth         */
                        k = i * j;
        exit(0);                                /* bye                  */
}
```

Sample Input And Output

A minimal, contrived C source listing is shown in Figure 6.1. The source file, named *sample.c*, was prepared using Epsilon with a standard 8 column hard tab setting. When displayed on the console, the file appears as shown in Figure 6.1. To generate this listing, *plist* was run on *sample.c* as follows:

```
plist -t8,8 sample.c >figure6.1
```

-t8,8 tells *plist* to preserve the original 8 column tab style in the translated (tabless) output. Because the hard tab setting was not changed, comments remain naturally aligned, as in the original source file.

To illustrate the effect of simple tab translation on comment alignment, Figure 6.2 was produced by the command:

```
plist -t4,8 sample.c >figure6.2
```

Figure 6.2

```
/*
    This is a sample test file for the plist program.
*/

main()                      /* this is a comment    */
{
    int i, j, k;
    printf("Hello\n");          /* this is another one  */
    for (i = 0; i < 8; i++)         /* here's a third   */
        for (j = 0; j < 8; j++)     /* and a fourth     */
            k = i * j;
    exit(0);                /* bye          */
}
```

As the output shows, reducing tab size shortens the listing and preserves code indentation. The comments, however, become misaligned relative to the original source file if tabs were used around or within those comments.

For the final example, Figure 6.3 was created via:

```
plist -n2 -t2,8 -c60 sample.c >figure6.3
```

The option *-n2* enables line number generation in a 2 column numeric field. *-c60* tells *plist* to right justify comments at column 60 (with automatic vertical alignment). By specifying a new tab size of 2 and the old size of 8 via *-t2,8*, I enabled *plist* to preserve the exact comment alignment of the original source code while recovering almost 75 % of the space originally consumed by tab indentation.

Figure 6.3

```
/*
   This is a sample test file for the plist program.
 */

main()                          /* this is a comment     */
{
   int i, j, k;
   printf("Hello\n");           /* this is another one   */
   for (i = 0; i < 8; i++)      /* here's a third        */
     for (j = 0; j < 8; j++)    /* and a fourth          */
       k = i * j;
   exit(0);                     /* bye                   */
}
```

By the way, Listing 6.1 (*plist.c*) was produced with:

```
plist -n3 -c78 plist.c >listing6.1
```

The *main* Program

Lines 66-98 of the program (Listing 6.1) process command line options. Except for the detail of the individual case statements, this is stock code I copy into any new application I write needing the ability to process options. It assumes options:

a) are always named by a single case insensitive character

b) are preceded by a dash

c) contain no white space

d) can all be processed before mainline program execution commences.

After each option is processed, the code in lines 94-97 removes it from the *argc/argv* parameter list. When the general usage check is reached (lines 100-102), the only remaining command line arguments are filenames or similar non-optional parameters not prefixed by dashes.

If the *-n* option was used to generate line numbers, then line 105 initializes the string *fmt* to the format specification that will be used for creating line numbers. This statement is tricky because it includes a format specification being used to create another format specification. The first two % characters generate a single % in the output, the *%d* sequence generates the value *numwidth*, and the final portion of the string, *"d: "* carries over literally. If run with a *numwidth* value of *3*, then *fmt* ends by containing the text *"%3: "* (minus the quotes, of course).

Lines 107-108 call *dofile()* for each input file named on the command line.

The *dofile()* Function

All file input and output housekeeping is performed by the function *dofile()*. Before any lines are processed, the variable *fpo* is initialized to the output stream handle. If the *-o* option was given, then an *.LST* file is created for each input file. If not, the standard output stream receives the processed text.

The loop in lines 145-147 calls *do_line()* once for each line of input text, and lines 149-151 clean up after the entire file has been processed.

Processing The Lines

The code to process each line of text is broken into two passes, performed by the functions *pass1()* and *pass2()*. *do_line()* ties them together and generates the leading line numbers (if needed).

Tab translation on a single line of input text is performed by the *pass1()* function. As a text line is processed from left to right, the variable *in_cmnt* records whether an open comment token (/*) has been encountered. (I've ignored close comment tokens, under the assumption that executable code always fully precedes comments on lines where both are present.)

The variables *col* and *old_col* track the current column number from the perspectives of the new and old hard tab settings, respectively. When a tab character is encountered in the input line, that tab is translated into spaces in one of two manners:

If *in_cmnt* is *TRUE* (we're in a comment), then the old hard tab value (*old_tab*) is used to control the number of spaces that are generated (lines 210-212).

If *in_cmnt* is *FALSE* (lines 201-208), then two things happen. First, the tab is translated as per the new hard tab setting (*tabstop*) in lines 202-204. Then, in lines 205-207, *old_col* is updated to represent the new column position as per the old tab setting. This step is the key to maintaining comment alignment. By knowing the precise column at which the comment began in the original text, *plist* can reproduce that comment in the output listing with the same total column width it previously had. When combined with right margin justification, these features insure that any input containing vertically aligned comments produces an output listing with those comments still aligned.

The function *pass2()* handles right margin justification after tab translation has been performed by *pass1()*. Wherever a comment is found, it is shifted right or left by just enough to make the total resulting line length equal exactly *cmnt_col* characters.

pass2() begins by checking to see if a complete comment is present (lines 237-238):

If opening and closing comment delimiters are not both detected, then all *pass2()* does for the current line is check its length against the value of the justification column, making sure the line is not too long for the desired maximum width. If it is too long, a warning message is issued.

If no complete comment was found, *pass2()* then returns, leaving the text unchanged. This exempts multiline comments (which usually begin at the left margin) from being right justified by *pass2()*.

If a complete comment is detected, then it is immediately copied to a holding buffer, *cmntbuf*, and its length is computed.

Lines 253-254 scan backward from the start of the comment, searching for the last character of executable code. A terminating null is installed immediately after that last character. There is now enough information available to determine if the comment can fit in the desired number of columns. Lines 258-264 detect the case where the comment will not fit and diagnose it.

When enough room is available for the comment, the necessary number of spaces are appended to the shortened input line (267-269), and then the saved comment text is appended onto that (line 270). Finally, a trailing newline is restored and the line processing is complete.

There is a case when applying *plist* might not yield the expected results. *plist* assumes that all tab characters appearing on a line of text always precede the text. In most of my C source files this is the case, but other styles of C programming involve more widespread use of tabs. The most obvious case involves writing a series of symbolic definitions where the symbols being defined have greatly varying lengths. Tabs, then, are often used to align the text to be substituted. Take the following code fragment for example:

```
#define FOO          100
#define A_LONG_NAME  50
#define X            25
```

If tabs were used after *FOO* and after *X*, then tab translation might alter the vertical alignment of the values in the right column. Because I could find no easy fix for this problem, the only way to preserve alignment in these cases is to write the lines without any tabs.

In the next chapter, I'll present another tool to help with trimming down source listings, a program that locates and displays the longest lines in a listing.

Exercise

The only comments supported by *plist* are the standard K&R style delimited by /* and */. Adapt the program to support C++ style comments, where the token // specifies the beginning of a comment that includes all text to the end of the line.

LISTING 6.1 plist.c

```
/*********************************************************
 *   plist.c:    Pre-publication Source Listing Processor
 *               Written by Leor Zolman, 2/91
 *
 *   Usage:
 *           plist [-t#[,@]] [-n[#]] [-c#] [-o] <file(s)>
 *
 *  Options:
 *   -t#[,@]:    sets new tab spacing to every # columns
 *                 if @ given, specifies OLD tab spacing
 *                 (Both # and @ default to TAB_SETTING)
 *  -n[#]:       geneate line numbers, using # as field
 *                 width (defaults to NUM_WIDTH)
 *  -c#:         Right-justifies comments to column #
 *  -o           Writes output into .LST file(s)
 *                 If omitted, output goes to stdout.
 *
 *  Compile:
 *       Borland C++:
 *           bcc plist.c [wildargs.obj]
 *       XENIX C:
 *           cc plist.c -o plist
*******************************************************/

#include <stdio.h>
#include <stdlib.h>
#include <ctype.h>
#include <string.h>

#define NEEDSTR     0                       /* 1 to use my strstr()     */
#define MAXLINE     200                     /* longest allowable line   */
#define TAB_SETTING 4                       /* default soft tab setting */
#define NUM_WIDTH   3                       /* default line # width     */
#define TRUE        1
#define FALSE       0

char *makofname(char *, char *);
void do_line(char *);
void dofile(char *);

#if NEEDSTR
    char *strstr(const char *, const char *);
#endif

void pass1(char *, char *);
void pass2(char *);

int docmnts = FALSE;                        /* do comments              */
int donums = FALSE;                         /* line numbering flag      */
int make_lst = FALSE;                       /* create .LST files        */
int numwidth = NUM_WIDTH;
```

LISTING 6.1 plist.c *continued*

```
int tabstop = TAB_SETTING;
int old_tab = TAB_SETTING;
int cmnt_col;                              /* col. to right-justify to */

char fmt[20];                              /* line numbering fmt spec  */
FILE *fpi, *fpo;                           /* Input and output ptrs    */
int lineno;                                /* current line number      */

void main(argc, argv)
int argc;
char **argv;
{
    int i, j;
                                      /* Process command line options: */
    for (i = 1; i < argc; i++)
        if (argv[i][0] == '-')
        {
            switch (tolower(argv[i][1]))
            {
                case 'n':   donums = TRUE;
                            if (j = atoi(&argv[i][2]))
                                numwidth = j;
                            break;

                case 't':   j = sscanf(&argv[i][2], "%d,%d",
                                &tabstop, &old_tab);
                            break;

                case 'c':   docmnts = TRUE;
                            cmnt_col = atoi(&argv[i][2]);
                            if (cmnt_col < 30)
                                fprintf(stderr,
                                    "WARNING: -c value small!\n");
                            break;

                case 'o':   make_lst = TRUE;
                            break;

                default:    fprintf(stderr, "Unknown option: '%s'\n",
                                        argv[i]);
                            exit(0);
            }
            for (j = i; j < argc - 1; j++)                 /* compress */
                argv[j] = argv[j + 1];                     /* arg list */
            argc--;
            i--;
        }

    if (argc < 2)
        exit(fprintf(stderr,
            "Usage: plist [-t#] [-n[#]] [-c#] [-o] files...\n"));
```

LISTING 6.1 plist.c *continued*

```

    if (donums)                    /* create line number format string */
        sprintf(fmt, "%%%dd: ", numwidth);

    for (i = 1; i < argc; i++)
        dofile(argv[i]);           /* process list of given files      */
}


/*
 * Process the named file.
 * If make_lst is true, create a .LST file for output.
 * Otherwise, write output to standard output.
 */

void dofile(fname)
char *fname;
{
    char linbuf[MAXLINE];
    char ofname[30];

    if ((fpi = fopen(fname, "r")) == NULL)
    {
        fprintf(stderr,
            "\aCan't open input file \"%s\"\n", fname);
        return;
    }

    if (make_lst)                           /* if making .LST files...  */
    {
        makofname(ofname, fname);           /* create output filename   */
        if ((fpo = fopen(ofname, "w")) == NULL)
        {
            fprintf(stderr, "\aCan't create \"%s\"\n", ofname);
            fclose(fpi);
            return;
        }
        fprintf(stderr, "Creating %s...\n", ofname);
    }
    else                                    /* write to standard output */
        fpo = stdout;

    for (lineno=1;
        fgets(linbuf, MAXLINE, fpi); lineno++)
                do_line(linbuf);            /* process each line        */

    fclose(fpi);                            /* close input file         */
    if (make_lst)                           /* and, if writing .LST,    */
        fclose(fpo);                        /*   then close that too    */
}

/*
 * do_line(): Process a line of text
 */
```

LISTING 6.1 plist.c *continued*

```

void do_line(cp)
char *cp;
{
    char result[MAXLINE], *resultp;

    resultp = result;
    if (donums)                       /* if we're generating line nos. */
    {
        sprintf(result, fmt, lineno);
        resultp += numwidth + 2;
    }

    pass1(cp, resultp);                    /* perform tab translation  */
    if (docmnts)
        pass2(result);                     /* right justify comments   */

    fputs(result, fpo);                    /* write finished line      */
}

/*
 * Perform tab translation for the line pointed to by cp.
 * Within comments, interpret soft tab as having spacing
 * of ORIGINAL soft tab setting, not the new tab setting.
 */

void pass1(cp, resultp)
char *cp, *resultp;
{
    char c;
    int col, old_col;                          /* current column no.   */
    int in_cmnt = FALSE;                       /* if in a comment      */

    col = old_col = 1;

    while (c = *cp++)
    {
        if (docmnts && !in_cmnt && c == '/' && *cp == '*')
            in_cmnt = TRUE;

        switch (c)
        {
            case '\t':                         /* process a tab:       */
                if (!in_cmnt)
                {                              /* if not in a comment  */
                    do                         /* then add real spaces */
                        *resultp++ = ' ';
                    while (col++ % tabstop);
                    do                         /* and log virtual ones */
                        ;
                    while (old_col++ % old_tab);
                }
                else                           /* if IN a comment,     */
```

LISTING 6.1 plist.c *continued*

```
                    do                             /* then translate as    */
                        *resultp++ = ' ';          /* per the OLD tab size */
                    while (old_col++ % old_tab);
                break;

            default:                               /* handle other chars:  */
                *resultp++ = c;
                col++;                             /* just pass on through */
                old_col++;
        }
    }
    *resultp = '\0';
}

/*
 * Justify comments to a common right margin.
 * Complain if there isn't enough room on a line to fit the
 * comment into the desired column width.
 */

void pass2(line)
char *line;
{
    char cmntbuf[MAXLINE];
    char *cmnt_start, *cmnt_end;
    int cmnt_len, code_len, col;

    if ( !(cmnt_start = strstr(line, "/*")) ||
                !(cmnt_end =   strstr(line, "*/")))
    {                    /* If no complete comment, just check length: */
        if (strlen(line) > cmnt_col)
            fprintf(stderr,
                "\aWarning: line %d too long.\n", lineno);
        return;
    }

    if (cmnt_start - line < 6)                     /* leave alone if the   */
        return;                                    /* line is all comment  */

    *(cmnt_end += 2) = '\0';                           /* found a comment  */
    strcpy(cmntbuf, cmnt_start);                       /* save the comment */
    cmnt_len = strlen(cmntbuf);                        /* get its length   */

    while (isspace(*--cmnt_start))                     /* find last non-   */
        ;                                      /* space before the comment */
    *++cmnt_start = '\0';                      /* and terminte the code    */

    code_len = cmnt_start - line;                      /* length of code   */
    if (code_len + cmnt_len > cmnt_col)                    /* comment fit? */
    {                                                  /* no. complain.    */
        fprintf(stderr,
```

LISTING 6.1 plist.c *continued*

```
            "\aWarning: comment on line %d doesn't fit.\n",
            lineno);
        strcat(line, cmntbuf);                     /* and concatenate it   */
    }
    else
    {                              /* comment will fit. Pad with spaces:   */
        for (col = code_len;
                col < (cmnt_col - cmnt_len); col++)
            line[col] = ' ';
        strcpy(&line[col], cmntbuf);                       /* add comment  */
    }
    strcat(line, "\n");
}

/*
 *  Create output file name by replacing extension of
 *  original filename with ".lst":
 */

char *makofname(dest, orig)
char *dest, *orig;
{
    int i;

    strcpy(dest, orig);
    for (i = 0; dest[i] && dest[i] != '.'; i++)
        ;
    strcpy(&dest[i], ".lst");
    return dest;
}

#if NEEDSTR
/*
 * Search for first occurence of substring s2 in s1:
 * Return a pointer to the first occurence, or NULL if
 * none was found.
 * (provided for Xenix only; this function is included
 *  with most ANSI-C distribution libraries)
 */

char *strstr(s1, s2)
const char *s1, *s2;
{
    int i, j, nposs;
    char *p1;

    int len1 = strlen(s1);
    int len2 = strlen(s2);

    if (len1 < len2)                /* can't have substring longer */
        return NULL;                /* than entire string!         */

    nposs = len1 - len2;            /* # of possible positions     */

```

LISTING 6.1 plist.c *continued*

```
    for (i = 0; i <= nposs; i++)
    {                                      /* check each possible position */
        for (j = 0, p1 = &s1[i]; j < len2;  j++)
            if (*p1++ != s2[j])
                break;                     /* break on 1st mismatch       */
        if (j == len2)                     /* if no mismatches,           */
            return &s1[i];                 /* then pattern was found      */
    }
    return NULL;                           /* didn't find the pattern     */
}
#endif
```

Chapter 7

Processing Code Listings for Publication Part II: Maximum Line Length

In the previous chapter I introduced *plist*, a program that translates tabs and realigns comments in C source listings. While *plist* effectively reduces the column width required to display a listing, it is the second of two programs I use to take a listing from conventional to "squashed" format. Now, I'll describe *plist*'s companion program, *maxl*. It's a tool that profiles the lengths of the longest lines in a source listing (or any text file) to localize the worst offenders in girth. With the longest lines of a file displayed, you can then decide how to obtain the largest reduction in code girth with the least editing effort.

The Strategy

If we start with the premise that input lines will remain below a reasonable maximum length (perhaps 300 characters), then the most efficient way to tabulate the lengths of all lines in a file is to use the value of each line's length as an index into an array of counters.

When the entire input file has been scanned, the information we'd like to have includes the complete text of the longest line(s), the location (line number) of those lines, and a frequency count for each of the largest line lengths encountered.

The fact that several pieces of information might need to be saved relating to each input line suggests the use of an array of structures (rather than an array of simple counter variables) for storing the required information. I've assigned a tag name of *line* to the structure definition and defined an array named *lines* to contain *MAXLINE* instances of this structure type (lines 34-38 of

Listing 7.1). Each element of the *lines* array therefore holds information pertaining to lines of a particular length (equal to the array element's index). This arrangement will support lines ranging anywhere from 0 to 298 characters in length. Note that two character positions are lost because of the need for both a terminating newline and a null byte at the end of each line read in through the use of the *fgets()* function.

The Variables

The *line* structure contains three elements: *first* records the line number of the earliest occurrence of a particular line length in the input file, *text* stores a pointer to a copy of the text corresponding to that first occurrence, and *how_many* counts the total number of lines found with that same length.

Unlike the *plist* program, *maxl* can operate on only one file at a time. *maxl* is designed for repeated use upon a single file, until that file is deemed sufficiently "squashed" for further processing with *plist*. There didn't seem much point, therefore, in supporting the ability to process an arbitrary number of filenames in one invocation.

maxl takes three optional command line parameters: *-t* allows you to enter the hard tab setting used in the creation of the input file (where the default is specified by the *DEFAULT_TAB* symbol), *-d* tells how many distinct line lengths to report on (default is *DIFF_SIZES*) and *-f* causes any lines longer than a specified length to be flagged. For example, you can write:

```
maxl maxl.c
```

or its equivalent, with the default option values written out,

```
maxl -t4 -d3 -f79 maxl.c
```

and get the results shown in Figure 7.1. Note that *maxl.c* refers in this example to the original C source file, not the listing file created by *plist* shown in Listing 7.1. Therefore, the line of length 70 showing up in the *maxl* output does not actually affect the width of the final printed listing, even if a maximum right margin value of 65 were specified to *plist*. This is because the comment alignment feature of *plist* removes enough of the whitespace between the code and the comment to keep the line from standing out.

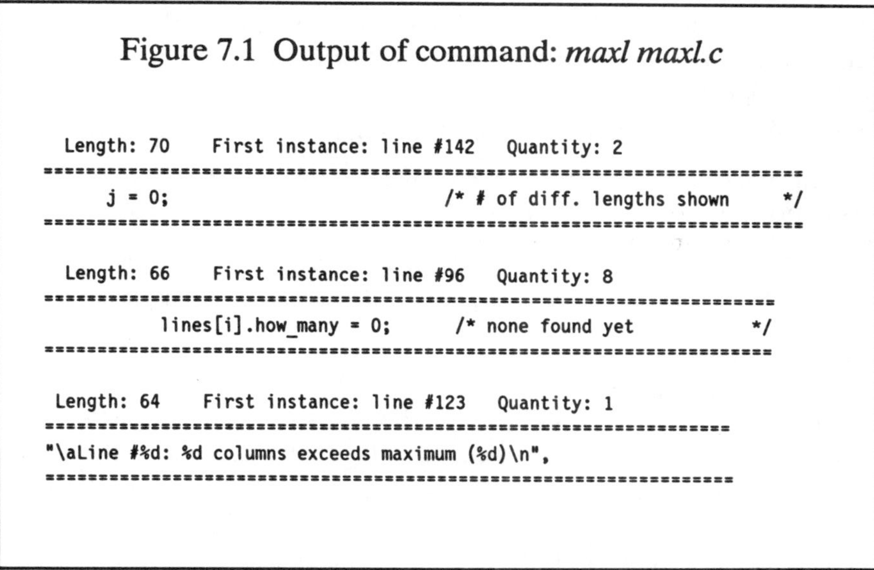

Figure 7.1 Output of command: *maxl maxl.c*

```
 Length: 70    First instance: line #142   Quantity: 2
======================================================================
     j = 0;                            /* # of diff. lengths shown    */
======================================================================

 Length: 66    First instance: line #96   Quantity: 8
==================================================================
          lines[i].how_many = 0;      /* none found yet          */
==================================================================

 Length: 64    First instance: line #123   Quantity: 1
================================================================
"\aLine #%d: %d columns exceeds maximum (%d)\n",
================================================================
```

Scanning a File

After processing command line parameters and opening the input file, *maxl* initializes the *how_many* counter for each index position in the *lines* array (lines 95-96. Note: this isn't strictly necessary, because external data should be automatically initialized to *0*, but making sure can't hurt. In the last step preparatory step, the line number counter *lineno* is initialized to *1*.

Lines 99-139 comprise the main processing loop. Each time through, a new line of input text is read into the *buf* character buffer. The length of that line is calculated by keeping track of a virtual column number in the local variable *v_col*, adjusting for hard tabs and carriage returns as the text is scanned from left to right in lines 102-119.

Either a newline or a null byte terminate the line scanning loop. When a tab character is found, *v_col* is incremented as necessary to simulate an advance to the next logical tab position according to the current hard tab setting, *tabstop*.

Carriage returns are not usually seen in the middle of normal lines of text. *maxl* displays a warning (line 113) when a CR is encountered, and sets the virtual column number back to *1*. (Remember that under DOS, the *fgets()* function returns a line of text where the CR of CR-LF pairs has been stripped out, leaving only the LF, otherwise known as a newline. Under UNIX-like systems, CRs are not part of the normal line termination sequence.)

All other characters cause *v_col* to be incremented to the next column (line 118).

After the line has been fully scanned, a test is made to see if the line exceeds the maximum allowed length; if it does, a warning displays (lines 121-124).

Now we have all the information we need to enter into the running store for this file. The value of *v_col* provides the index into the *lines* array element that interests us, so the expression *lines[v_col]* evaluates to the structure containing information about all lines of length *v_col*. The member *how_many* of that structure tells how many lines of that length have been previously encountered. The expression in line 126 tests whether a previous line had been found by returning a value of *1* (true) if the value of the *how_many* element is *0*. It then increments *how_many* regardless of its previous value.

If this is the first instance of a line of lengthy *v_col*, then the statements in lines 128-136 serve to save the line number and complete text of the line in the structure, *lines[v_col]*.

And The Winners Are

After all input text have been processed, lines 142-154 display the results. The loop iterates through the structures in the *lines* array, from last (highest index value) backward. Any entry with a *how_many* value of *0* is skipped over completely (lines 145-146). Every time an entry with a nonzero value for *how_many* is found, all required information is displayed and the counter *j* is incremented. When *j* reaches the value of *diffsizes* (the number of different sizes to display), then we're finished.

The `putline()` function displays a line of text, performing tab expansion in the process. `putline()` calls `putrule()` before and after the line is displayed, to provide a visual reference for the exact physical length of the line. `putrule()` displays a line made up of exactly the supplied number of `'='` characters. If the trailing characters of a text line are spaces or tabs, the rule line will extend beyond the apparent end of the text line to reveal the superfluous trailing spaces.

LISTING 7.1 maxl.c

```
/***********************************************************
 *  maxl.c: Analyze line lengths to help slim down
 *      code listings for publications such as CUJ
 *  Written by Leor Zolman, 12/89, 2/91
 *  What it does:
 *   Scans the input file, keeping track of the number of
 *      lines of each varying length encountered
 *   Displays first instance of each of the n longest
 *      line lengths encountered, along with frequency
 *   Hard tab interpretation may be set to any value.
 *
 *  Usage:  maxl [-t#] [-d%] [-f$] filename
 *          # = soft tab setting (defaults to 4)
 *          % = how many different lengths to display (def. 3)
 *          $ = flag lines longer than this length (def. 79)
 *  Compile:
 *      Borland C:
 *          bcc maxl.c
 *      Xenix C:
 *          cc maxl.c -o maxl
 ***********************************************************/


#include <stdio.h>

#define MAXLINE 300                     /* longest allowable line   */
#define DEFAULT_TAB 4                   /* default soft tab setting */
#define DIFF_SIZES  3                   /* # of diff. sizes to show */
#define DEF_FLAG    79                  /* flag lines longer than...*/

void putrule(int);                      /* draw a horizontal line   */
void putline(char *, int);

struct line {
    int first;                          /* line # of first instance */
    char *text;                         /* the text of 1st instance */
    int how_many;                       /* # of lines that length   */
} lines[MAXLINE];                       /* one for each length      */

int tabstop = DEFAULT_TAB;
int diffsizes = DIFF_SIZES;
int flaglen = DEF_FLAG;

void main(argc, argv)
int argc;
char **argv;
{
    int v_col;                      /* virtual column number        */
    int lineno;                     /* line number of current line  */
    char lbuf[MAXLINE];             /* input line buffer            */
    char c, *lp;
    FILE *fp;
    int i, j;

```

LISTING 7.1 maxl.c *continued*

```
    for (i = 1; i < argc; i++)
        if (argv[i][0] == '-')
        {
            switch (tolower(argv[i][1]))
            {
                case 't':   tabstop = atoi(&argv[i][2]);
                            break;

                case 'd':   diffsizes = atoi(&argv[i][2]);
                            break;

                case 'f':   flaglen = atoi(&argv[i][2]);
                            break;

                default:    printf("Unknown option: '%s'\n",
                                    argv[i]);
                            exit(0);
            }
            for (j = i; j < argc - 1; j++)
                argv[j] = argv[j + 1];
            argc--;
            i--;
        }

    if (argc != 2)
    {
        fprintf(stderr,
            "Usage:  %s [-t#] [-d#] [f$] <filename>\n",  argv[0]);
        fprintf(stderr,
            "-t#: Set hard tab value\n");
        fprintf(stderr,
            "-d#: Set number of different lengths to show\n");
        fprintf(stderr,
            "-f#: Flag lines longer than # characters\n");
        exit(1);
    }

    if ((fp = fopen(argv[1], "r")) == NULL)
        exit(printf("Can't open %s for input.\n", argv[1]));

    for (i = 0; i <= MAXLINE; i++)
        lines[i].how_many = 0;              /* none found yet           */
    lineno = 1;

    while (fgets(lbuf, MAXLINE, fp) != NULL)
    {
        v_col = 1;                          /* track virtual column #   */
        for (lp = lbuf; c = *lp; lp++)
        {
            if (c == '\n')                  /* newline is end of line   */
                break;
```

LISTING 7.1 maxl.c *continued*

```

            if (c == '\t')                  /* tab is interpreted as a  */
                while (v_col++ % tabstop)         /* number of spaces */
                    ;
            else if (c == '\r')             /* return w/o newline is a  */
            {                               /* special twisted case     */
                fprintf(stderr,
                  "WARNING: CR before newline in line %d\n",
                            lineno);
                v_col = 1;                  /* back to the left margin  */
            }
            else
                v_col++;                    /* all printing chars       */
        }
        v_col--;                            /* adjust to ending col. #  */
        if (v_col >= flaglen)
            fprintf(stderr,
                "\aLine #%d: %d columns exceeds maximum (%d)\n",
                        lineno, v_col , flaglen);
                                            /* bump counter for length  */
        if (!lines[v_col].how_many++)              /* first time for   */
        {                                   /* this length? if so...    */
            lines[v_col].first = lineno;               /* save line #, */
            if ((lines[v_col].text =                   /* & save text  */
                (char *) malloc(strlen(lbuf) + 1)) == NULL)
            {
                fprintf(stderr,
                    "Out of memory in line %d\n", lineno);
                exit(1);
            }
            strcpy(lines[v_col].text, lbuf);
        }
        lineno++;
    }

    printf("\n");
    j = 0;                              /* # of diff. lengths shown     */
    for (i = MAXLINE - 1; i > 0; i--)                /* display results  */
    {
        if (!lines[i].how_many)
            continue;
        printf("Length: %d    First instance: line #%d",
                i, lines[i].first);
        printf("   Quantity: %d\n", lines[i].how_many);
        putline(lines[i].text, i);
        if (++j == diffsizes)
            break;
        printf("\n");
    }
    fclose(fp);
}
```

LISTING 7.1 maxl.c *continued*

```


/*
 * putline(): Display a line of text, with rule line
 *            before and after
 */

void putline(line, length)
char *line;
int length;
{
    char *lp, c;
    int v_col;

    putrule(length);
    for (lp = line, v_col = 1; c = *lp; lp++)
        switch (c)
        {
            case '\t':                      /* translate tabs to spaces */
                do
                    putchar(' ');
                while (v_col++ % tabstop);
                break;
            default:
                putchar(c);
                v_col++;
        }
    putrule(length);
}


/*
 * putrule(): display a horizontal line so trailing
 *            whitespace is detectable
 */

void putrule(ncols)
int ncols;
{
    int i;

    for (i = 0; i < ncols; i++)
        putchar('=');
    putchar('\n');
}
```

Chapter 8

A Portable Menu Compiler: Implementing a Small Language Translator

Here at **The C Users Journal**, we do most of our internal data processing on a single SCO XENIX/386 system running the latest available releases of the Informix database system for XENIX. There may be up to thirty users sharing the system. Many of those users run under the FACET/TERM software package to launch multiple login sessions on their individual serial terminals. It is not unusual to see as many as fifty logical users, and perhaps 150 system processes active at any time during the business day. Despite the load, the system response time experienced by our users is pretty darn good.

Now, for the punch line: our CPU is an inexpensive 386/25 Taiwanese clone. Even with 12 Megabytes of RAM, these system units sell for about half the price of the 10 Megabyte hard disk drive I purchased in 1980. My intention isn't necessarily to tout the cost effectiveness of imported hardware; I think it is remarkable how well a contemporary entry level CPU can perform. A system load like ours could have brought a minicomputer system to its knees not long ago.

One way we've streamlined our system is by eliminating as many CPU intensive tasks as possible from the business hours load. We did this partially through the design of a general purpose sequential overnight job spooler. We looked for the worst bottlenecks among our routine daily tasks. We then modified the shell scripts controlling those programs to allow users to schedule overnight execution.

In this chapter, I'll describe the CMENU menu system, originally created as part of our effort to reduce the daily system load. CMENU also brought some welcome spin-offs. It significantly reduced the Technical Department's maintenance requirements and enhanced the usability, speed and efficiency of the menu system for our users.

The Fifty Percent Solution

R&D's entire internal business management system revolves around menus. All the menus stem from two root menus invoked from the system prompt. The first of these two menus contains all invoice processing and customer related tasks. The second main menu handles our advertising subsystems and personal utilities (E-mail, calendar maintenance, business letter generation, etc.,). Counting all the submenus and sub-submenus, there are approximately 300 distinct menu options in the system. Many of these are shell scripts that manage standardized parameter entry and invoke Informix report generators.

Before CMENU, this entire menu system ran under Informix's own menu processing scheme. Menu headers and their associated lists of menu items existed as database tables in a master/detail relationship. The mechanism supplied by Informix for creating and maintaining the menu system relied on a screen form built to work with Informix's general purpose table query tool, Perform. This screen form, unfortunately, allows only one menu selection to appear on the screen at a time. This made online searches for a particular item in the menu hierarchy a repetitive, time consuming operation.

Informix integrated their menu maintenance programs into their new generation SQL runtime module, but imposed the limitation that each database can contain only a single associated menu system. Because there were two distinct menu hierarchies used with our one major database, we had to create a dummy database to support the existence of a second independent menu hierarchy. Each time a user invoked a menu, the menu program launched two system processes. The first was an SQL interpreter to run the user interface portion of the menu. The second was a back-end SQL engine that interfaced with the actual database. Then, in the cases where we had logically isolated some additional menu subsystems from the main menus (as when developing new subsystems, or when we had not yet ported an existing application from our old Informix 3.3 system and the menus were still in the old format), any invocation of an external nonintegrated submenu from the main menu meant:

1) all the processes from the main menu were still active,

2) a new set of processes was launched to handle the new menu, and

3) more processes came along when the user made a selection from the new menu.

This was not an effective use of system resources.

In contrast to the clumsy internal implementation and maintenance difficulties of Informix's menu system, the enduser interface portion of the Informix system is remarkably clean, intuitive and generally user friendly. I chose to retain much of the look and feel of their user interface in designing CMENU as a replacement for their menu system. This would allow a changeover at R&D to take place in the office with a minimum of retraining. After installation of the new CMENU system, a short E-mail message to all users sufficed for retraining. That message outlined CMENU's few extensions to the Informix menu system's user interface, because the basic operation involved familiar features.

The Best of Both Worlds

To the enduser, CMENU based menus appear similar to their Informix based predecessors. Internally, however, CMENU works differently. CMENU, not built on top of a complex database package, is a standalone system using a precompilation scheme to make execution (interpretation) of menus as efficient as possible.

The menu compiler module, named *cmenu*, compiles an ASCII format menu specification file containing any number of menu screen specifications into an intermediate binary object format. The menu runner module, *rmenu*, loads the intermediate file(s) into RAM and executes the menu system as specified.

The advantage of precompiled menu specifications is that most of the work of parsing the source code and compiling it into a form suitable for efficient runtime interpretation happens only once, at compilation time. When *rmenu* is invoked, it has only to display the text on the screen, interpret the user's keystrokes, process menu navigation commands, and submit the action commands associated with selected menu commands to the operating system for execution.

To reduce the number of processes launched by the runtime menu system, *rmenu* employs a recursive data structure. Separate screens of a menu system may be compiled either together in one source file or separately in distinct physical source files. At runtime there is no need to spawn additional processes to traverse up and down through the menu structure, even when that structure contains separately compiled menu files. A single process coordinates all the dynamic loading and menu navigation operations.

A rich, powerful repertoire of options in the CMENU specification language provides a high level of control over menu behavior in response to the varying requirements of application programs and shell scripts. Some applications, for example, may require a prompt after their completion allowing users to read vital information left on the screen immediately before the application terminated. Other applications never leave any useful information on the screen and do not require a prompt. Other applications may sometimes require a prompt, and sometimes not, based upon their exit status code. Any of these cases can be handled easily by CMENU (at least the UNIX version) through appropriate use of the specification language.

Two Programs, Two Personalities . . .

The *cmenu* and *rmenu* programs share a common intermediate menu object format, and not much else. Each evolved in its own necessarily distinct style of programming, because of the disparate natures of the two connected tasks.

The menu compiler, *cmenu*, operates as an iterative state machine. It processes the source file text sequentially and maintains all state information in global data shared by all the token processing functions of the program.

To understand why such a scheme is appropriate for the *cmenu* program, note that the CMENU specification language, like C itself, is not block structured. In C, you define all functions at one top level, and can't define functions within functions (although you can reference functions from within other functions). Other constructs in C, such as expressions, do have a recursive nature; there are no such recursive expression structures in a CMENU specification.

Thus, a sequential approach works well for parsing CMENU source code and also makes the program less complicated.

The simplicity inherent to *cmenu* however, wouldn't work for *rmenu* without severely limiting its power. At run time, menus must be callable from other menus, and there should, ideally, be no structural limitation on the depth to which menus nest. In practice, of course, memory may eventually run out.

Several steps can be taken to increase the practical limit on the number of menus and/or total menu items a single logical menu system can contain. The first is to design a longitudinal menu tree structure, to take maximum advantage of the dynamic loading features of CMENU. The second is to compile the CMENU program using the huge memory model, eliminating array size limitations. For efficiency, all my testing was performed with the CMENU programs compiled with the default small memory model.

One way *rmenu* differs from *cmenu* is that *rmenu*'s menu processing functions support recursion. There is only one trivial case where *rmenu* would not actually employ recursion in the process of interpreting a menu's specification. That is when a complete menu system consists of only a single menu file, and that file contains only a solitary menu definition with no submenu references. In any other configuration, recursive calls will always occur.

. . . And At Least Two Operating Systems

Platform dependence varies between the two programs. Both support C compilers of varying ANSI compliance; aside from that *cmenu*'s code is pretty much system independent. Because *cmenu* simply compiles a text file into a binary file, the issue of realtime user interface management does not arise.

rmenu, however, must deal with the user's screen. Pandora's box immediately opens, because DOS and UNIX systems have completely different ideas regarding the user's terminal. UNIX sees terminals as serial devices, while DOS sees them as direct memory mapped devices (that is an over simplification, but it'll suffice for present purposes).

There is a standard utility library available with most UNIX-like systems for managing the screen. Its name is "Curses." The Curses library represents enough of a standard that several PC based implementations have even popped up. I chose to use one such PC Curses package that we distribute through our

C Users Group library. It's name is, appropriately, "PC Curses" (CUG volume 298), written by Jeff Dean. (Jeff volunteered extensive assistance to me in checking the CMENU package for bugs and portability issues. Thank you Jeff!)

PC Curses allows the CMENU system to be compiled under DOS with very few conditionally compiled variations in the terminal handling code. This is possible because Jeff's library uses the same standard function names as the UNIX versions of Curses.

There are some minor variations between the UNIX and DOS flavors of Curses. There are also other areas of the CMENU system that must be handled differently between UNIX/XENIX and DOS. The most irritating one involves the "current working directory," or CWD, and how the CWD can change unexpectedly after submitting command strings to the respective operating system's command processors.

Under UNIX, a subshell can never alter the parent shell's current working directory. There are subtle tricks for letting a child process have a say in setting the CWD of its parent. Ultimately, however, the parent is always in control of its own CWD.

Not so under DOS. Once you pass an unknown command string to the command processor under DOS, you can't know for sure where the CWD will be upon return. The current working directory and currently selected drive (two distinct global modes, as described in Chapter 1) must be saved before making any system calls. Then, upon return from system calls, those settings must be restored.

Finally, screen and terminal characteristics may vary from system to system. Features such as lines per screen, column width, and operation of certain keys are terminal dependent. Under UNIX, for example, some versions of Curses support predefined cursor key codes and certain others do not. Under XENIX, at least one Curses library function name is different from the equivalent Curses function name on other UNIX variants. CMENU's header files try to handle known variations such as this, to keep the program text as uncluttered with conditional compilation directives as possible.

The CMENU system may be compiled interchangeably under either DOS or XENIX without requiring any changes to the code. Use the appropriate *makefile* for the target operating system. Figure 8.1 shows the *makefile* for

Figure 8.1 DOS Makefile

```
#
# Make file for CMENU Menu compiler system
# For use with Borland/Turbo C++
#

CC = bcc                        # command-line compiler name
DEBUG = -v                      # enable imbedded debug info
SHUTUP = -w-pia                 # supress obnoxious warnings
CULIBS = tscurses.lib           # curses libraries

#
# From this point on, no changes should be necessary.
#

COPTS = -DDOS=1 $(DEBUG) $(SHUTUP)
CFILES = cmenu1.obj cmenu2.obj cmenu3.obj
RFILES = rmenu1.obj rmenu2.obj  rmenu3.obj rmenu4.obj

all: cmenu.exe rmenu.exe dmenu.exe

.c.obj:
    $(CC) -c $(COPTS) {$< }

cmenu.exe: $(CFILES)
    $(CC) $(DEBUG) -ecmenu $(CFILES) wildargs.obj

rmenu.exe: $(RFILES)
    $(CC) $(DEBUG) -ermenu $(RFILES) $(CULIBS)

dmenu.exe: dmenu.c cmenu.h
    $(CC) $(COPTS) -edmenu dmenu.c

$(CFILES): ccmenu.h cmenu.h

$(RFILES): rcmenu.h cmenu.h
```

Figure 8.2 UNIX/XENIX Makefile

```
#
# Make file for CMENU Menu compiler system
# For use under Unix/Xenix
#

CC = cc

# Operating System (Uncomment one only):
#SYSTEM = UNIX
SYSTEM = XENIX

CULIBS = -ltcap -ltermcap       # curses libraries

#
# From this point on, no changes should be necessary.
#

COPTS = -D$(SYSTEM)=1
CFILES = cmenu1.o cmenu2.o cmenu3.o
RFILES = rmenu1.o rmenu2.o  rmenu3.o rmenu4.o

all: cmenu rmenu dmenu

.c.o:
    $(CC) -c $(COPTS) $<

cmenu: $(CFILES)
    $(CC) -o$@ $(CFILES)

rmenu: $(RFILES)
    $(CC) -o$@ $(RFILES) $(CULIBS)

dmenu: dmenu.c cmenu.h
    $(CC) $(COPTS) -odmenu dmenu.c

$(CFILES): ccmenu.h cmenu.h

$(RFILES): rcmenu.h cmenu.h
```

DOS. This version works specifically with the Borland C++ *make* program, but can easily be adapted to other dialects of *make*. Figure 8.2 shows the UNIX/XENIX version of the *makefile*.

Each *makefile* uses the C compiler's *-D* command line option to define the target operating system and cause the appropriate variations of system dependent code to be compiled. Several lines at the top of the *makefile* may be customized as needed to configure CMENU for the desired target environment.

There may be issues with UNIX variants (other than XENIX) that I haven't foreseen. The way the *makefile* specifies the names of the Curses library object files will need changing for other UNIX systems. It works as supplied on XENIX, but I make no other guarantees.

The CMENU language

Figure 8.3 shows a modified BNF specification of CMENU's menu definition language. Here is a detailed English explanation of that specification.

A CMENU description file has one or more menu definitions. The first menu appearing in the file is always the main menu for that file, and need not have a name. Additional menus appearing in the same file can only be accessed by name via the *lmenu* (local menu) option in the main menu. Such additional menus, therefore, must all be given unique names.

Each menu definition begins with a menu clause, consisting of the keyword *menu*, an identifier (optional only for the main menu, required otherwise), and an optional colon. After the menu clause come any desired menu options, followed by the item definitions. The menu definition is complete when the *endmenu* keyword appears.

A menu system may consist of any number of separate menu files (or compiled units). Traversal across compiled units at runtime is totally transparent from the user's point of view. Selecting and returning from an external menu (separately compiled unit) appears the same, to the user, as selecting and returning from a local menu. The user receives no indication that another compiled unit has just been dynamically loaded. Within a single menu definition, global menu options may be specified immediately after the opening *menu* clause, but before the first *item* has appeared. If such options appear in a

Figure 8.3 Modified BNF description of CMENU Specification Language

---

```
Explanation of my "loose BNF" form:

 := reads "is defined as".

 Terms in <>s are syntactic objects.

 Terms in CAPITALS are keywords.

 An item in [] is optional

 If a set of items is enclosed in {} with | between
    each item, or a range is shown using the - character,
    exactly one of those items must be picked.

 * to the right of an object denotes 0 or more occurrences.

 + to the right of an object denotes 1 or more occurrences.
```

```
<cmenu-source-file> :=
    <menu-defn> +

<menu-defn> :=
    MENU [<identifer>] :
        <menu-option> *
        <item-defn> +
    ENDMENU

<identifier> :=
    { a-z | A-Z | _ }+  { a-z | A-Z | 0-9 | _ } *

<menu-optiion> :=
    PATH <text>
    ALIGN { LEFT | CENTER } |
    ESCAPE |
    NOESCAPE |
    SPACING { 1 | 2 } |
    COLUMNS <integer>

<integer> :=
    {0-9} +
```

Figure 8.3 Modified BNF description of CMENU Specification Language *(continued)*

```
<text> :=
    "<ascii-string>"  |
    '<ascii-string>'  |
         <no-space-string>

<item_defn> :=
    ITEM [<identifier>] : [<text>]
    [<item-option>] *
    <action-code>

<item-option> :=
    NEXTITEM
        {
            <identifier> |
            FIRST  |
            LAST  |
            NEXT
        }  |
    TEXT <text> |
    HELP <text>  |
    PATH <text> |
    PROMPT  |
    NOPROMPT  |
    PAUSE  |
    NOPAUSE  |
    NOPRECLEAR  |
    PRECLEAR

<action-code> :=
    ACTION  <text> |
    EXIT |
    LMENU <identifer>  |
    EMENU <text>

<ascii-string> := string containing any ASCII characters,
    delimited by either single (') or double (") quotes.
    Line continuation is NOT permitted.

<no-space-string> := string without quotes, containing no
    whitespace characters whatsoever. Terminated by first
    whitespace character.
```

Figure 8.3 Modified BNF description of CMENU Specification Language *(continued)*

```
Notes:
The <text> displayed for any one item may be specified
    either as an <item-option> (the TEXT clause) or
    immediately following the colon after the ITEM
    declaration. Exactly ONE of these methods must be used
    for each item in the menu file.

 Wherever a separator is necessary to delimit tokens, the
    characters ';' and ',' are both valid separators along
    with the usual whitespace characters (space, tab
    and newline.)
```

menu, they control screen processing for the entire menu (but not for any sub-menus that might be invoked). The available menu options are:

path	defines the default path for all action items in the menu
escape, *noescape*	tells whether to allow shell escapes
spacing	sets vertical spacing between items (single or double)
columns	tells number of horizontal columns to be used (1-6).

Code supporting the compilation of a text alignment option is present, but currently there is no runtime support for this option. There didn't seem any need for it. In case someone wants to add customized options to CMENU, I've left the code in as a template for work on such extensions.

After all desired menu options have been specified, the item definitions follow. Each item definition begins with an *item* clause, consisting of the keyword *item*, an optional item identifier, an optional colon, and an optional text string. The text string is only optional because the item text may alternatively be specified in its own *text* clause later in the item definition.

Not all components of the item clause are completely optional. If there is no item identifier but the text appears directly in the item clause, then a colon must separate the *item* keyword and the text string. This keeps the text string from getting parsed as an item identifier. When both an identifier and item text are present, the colon may be omitted.

The only strict requirement for each item definition, other than the item clause itself, is an action clause. The action clause must be one of the following:

action	execute a system command, or set of commands
lmenu	run a local menu (one in the same compiled unit)
emenu	run an external menu (separate compiled unit)
exit	return to the previous menu, if none, exit.

A menu does not require an *exit* action, because the user may directly exit a menu anytime via the *e* or *x* runtime keystroke commands. Displaying the *exit* option on the screen with other menu items can sometimes be useful. I've included the *exit* action code to provide that capability.

Before or after the action code some item options also may appear. Many of these item options have default behaviors that apply in the absence of explicit directions. Such defaults are hardwired at *rmenu* compile time by definitions in the *rmenu.h* header file. They may be chosen to suit the specific requirements of your user environment. Any item options stated explicitly in a CMENU specification always override the defaults. These are the available item options:

text	if the text isn't part of the item clause, a text clause must be provided
help	a help message, appearing only when the highlight bar is on the associated item
path	a full pathname overrides the default path; a relative pathname is appended onto the default path
prompt, *noprompt*	controls whether the system pauses for a keystroke following termination of an action item

pause, *nopause*	equivalent to *prompt/noprompt* above (I couldn't decide which terms were clearer, so I left them both in.)
preclear, *nopreclear*	controls whether an explicit screen clear occurs before execution of an action item. (I've never needed this, but perhaps someone else might.)
nextitem	tells where to send the highlight after the current item has been executed. Options are:

first	to the first item in the menu
last	to the last item in the menu
next	to the next item in sequence
<ident>	to the item with the given identifier.

If no *nextitem* clause is present, the highlight bar remains on the item just run.

The *path* string, if specified, causes a *cd* command to be prepended to the action string when running under a UNIX variant. If running under DOS, then both a *cd* and a drive selection operation are performed. This ensures that the named drive/directory is made current before the associated action statement executes.

Under UNIX, the *action* clause (possibly with prepended *cd* statement) is passed directly to a *system()* call. DOS does not support multiple commands on a single command line as UNIX does, but some special processing supports compound statements under DOS. This code begins by scanning the action text for semicolons. If it finds any, it breaks the action text into a set of individual subcommands as delimited by the semicolons. Each subcommand is then processed by an independent *system()* call. This allows several DOS commands to be chained together in a single *action* clause text string.

Upon completion of all listed actions, the original drive and path are restored under DOS. Under UNIX, this isn't necessary, because a child shell cannot alter the parent's current directory.

An item definition implicitly ends when either another item clause or an *endmenu* keyword is encountered.

CMENU Language Minutiae

That sums up the high level structure CMENU language. There remain a few syntactic details to mention before moving on.

Tokens in the CMENU language are delimited by one or more of the following: any whitespace (space, tab or newline), **;** (semicolon) or **,** (comma) characters. Figures 8.2 and 8.3 illustrate the format I use. There is, however, no reason (syntactically) why you couldn't create something to rival Don Libes's "Obfuscated C Code" winners if you wished. (In **The C Users Journal**, Don Libes published a series of columns showing how badly a program can abuse syntax rules and still compile successfully.)

The parser considers a string to be any sequence of printable characters that is neither a keyword nor contains any whitespace. Strings are legal as the operand of a *path*, *text*, or *action* clause, and as labels when needed. Single or double quotes may be used to delimit a string and, except in the case of labels, it is prudent to do so. The quotes, however, are not strictly required if the string contains no whitespace. I have, in a rush, written lines such as

```
action mail
```

with only a token amount of guilt (sorry) for omitting the quotes around mail. Within a string, all characters are taken literally. The backslash character (\) is no exception. There is no provision for specifying control characters. There is only one restriction on allowable character codes within a string: single and double quote characters cannot both appear within the same string. If you need to include double quotes within a string, delimit that string with single quotes (and vice versa).

If your editor can generate control characters, you can put them into CMENU strings. In practice, however, I've never run across the need to insert a nonprintable character into any CMENU text string.

Identifiers, used to assign labels to menus and items, follow the same naming rules as C variables, with one exception: case is insignificant. Internally, all identifier names are represented by lowercase characters.

Any token beginning with a digit is parsed as the beginning of a decimal integer value (and as the end, because meaningful values are all single digit here), appropriate only as the operand to either the *spacing* or *columns* options.

Finally, the # character (except inside a quoted string) denotes a comment. All characters from # to the end of the line are ignored. A line may begin with #.

The Saga of Pathname Delimiters

After years of programming in C under DOS, I still occasionally forget to double up the backslashes in pathname strings. For example, I may have a statement at the top of my C program that looks something like:

```
#define PATH "c:\foo\bar"
```

The compiler sees a string containing *c:*, a formfeed, *oo*, a backspace, and *ar*. This is clearly not the intended result. What I really meant to write was:

```
#define PATH "c:\\foo\\bar"
```

This kind of goof draws no compilation errors. Often, it isn't until after I've become thoroughly confused and fired up the debugger that I find the error. To allow the use of the single backslash character in CMENU source files and avoid the need for the double backslash notation, I decided that the backslash character would not have any special meaning in the CMENU specification language. As described above in the section on strings, there is no notation for escape sequences and single backslashes in pathnames are taken literally.

While DOS uses the backslash (\) to delimit subdirectories in pathnames, UNIX systems use the forward slash (/). The CMENU language supports the use of the forward slash (/) to delimit pathnames under DOS as well. The *rmenu* program processes all DOS pathname strings through a function named *trans_slash()* (Listing 8.11, lines 94-112) to convert forward slashes into backslashes. This reduces the amount of revision required to move a CMENU specification between DOS and UNIX systems.

To allow the forward slash character to appear in system commands (for example, as part of an option string to a DOS application program), action text is not processed by *trans_slash()*. A pathname written with forward slashes is acceptable in a DOS *path* statement, but will not work in a DOS *action* clause.

The result is the following rule of thumb: under DOS, to be absolutely safe always use backslashes. If you prefer to use forward slashes, then use them only in *path* clauses, never in an *action* clause.

A Sample Menu System

Figures 8.4 and 8.5 represent a small scale menu system illustrating most of CMENU's features. I've arbitrarily chosen a UNIX based example, but a DOS version would not be much different.

In *t.mnu* (Figure 8.4), the main menu has no identifier label (acceptable for the initial menu in a file), allows shell escapes, and is to be displayed with double spacing on the screen. There are nine items in this main menu.

The first item illustrates the automatic prompting feature of CMENU that is in effect when the *DEF_PROMPT* symbol (to be covered later in the *rmenu* section) is set to *ON_ERROR*. This causes *rmenu*, in the absence of an explicit *prompt* or *noprompt* option, to prompt after an action has been completed if, and only if, the status returned by that action is nonzero. In this example, a prompt is issued only if the user typed an *e* in response to the prompt displayed by the *test.sh* shell script (Figure 8.6). Upon return from *test.sh*, the highlight bar moves over to the item labeled *"zot"* below.

DOS systems do not provide standardized support for direct return values from system calls. Therefore, the *ON_ERROR* option for the *DEF_PROMPT* feature is only meaningful under UNIX. Under DOS, *DEF_PROMPT* may be set to either *YES* or *NO*. Individual menu items may always override that default by including the *prompt* or *noprompt* options.

The second item in the main menu calls up an external menu, *t2.mnc*, located in subdirectory *test*. The item path is given relatively (that is, no leading / character or, if it were under DOS, no drive letter either). The path, therefore, is treated as a subdirectory of the current default menu path. Be-

Figure 8.4 t.mnu test system

```
#
# t.mnu (compiles into t.mnc):
# Top level menu for CMENU test system. To test this menu,
# start in a test directory /u/myname/menu, and
# put the command script "test.sh" into the this directory.
# Then create a subdirectory named "/u/myname/menu/test"
# and put the  object file for menu t2 (t2.mnc) in it.
#

menu:
    title "The MAIN Menu"       # menu title appears at top
    escape                      # allow shell escapes
    spacing 2                   # double space the entries

    item:
        "Run test.sh"
        help 'next item is "zot"'
        action "test.sh"        # after the "speed" program runs,
        nextitem zot            # item "zot" (below) is highlighted

    item:
        "Run External Menu t2"
        path "test"             # run menu "t2", found in
        emenu "t2"              # subdirectory "test".

    item:
        "run a Unix shell"
        action "exec sh"        # most efficient with "exec"

    item:
        "run shell, no exec."   # creates an extra process.
        action sh               # (note: quotes not really needed)

    item zot:
        'ITEM "Zot": list the directory (in reverse chron. order)'
        help 'this is a help line for #5, "ZOT"'
        action "ls -t"
        prompt                  # prompt user before continuing

    item
        text "Do a long directly listing (no prompt)"
        help "the next item should be zot"
        action "l"
        nextitem zot

```

Figure 8.4 t.mnu test system *continued*

```
    item
        text "GO TO MENU BAR"   # invoke a locally defined menu
        lmenu bar

    item
        text "filler"           # clone this entry several times
        action "ls"             # to see automatic multiple columns

    item
        text "filler"           # clone this entry several times
        action "ls"             # to see automatic multiple columns
endmenu


menu bar:
  title "This is local menu BAR.  shell escpaes won't work."
  noescape
  path "/usr/bin"

    item
        text "here is the first item of menu BAR"
        action "ls"; prompt     # semi OK as separator

    item
        text "here is the next item of menu BAR"
        action "ls" prompt      # so is a space

    item
        text "here is the LAST item of the menu BAR (with help)"
        help "this is help for the LAST item of menu BAR"
        action "ls"
endmenu
```

Figure 8.5 t2.mnu second test system

```
#
# Second test menu: t2.mnu (compiles into t2.mnc)
#

menu foo:
    title "The MAIN Test Menu for my SECOND menu file"

    item fraz:
        text "This is item FRAZ: run the pwd program (next is zot)"
        help "This is a HELP line for item 1 - next item is zot"
        action "pwd"
        prompt
        nextitem zot

    item:
       text "This is item #2: run the editor on file foo (next is FRAZ)"
        action "e foo"
        nextitem fraz

    item zot:
        text "item ZOT: list the directory (prompt)"
        help "this is a help line for #2 "
        action "dir"
        prompt

    item text "GO TO MENU #2"
        lmenu bar

endmenu


menu bar:
  title "This is the SECOND local menu in the SECOND test file"

    item text "here is the first item of the 2nd menu"
    action "dir"

    item text "here is the SECOND item of the 2nd menu (with help)"
    help "this is help for that second item of menu #2"
    action "dir"
endmenu
```

Figure 8.6 test return status

```
#!/bin/sh
# Unix script to test return status feature of CMENU
#

cat <<END
This is test.sh running, to test the error status
feature of the CMENU system.

If you type 'e' to return an error status, rmenu should
prompt before returning to the menu. Otherwise, no prompt
should appear issued:

Press just return for normal exit,
or else press 'e' and then the Return key:
END

read char
[ "$char" = e ] && exit 1
exit 0
```

cause no *path* clause was specified in the menu options section, the default menu path is the current working directory at the moment of *rmenu* invocation.

The third and fourth items illustrate different ways to invoke an action. Using the *exec* command (UNIX only) saves a process.

Item *zot* (lines 34-38) contains help text. This text is displayed on the screen only when the highlight bar is on that item. To display the double quotes around the word *"zot"*, the entire help text is delimited by single quotes.

Finally, the *prompt* command in menu item *zot* causes a prompt to be issued after the action is executed. This forces the user to press a key before the information left on the screen is erased and the menu screen is redisplayed.

The next item illustrates how *nextitem* specifications may be backward references as well as forward references.

The next item invokes the local menu named *bar* at the end of the file. The last few items are filler to illustrate what happens when the total number of items exceeds the capacity of the default screen arrangement. Since there are eighteen lines available for item information in the standard twenty-four line screen setup, double spacing the items means that only nine would fit in the single column format. If additional menu items were created by cloning the filler items, for example, then *rmenu* would automatically select two column mode to preserve the double spacing specified in line 13. If the spacing were set to one or omitted entirely, *rmenu* would select single spacing mode and remain in single column mode. There is a function in *rmenu* devoted entirely to determining the appropriate screen arrangement for any given menu. That function uses a heuristic based upon the number of items in the menu and any explicit *spacing* and *column* directives given. I'll cover this, in gory detail, when discussing the *rmenu* program later in the chapter.

Following the *endmenu* keyword, the second local menu, *bar*, is defined. The local menu options serve to disable shell escapes and set the default path for actions in this menu to */usr/bin*. Setting a path this way merely generates a *cd* statement before running an action. A named action, therefore, need not reside in the directory specified in a *path* clause, as long as the program can be found somewhere along the default system path. In many system paths, the current directory is searched first. If this is the case on your system, any executable commands in the directory named by a *path* clause take precedence over similarly named commands residing elsewhere along the system path.

There is nothing shockingly new about the three items in the *bar* menu. I used semicolons instead of newline to separate some clauses, to show that it's permissible.

The second menu file, *t2.mnu* (Figure 8.5) also lacks any particularly interesting features. It is there to complete the illustration of a two file menu system. The default path for all actions is the same as the default path of the calling menu. In this case, the path is specified by the second item in the first menu of the *t.mnu* file because menu *foo* contains no explicit *path* clause to override that default path.

One final note. An action clause may contain explicit commands to change the path, effectively superseding all previous default paths. An extraneous *cd* command may be executed if a *path* clause is given and an explicit *cd* command is present within the action text. Such extra *cd* commands generate a negligible quantity of CPU overhead and may be ignored.

Common Menu Data Structures

There are three header files in the CMENU package. The master header file, *cmenu.h*, contains the symbolic constant definitions (*#define* statements) controlling common data structures and operating system specific code for both *cmenu* and *rmenu* programs. *cmenu.h* is included by all program modules, so it performs the inclusion of the standard C header file, *stdio.h*.

Besides including *cmenu.h*, the *cmenu* and *rmenu* programs have their personal header files, named *ccmenu.h* and *rcmenu.h* respectively. Both header files use the symbolic constants and data types defined in *cmenu.h* to build the actual data structures needed to perform their specific tasks.

We'll look first at the common, elementary structures defined in *cmenu.h*, and later examine how *cmenu* and *rmenu* build upon them.

The Basics

As noted earlier, *cmenu* and *rmenu* share the intermediate *.mnc* file format. Consequently, most of *cmenu.h* (Listing 8.1) is devoted to declarations of the structure types used in that format. The two major structures are named *MENU* and *ITEM*. Within these two structure types, string elements are all defined as *char* arrays (as opposed to pointers), Boolean elements have type *BOOL*, (really just *char*), logical and multiple choice elements have type *char*, and numeric elements have type *int* (though they would never be negative and probably never exceed a value of 255).

The logical elements have three possible values: *YES*, *NO* and *DEFAULT* (as opposed to the Booleans, which can only be *TRUE* or *FALSE*). *YES* and *NO* values appear when an explicit option was written for that element in a menu or item definition. The value *DEFAULT* signifies that no explicit option was written, so the *rmenu* program performs the actions dictated by a set of default action definitions, specified in the *rcmenu.h* header file.

If a text element is not specified, it is represented as the zero-length string (first character is a *'\0'*). If a numeric element is omitted, the value inserted is *DEFAULT*, as described above.

A *MENU* (actually, an object of type *struct menu*) contains the following elements:

title	the menu title, displayed at the top of a menu screen
path	the default action path for all items (absolute or relative)
nitems	the number of items present in the menu
align	(not used)
columns	number of columns specified for the item display
spacing	spacing specified for the column display
widest	length of the widest item text (in characters)
escape	whether shell escapes are permitted

An ITEM (really *struct item*) contains:

text	the text to be put up to represent that item (may be truncated if the space is needed for multiple columns)
path	the path for the item (absolute or relative)
action	the text of the command(s) to be submitted to a *system()* call when the item is chosen to be run, or the name of an external menu if the action is *emenu*.
help	the text of any help info, put up on the screen when the item is under the highlight bar (never truncated)
pre_clear	*(logical)*: to clear the screen before the action
post_clear	*(logical)*: to clear the screen after the action
prompt	*(logical)*: to pause before returning to menu
acttyp	*(multi-choice)*: tells what brand of action to perform. Choices: a system command, local menu, external menu, or exit (represented by the ACT_* symbolic constants)

lmenunum	if the *acttyp* is *ACT_LMENU*, this specifies the index value of the specified local menu in the menu table
nextcode	*(multi-choice)*: tells how the next item is to be determined, choices are: first, last, next, or direct (*NXT_** symbols)
nextitem	if nextcode is *NXT_DIRECT*, this contains the index of the next item to be highlighted.

cmenu.h does not specify how *MENU* and *ITEM* objects are combined into bigger data structures because *cmenu* and *rmenu* use different combinations. First, I'll focus on the *cmenu* program and its data structures.

The *.mnc* Format

The format of compiled *.mnc* files is summarized by the comments in lines 237-258 of Listing 8.3. Remember, this is a binary format, not an ASCII one.

The first item in an *.mnc* file is an integer value that tells how many (local) menus are defined in the file. Immediately after this count is the *MENU* structure for the first menu, followed by the *ITEM* structures for each item in the menu. The number of items in each menu is part of the information stored in the associated *MENU* header. There is no need to store separate item counts in the file format.

That's it. The *.mnc* format is fairly simple; generating it is more complex. Now the real fun begins.

At Last, *cmenu*

The *cmenu* program is essentially a big state machine. It's purpose is to scan through the sequential ASCII token stream of one or more CMENU specification files, and produce a correctly compiled *.mnc* output file for each input file.

At the heart of *cmenu*'s operation is a structure named *keywords*, defined in *ccmenu.h* (Listing 8.2, lines 190-228). *keywords* defines two attributes for each possible keyword token. The tokens represent each symbol, keyword or special condition (such as *EOF)* that the CMENU language recognizes.

The first attribute, *keyword*, is the text of the keyword itself. For tokens that have no printing text associated with them, I've contrived some special identifying sequences (see lines 191 and 223-226) that assisted me during interactive debugging of the *cmenu* program.

The other attribute is a pointer to the processing function called when the associated token shows up in the input stream. All token processing functions are named *do_whatever*, where *whatever* is the name of the token. There are also additional *do_whatever* functions not tied to a particular token, but called occasionally under special circumstances.

An enumeration constant list (lines 43-58) defines a symbolic name for each keyword. These symbolic names appear in the same order as their corresponding *keywords* table entries. Thus, the symbolic name for each token has a value equal to that token's physical index position in the *keywords* array. Because the symbolic values are used to represent tokens during the parsing of input text, this arrangement has a side effect that facilitates debugging of the *cmenu* program: you can keep a running display of the ASCII string associated with the most recently parsed token by placing the expression

```
keywords[token].keyword
```

into a watch window.

For compilers that do not support enumeration constants, the old fashioned way of defining a set of sequential symbolic values is shown in lines 60-99. This section of conditionally compiled code is used instead of the *enum* section when __STDC__ (a predefined symbolic constant indicating ANSI compliance) is undefined.

There are a couple of key global state variables that describe which portion of a menu definition is currently being processed. The first of these is named *in_menu*, a simple Boolean variable telling whether a menu definition is being processed. *in_menu* remains *FALSE* until the first menu clause is encountered. From that point on, *in_menu* is *TRUE* between each menu clause and *endmenu* keyword, *FALSE* if not.

The other critical state variable is *in_item*. This one is set to *TRUE* every time the first item clause of a menu is encountered, and reset to *FALSE* (along with *in_menu*) each time *endmenu* is processed.

Both state variables are initialized to *FALSE* near the start of *do_menu()*. Thereafter, their values toggle as necessary under control of the appropriate token processing functions.

With the *keywords* structure and state variables all in place, *cmenu*'s main processing loop can be simple. Lines 71-81 of *cmenu1.c* (Listing 8.3) make up this entire loop. The code relies, however, on the token scanning function *gettok()* to parse the next little piece of the input stream into a token value and associated detail values.

If the next token is a string, for example, then *gettok()* returns the token value *T_STRING*. The actual text of the string is stuffed into a global character array named *tparam*.

The main loop can prevent each token processing function from needing to perform one common error checking test by assuring that the *menu* keyword is the next token scanned, when not currently within a menu (i.e., *in_menu* is *FALSE*). Whenever any token other than *menu* is encountered outside of a menu definition, an error is reported (line 75) and processing of the current file terminates.

No other error condition is as universally easy to detect; any further error diagnostics are relegated to the token processing functions. Lines 78-80 dispatch control to the appropriate processing function and, upon return, check for the possibility of a fatal error before continuing on to the next token.

Information Economy

Now return to the *ccmenu.h* header file and consider some new data structures.

The CMENU language supports forward references in both menu and item label references. We need some way of keeping track of which menus and items have been defined thus far, which ones have not, and where those references came from so they can be resolved or diagnosed as unresolved reference errors.

There is also the matter of the menu and item identifier names. There is no place for identifiers in the *.mnc* file format. By the time the *.mnc* file is written, each symbolic reference to a menu or item has been resolved into an integer index value that allows direct access to the menu or item desired through a simple indexing operation.

A set of data structures is needed containing the elementary *MENU* and *ITEM* structures as subsets of larger structures. These larger structures add the additional pieces of data necessary to support the compilation process, but still allow the essential *MENU* and *ITEM* information to be extracted in the required elementary format when the time comes to write an output file.

The *typedef*s for just such a set of incremental structures can be found in lines 27-37 of Listing 8.2. The first definition, *IINFO*, is a structure containing two elements: a name string and an *INFO* structure. The second *typedef*, *MINFO*, is a structure containing a name string, a *Processed* flag to indicate completion of menu processing, a *MENU* structure describing the properties of the menu, and an array of pointers to the *IINFO* structures making up the individual items associated with the menu.

Much trial and error resulted in the decision to use an array of pointers to structures in the *Items* array, but actual instances for the other structure elements (*Item* and *Menu*). My goal was to find an ideal balance for this application between memory efficiency and coding clarity. In C, unfortunately, those two properties tend to unfold in inversely proportional quantities within any sufficiently complex application. Finding the right balance can be a challenging task.

To make efficient use of available memory when the size of an array is not fixed at compile time, we need dynamic memory allocation to obtain exactly the needed quantity of memory (and no more) at run time. When the storage for an object is allocated dynamically, then pointers must be used to access the data. Manipulating pointers to objects is usually more complex than directly manipulating the objects themselves.

If more than one level of dynamic arrays are involved, things get twisted. In my first design for *cmenu*, I attempted to use a data structure that had multiple levels of dynamically allocated arrays. (Remember the tricky dynamically allocated arrays from the Mini-Database System in Chapter 3? That was only one level!) It was a mess. I learned, however, that it was still possible to run CMENU in a small model memory space without such excessive use of dynamic allocation tricks. Most of the memory goes to hold *ITEM* information, so dynamic allocation can be restricted to only the memory needed for *ITEM* structures. The resulting code is much easier to document and understand than my earlier multilayered dynamic scheme.

Each *MINFO* structure applies to a single menu only, so there is an array of *MAX_MENUS MINFO* structures defined in line 235 (Listing 8.2) as *MInfo*. The dimension of *MAX_MENUS* limits the number of structures that may be defined within a single source module. If long menu source files give you memory problems, reducing the value of *MAX_MENUS* offers quick memory relief (but might make it necessary to split some large *.mnu* files into smaller pieces).

The final major data structure in the *cmenu* program is the forward reference table *fwd_refs*, defined in lines 241-245. This table performs the task of tracking forward references to named items in a menu. There is, however, no such corresponding table needed to handle forward menu references, because the order of items within a menu is significant. They should appear on the screen in the same order as their specification in the source file. But how is the compiler to behave when a reference is made to an, as yet, undefined item, one that could appear anywhere from the current point in the menu source to the end of the menu? Does the compiler immediately create an item record reserved for the future item and add it to the array of items? If so, the physical order of the items gets messed up. (This isn't an obvious side effect. My first stab at this code utilized an *IINFO Processed* flag similar to the *MINFO* flag of the same name, without taking the aforementioned phenomenon into consideration. Surprise, I couldn't get forward references to work!)

Rather than creating an *IINFO* structure when a forward reference in encountered, the present scheme simply registers the reference into the *fwd_refs* table (including the line number of the reference, for diagnostic purposes), and goes on processing more menu items. Whenever a new labeled item definition is encountered, *cmenu* makes a quick check to see if any references have been made to that item label. If found, the references are resolved by copying the index number of the new item definition into the location whose address was saved in the forward reference table. If any unresolved references remain at the end of the menu definition, the precise line number of the reference can even be supplied in the error diagnostic. The code that handles this is not very complicated, but it is immensely effective. If I were smarter, I would have written it this way in the first place, (but I would have missed another opportunity to play with Turbo Debugger).

The remaining definitions in *ccmenu.h* are for miscellaneous scratch pointers, global variables and constants. Now we'll journey through the rest of *cmenu's* procedural code.

Doing Files

cmenu's main function passes the name of each file to be processed, in sequence, to the *dofile()* function.

dofile() (beginning at line 40 of Listing 8.3) processes a CMENU specification file from start to finish. The first few lines chop off the *.mnu* extension in case the user included it in the filename. Two copies are then made of the base filename. One (*src_name*) gets the source file extension appended onto it, and the other (*obj_name*) gets the object file extension.

If opening the source file succeeds, lines 62-65 initialize some global modes and counters, and the file is entirely processed within the token loop described earlier.

After an *EOF* is encountered and the main loop terminates, the file is closed and several checks for possible error conditions are performed. In line 85 we make sure that at least one menu was defined, or there wouldn't be much point in writing an output file.

Lines 88-93 check if the last menu terminated correctly. If the value of global *in_menu* is *TRUE*, then there was an *endmenu* keyword missing. At this point, we also call the *itemcheck()* function to see if the last item in the last menu was similarly incomplete (an item isn't complete until both text and action clauses for that item have been processed).

The last piece of error checking is performed in lines 95-101, a test for unresolved forward menu references. The *MInfo* array is scanned for entries having a *Processed* flag still set to *FALSE*. Menu entries are created as soon as they are first referenced (unlike item entries, for the reasons given above). It is, therefore, possible that a menu entry referenced in an *lmenu* statement was never defined or the identifier was misspelled somewhere. Either way we get an unresolved menu reference.

Finally, if there weren't any fatal errors encountered, the object file for the current menu is written to disk and *dofile()* returns.

Utilities, Utilities

The remaining functions in *cmenu1.c* provide support for creating entries in the menu and item info tables, searching for those entries by label name, checking for item completeness, writing the output file, string matching, and reporting errors and warnings.

Menu info table management is performed by *create_menu()* and *find_menu()*. Because *MENU* structures are stored directly, there is no need to worry about memory allocation when creating a new *MINFO* entry. *create_menu()* defines a local *MINFO* structure, initializes it appropriately, and returns it by value to the calling routine. To find a given *MINFO* entry, *find_menu()* iterates through the *MInfo* array, comparing the name of each registered entry with the name string supplied. When a match occurs, a pointer to the structure having the matching name is returned.

The item info table is managed by *create_item()* and *find_item()*. *find_item()* works like *find_menu()*. Because *IINFO* structures are stored by reference (to reduce memory requirements), *create_item()* must allocate a memory block for the new *IINFO* structure and return a pointer to that block. Provided there wasn't any problem with obtaining the memory, both the *IINFO* structure and its member *INFO* structure get initialized with all the default values appropriate to an unprocessed item entry.

The *itemcheck()* function is called from a few places in *cmenu* to make sure both required portions of an item definition, the text and an action clause, have been specified.

When a menu specification file has been completely processed and no fatal errors occurred, the *write_file()* function is called to create the output file on disk. After creating the output filename and opening the file for writing (in binary mode), the first thing *write_file()* actually writes is the value of the global menu count, *n_menus*. Each menu is then written to the file in a format consisting of the *MENU* structure first, then each associated *ITEM* structure. There is no need to write an explicit item count for each menu because that information is already part of the *MENU* structure, and *rmenu* can obtain that value dynamically when the *.mnc* file is loading for execution. To insure portability across machines with different storage requirements for various variable types, all reads and writes involving the *.mnc* file are performed using the *sizeof* operator to determine how many bytes to transfer. Even writing a simple integer value, such as the menu count (line 273), should employ *sizeof* rather than a constant byte count value such as 2 or 4.

After each item is written to disk, its memory block is freed (line 299). If there are many menu definitions in a single menu specification file, then many blocks of item memory will end up having been allocated and freed repetitively. Since, however, *cmenu* is only run occasionally, the extra overhead this repetition entails isn't enough to have a noticeable effect on performance.

In *rmenu*, realtime efficiency is far more critical because many processes may be active simultaneously. (I often see between ten and fifteen *rmenu* processes running concurrently at the office.) Later we'll see how *rmenu* employs a slightly more complex allocation strategy to avoid the memory thrashing problem.

Error Reporting

The next set of functions in *cmenu1.c* are *warning()*, *error()*, and *fatalerr()* (lines 307-387). These represent variations on a single theme: display a diagnostic message on the standard error device (usually the user's terminal). All three functions take a variable number of arguments, allowing format conversions like *printf()* to be supported. Since pre-ANSI and post-ANSI C differ in their provisions for functions that accept a variable number of arguments, I found it necessary to include two different versions of the starting sequence in each of the three error reporting functions.

ANSI C function headers allow the specification of ellipses (...) to indicate a variable number of arguments in a function header or prototype. The macros *va_list* and *va_start*, used in the processing of the variable length argument list, are taken from the <*stdarg.h*> standard header file (see line 16).

Pre-ANSI C, on the other hand, cannot handle ellipses in function definitions. Before the existence of ellipses and <*stdarg.h*>, functions taking a variable number of arguments were processed with the macros defined in <*stdarg.h*>'s predecessor, <*varargs.h*>. <*varargs.h*> contains alternate versions of the macros *va_list* and *va_start*, plus an additional macro named *va_alist* that is used in function headers as the placeholder for optional arguments.

The usages of *<varargs.h>* and *<stdarg.h>* differ only up to (and including) the appearance of the *va_start* macro. After that, the methods are equivalent, so the conditional portions of the three error reporting functions end at that point.

Each diagnostic function passes the values of its first three arguments to *fprintf()* to print out the supplied diagnostic information. This text is always preceded by the name and current line number of the source file involved. The only difference between the three functions is in the way they affect the global error flags. *warning()* sets no flags. *error()* sets only *err_flag*. *fatalerr()* sets both *err_flag* and *fatal*. Setting the *fatal* flag causes processing of the current source file to be terminated immediately upon return to the main processing loop, while *err_flag* is sampled only after the current source file has been completely processed (without fatal errors) to determine if an object file should be written.

String Matching

The *matchkey()* function searches the keyword table to see if a keyword exists matching the given string, and returns the token value for that keyword if a match is found.

The *strstr()* function tests if one given string is a subset of a second given string. *strstr()* is supplied in case your library does not already include it. Compilation of *strstr()* is conditionally controlled by the *NEEDSTR* symbolic constant defined in the makefile.

Parsing the Input Stream

The two major components of *cmenu* remain to be discussed: token parsing, and token processing. Because tokens must be recognized before they can be processed, I'll begin with a description of the token parsing process. I'll then tackle token processing to tie everything else together.

Tokens are the basic syntactic objects manipulated by *cmenu*. Each token is represented by an integer value, sometimes in conjunction with the value of an auxiliary variable. If the token represents a keyword or special condition, then the integer value alone is sufficient to qualify it. If the token represents a string or a numeric value, then the token value *T_STRING* or *T_VALUE* in conjunction with the text in global array *tparam* (for strings), or the integer value of the global *vparam* (for values) is needed to fully qualify the token. You'll find definitions for *tparam* and *vparam* in *ccmenu.h* (Listing 8.2, lines 253-254). The token values are defined in lines 41-99.

The token parsing code resides in *cmenu3.c* (Listing 8.5). There are three functions in this source file, two of which are called from other parts of the program: *gettok()* to get the next token, and *ungettok()* to "unget" a token. The last function, *getword()*, is called only by *gettok()*.

getword(), the Workhorse

getword() does all the grunt work in the token parsing process. It recognizes and skips over comments and whitespace, keeps track of the current line number, recognizes both quoted and unquoted text strings, and maps unquoted text strings into lowercase. *getword()* returns a pointer to a statically allocated text string containing the text of the next token from the input file without making any attempt to distinguish a keyword string from straight text (that job is handled by *gettok()*). Starting in line 126 (of Listing 8.5), *getword()* checks for all the special cases just mentioned. Newlines cause the *lineno* global to be incremented, while other whitespace is ignored (including commas and semicolons). The only nonalphabetic keyword, the colon, requires a special case. This simplifies the code to recognize other tokens (lines 146-147).

Comments are handled by *getword()* in lines 149-162: all characters after the leading # are ignored until a newline is encountered (or *EOF*, should the trailing newline be missing). The line count is then incremented.

Lines 164-200 process quoted strings. First, the *quoted_text* flag is set to *TRUE* so *gettok()* will know a string has been found. Then the string is collected into the *tok* array, with appropriate action being taken when certain special characters are encountered. Because multiline strings are not supported, a newline in a string is treated as an error, as is an *EOF* condition. If a double quote is encountered, the string is terminated with a zero byte and a pointer to the string is returned to *gettok()*.

Finally, an unquoted string (probably a keyword or an identifier, but possibly a short action string or a pathname) is processed in lines 202-211. Any of the usual separators or a colon terminate such a string. While it is being collected up into the *tok* array, the string is converted to lowercase. As soon as an illegal character is found, it is "ungotten" and a pointer to *tok* is returned.

Back to *gettok()* and *ungettok()*

At the top of *cmenu3.c* (lines 14-19), several items of static data are defined to support the unget feature for tokens. This is a necessary feature for a simple language processor like *cmenu*, because in some cases the code must scan past the end of a clause to determine that the clause has come to an end. The unget feature allows any token processing function to give back the extra token. Then, next time the *gettok()* function is called to get a token from the input stream, the ungotten token will be returned again. Only a single level of ungetting is needed to process the CMENU syntax.

When *gettok()* is called it first checks for an active ungotten token. If found, all the saved static token detail variables are copied into their global counterparts and *gettok()* returns the saved token value.

If there wasn't an active ungotten token, it is time to get a new one. The global detail variables *tparam* and *vparam* are cleared, and *getword()* is called to fetch the next syntactic object from the input stream. Lines 85-98 handle the easy kinds of tokens: *EOF*, quoted string, colon, or simple reserved word (in the case of quoted text, the text needs to be copied into *tparam*). Lines 100-104 process integer values by setting *vparam* if a leading digit is detected and returning *T_VALUE*. If we reach line 105, the token is treated as an unquoted string: the text is copied into *tparam*, and *T_STRING* is returned.

The *ungettok()* function (lines 29-49) first checks to make sure there isn't already a token pushed back (there shouldn't ever be if the program is working correctly; this test was put here only to catch possible development bugs). Then all the token detail values are saved in the static variables.

Token Processing

The *cmenu* code discussed up to this point all plays a supporting role to the actual token processing functions in *cmenu2.c* (Listing 8.4). The call to each token processing function is placed indirectly through the function pointers stored in the *keywords* table. The dispatching takes place in the main processing loop in *cmenu1.c*.

As each token processing function receives control, it can count on the availability of certain information through global variables. We've already seen how most of these global variables are managed. There's one more, named *token*, that contains the most recently scanned token value (responsible for arrival at a particular function in *cmenu2*). This variable is assigned in the main processing loop, immediately before the dispatch is performed. We need to know this value, because some token processing functions can handle more than one token, and they examine the value of *token* to determine which token they have been called to process.

The Menu Clause

Starting at the beginning, the *do_menu()* function (Listing 8.4, line 20) handles the start of a menu definition. The first thing that happens is a check to see if the previous menu in the program was properly terminated with *endmenu*. If it wasn't, then *do_endmenu()* is called and a warning is issued. If it was just a missing *endmenu* statement, the compilation will still (begrudgingly) succeed.

do_menu() then checks for the existence of a menu label by calling *get-tok()* and seeing which token turns up next. If it is not a string, then no label was given. This is only tolerated at the start of the file, because the omission of a label in subsequent menus would prevent that menu from ever being accessible (via the *lmenu* action). If the first menu is missing a label, a dummy label is stuffed into *tparam*.

If the label is too long it is truncated (lines 38-43), and then a check is made to see if the name appeared previously. If not, then we have the simple case of a new definition, and lines 47-49 create an entry for it in the *MInfo* array.

If the name has been used before (i.e., there's already an entry in *MInfo* for it), then there are two possible explanations. Either it was used in a forward *lmenu* reference, which is legitimate, or the label has already been used in the definition of a previous menu, constituting an error (line 55). We can tell which case it is by examining the *Processed* flag associated with that *MInfo* entry.

When we get to line 57, *MIp* points to the *MInfo* entry for the new menu. We now need to modify a group of elements of the *Menu* structure that is itself an element of the *MInfo* entry. So, we assign the address of the *Menu* structure to the pointer *Mp*, and then initialize everything in the *Menu* structure through that pointer. *Mp* remains a valid pointer to that *Menu* structure after return from *do_menu()*; several other functions will take advantage of it.

After all the attendant mode and structure initialization, we check for a trailing colon in lines 68-69 and, if found, ignore it.

Menu Options

The next six functions (lines 75-257) deal with all the possible menu option statements that, if present, must appear before the initial item clause.

do_title() and *do_path()* are very similar, each verifying the existence of its required text string parameter, making sure the option hasn't appeared before, and stuffing the string into the appropriate element of the current *Menu* structure (*Mp* comes in handy here).

do_path() performs all the steps above, plus one more: it deletes any trailing path delimiter character (slash or backslash) found at the end of the path text. This prevents two consecutive path delimiter characters from appearing in a path string when incremental paths are glued together.

The *do_align()* function was originally intended to support alternative ways of aligning the item text on the screen. I later changed my mind about the usefulness that option and never taught *rmenu* how to recognize it. The *cmenu* code for processing the option remains, if someone thinks of a reason for *rmenu* to use it.

do_spacing() and *do_columns()* are similar to *do_title()* and *do_path()*, but they take an integer instead of a text string for their parameter. I don't think they require any further annotation.

The *do_escape()* function handles both the *escape* and *noescape* options, checking for the usual error conditions and then setting the *escape* flag in the *Menu* structure to either *YES* or *NO*. If this option does not appear, the default value for the escape flag ends up being *DEFAULT*, which has a very different meaning from both *YES* and *NO*.

The *do_endmenu()* function pulls clean-up duty after a menu definition. If no items were found, that merits an error message. The forward reference table is then checked to make sure all references have been resolved. If an unresolved reference is found, then a little shuffle-play is performed involving the global line number variable, *lineno*. This forces the error message function to report the line number where the unresolved reference was made, instead of the current line number.

Finally, global modes are reset in lines 284-287 with values indicating a "not in menu" status. The *Processed* flag is set to show that the menu has now been defined, and the number of items found is stashed away in the *Menu* structure (squeezing some final mileage out of old venerable *Mp*).

The Item Clause

There is a lot of parallelism between the set of functions that process item related statements and the set we just saw for handling menu related ones. I suppose one could even describe the relationship between menus and items as fractal, because the structure somewhat repeats itself. There is an item clause with an optional identifier, followed by a set of item options, some of which are required and some are optional. In the case of item definitions, however, there is no requirement that the optional clauses precede the required ones (the way menu options must precede all menu items).

There is no explicit keyword to mark the end of an item definition. The first thing, therefore, the *do_item()* function (lines 291-357) must do is check that the last item, if any, defined in the current menu included its required clauses. The call to *itemcheck()* in line 303 does this.

Next, we test if a label is attached to the item definition. If not, a dummy name is constructed; if so, the identifier name used is checked for legality in lines 311-326.

Lines 328-329 make sure that the label name has not been used before in the current menu. Even if a forward reference has been made to this label, it will not show up in a call to *find_item()* because the forward reference information has all been segregated into the *fwd_refs* table (to be examined shortly).

Now we can create an entry for the new item, and place a pointer to it in the *Items* array. The *create_item()* function (Listing 8.3, lines 160-192) allocates memory for the new item info structure, initializes its members, and returns a pointer to the structure. If there is a problem creating the array, *create_item()* returns *NULL* and the process is aborted.

Having survived to line 335, the global mode *in_item* is set and a handy *ITEM* pointer, *Ip*, is set to point to the *ITEM* structure element of the *IINFO* structure just created. *Ip* may then be used throughout the remainder of this item's processing.

Lines 338-340 resolve any possible forward references to the new item. The *fwd_refs* table is scanned for an entry whose name matches the new item's. If one is found, the *lmenunum* element of the item where the reference was made is set (indirectly, through the *refp* pointer) to reflect the new item's index value. This overwrites the previous item's *lmenunum* value of *UNDEF_FWD*, thereby resolving the forward reference.

The last part of the *do_item()* function checks to see if the item text is present as part of the item clause. To prevent ambiguity, I've required a colon to precede any item text included directly in an item clause. Without this restriction, the parser couldn't know if text found after the *item* keyword was meant to be a label or an item text string. At this point in *do_item()* (line 344), anything other than a colon terminates the item clause processing.

Even if a colon is spotted, there may not be any item text given. Lines 350-351 check for the item text and register it via *do_text2()* if present.

Item Options

The next six functions handle the various item options and the required action clause. By now the pattern of these token processing functions should be familiar. I'll skip the routine details and point out the highlights.

The *do_opts()* function handles a whole slew of trivial binary options by setting *Item* flags to values triggered directly by the option tokens. There are three functional categories processed by *do_opts()*: prompting, pre-clearing and post-clearing. Only one option from each of those three categories is permitted to appear within any one item definition. The flag associated with each category is initialized to the value *DEFAULT*. It keeps that value until the appropriate statement forces the value to either *YES* or *NO*.

The *do_nextitem()* function processes the *nextitem* clause, so the user may alter the menu system's flow of control. One of four variations must be used. The last is to supply a label for the next item to be highlighted. If the next token after *nextitem* is a string, then *find_item()* is called to see if the item has been defined. If it has, its index is inserted into the *nextitem* element of the *Item* structure and no forward referencing is involved. If *find_item()*

couldn't find it, lines 432-437 install the item reference into the forward reference table, for resolution when the item definition with the given label finally appears. If you missed it, see **The Item Clause** section above for related details.

If the screen text for the menu item was not specified in the item clause, it must appear in a subsequent *text* clause. The *do_text()* and *do_text2()* functions process this option. After *do_text()* has checked the basics, *do_text2()* tests whether the string is too long to store in the available space. If it's too long, a message is printed and no attempt is made to copy the string into the *ITEM* structure.

After copying a reasonable length string in through the *Ip* pointer, the flag named *widest* (in the *MENU* structure) is updated to reflect the length of the longest item text seen so far. This value will be used by *rmenu* when it comes time to decide how all the menu items will be arranged on the screen.

Springing Into Action

There must be exactly one action associated with each menu item, from a choice of four possibilities. The *do_action()* function is set to process all four actions, each using a different token sequence.

The *exit* action may be specified either with or without the *action* keyword preceding it. Both forms are legal.

The basic action clause is specified by the *action* keyword and a text string. The string represents an operating system command (or sequence of commands separated by semicolons). All *do_action()* does is copy the string (through *Ip*) into the *action* element of the current *ITEM* structure (line 527). The *emenu* action, which calls an external menu, is processed in the same way, except that the *acttyp* element of the *ITEM* structure is set to identify the *action* string as an external menu name rather than a command to be passed to the system's command interpreter.

The fourth type of action is the *lmenu* clause, specifying a local menu to run. If no menu by the given name is found in the file, a menu structure is created and added to the *MInfo* array, and the index number of the new menu entry is plugged into *lmenunum* element of the item being processed.

There is nothing new to say about the *do_help()* function, so I won't.

The final function in the module, *do_err()*, gets called whenever a keyword is encountered unexpectedly (for example when the *first* keyword is seen without a leading *nextitem*). In the keywords table array, any keyword that does not represent the beginning of a legitimate option sequence is assigned *do_err()* as its processing function. By calling the *fatalerr()* function to print its error message, *do_err()* forces compilation to be terminated immediately after the error message is printed, allowing the user to fix the syntax without having to deal with additional spurious error messages.

Intermission: *dmenu*

This concludes the *cmenu* tour. Before delving into *rmenu*, I'd like to introduce a little diagnostic utility named *dmenu*. I wrote this short program after eliminating the simple syntax errors from my initial stab at the *cmenu* code, but before *rmenu* was written. At that point, I needed a quick, easy way to examine *cmenu*'s output files for debugging purposes. *dmenu* reads an *.mnc* file and disassembles it into human readable form, providing a complete picture of a compilation job performed by *cmenu*. With the help of *dmenu*, I was able to debug *cmenu* quickly, without even needing to have *rmenu* available. The process of reading in an *.mnc* file is similar for both the *dmenu* and *rmenu* programs. Stay tuned for the discussion of the *rmenu* loading process.

The code for *dmenu.c* is shown in Listing 8.6.

Introducing *rmenu*

When a CMENU specification file has been successfully compiled by *cmenu*, the menu is ready to be run (or interpreted, to be more precise) by the *rmenu* program. Interpretation of intermediate code often carries a connotation of inefficiency. Perhaps this is based on many experiences with early BASIC interpreters that were inefficient when compared with compiled programs. Interpretation, however, can be implemented efficiently when

1) the primary objects of manipulation are addressed directly (as opposed to symbolically or associatively), and
2) the primary operations on those objects are I/O bound rather than computation intensive.

Based upon those criteria, I chose to implement the CMENU system as a pseudo-compiler/interpreter program pair. The *cmenu* menu compiler was the subject of the first part of this chapter. Now, we'll take a closer look at the *rmenu* interpreter.

rmenu Basic Operation: An Overview

From the user's perspective, *rmenu* runs a precompiled menu system made up of one or more menu specification files (having the filename extension *.mnc*). While any single *.mnc* file may contain more than one menu definition, it is always the first menu of the file named on the command line that appears on the user's screen at the start of an *rmenu* session. Other menus of the system, if any, can only be accessed by making the appropriate selections from the top level menu.

The command line syntax for invoking *rmenu* is:

```
rmenu [menufile]
```

menufile is the name of the *.mnc* file that is the root node of a compiled menu system (i.e., all other menus of the system may be accessed through that file). If the filename is omitted altogether, *rmenu* looks for a specification file named *menu.mnc* in the current directory. If found, it runs that file by default.

Once the root specification file has been found, the first menu contained therein is placed up on the screen.

The menu title appears at the top of the screen. The menu items are arranged in a rectangular array. The exact configuration depends upon the number of items present and the options specified in the menu definition. The items are numbered sequentially, and a highlight bar is placed on the first menu item. A prompt line at the bottom of the screen lists all the available commands and the keys to control them. At the end of the prompt line, the number associated with the highlighted item (1, for starters) is shown with the cursor sitting to its immediate right.

If the first menu item has any help text associated with it, then the message *HELP:* appears on the screen below the item array, and the help text associated with that item appears highlighted on the following line.

After displaying the initial screen configuration, *rmenu* waits for the user to make a menu selection. The user does this by moving the highlight bar to the desired item and pressing the ENTER key. There are several ways the highlight bar may be moved:

1) using the arrow keys

2) using the space bar (equivalent to the down-arrow)

3) entering an item number directly through the numeric keys.

The arrow keys and space bar work as might be expected. When they reach the end of a row or column, they wrap around to the opposite side of that row or column.

The direct numeric addressing option tries to be intelligent about the selection value entered. A string of digits is considered part of a single selection value as long as there is an item on the screen labeled by that value. As soon as a key is pressed that would make the selection value too large, the old selection value is discarded and the new digit alone represents the new selection value. If even that single digit is greater than the number of items on display, the bell is rung and the key has no effect on the current selection value.

Every time the selection value changes, the highlight bar is moved from the item represented by the old selection value over to the item represented by the new one. To execute a menu item, the user presses the ENTER key when the highlight bar is positioned on the desired choice.

There are four types of menu items:

1) an executable system command

2) a local menu

3) an external menu

4) an exit item.

The last type of menu item, the `exit` item, need never explicitly appear because there are built-in commands (*e* and *x*) for exiting the current menu. It is provided only for supporting additional help text to describe the exit option (for example, a reminder to the user of the parent menu's content).

When an executable action command is run, *rmenu*'s exact behavior is controlled by option specifications on two different levels. On one level, the CMENU specification file may contain item options to explicitly determine:

1) how *rmenu* handles screen clearing before a menu action is executed
2) whether *rmenu* prompts for a keystroke after the item completes execution
3) which menu item is the next to be highlighted after all processing for the current item is completed.

On another level, the source code to *rmenu* itself contains a configuration section that specifies defaults for the behavior of the above mechanisms. These defaults apply whenever any of the options that control those mechanisms are omitted from an item specification (i.e., most of the time if the defaults are chosen appropriately).

When a local or external menu is chosen, the specified submenu is called with the state of the current menu preserved. Upon return from the submenu, processing of the current menu resumes. There is no apparent difference to the user between a call to a local menu (one specified within the same physical *.mnc* file as the currently active menu) and a call to an external menu (another *.mnc* file).

The hardwired options available on every menu screen, in addition to ones described above to move the highlight bar, are:

e Return to the previous menu, or exit *rmenu* if currently in the root menu

x Exit *rmenu* immediately, no matter how deeply nested in submenus

! Escape to a system prompt (may be optionally disabled)

Beyond the User Interface

The above description of *rmenu* could serve as a user's guide. Now, we'll delve into *rmenu*'s implementation.

First, some guideposts to the source code; the *rmenu* source consists of four major program files (*rmenu1.c* through *rmenu4.c*), *rmenu*'s personal header file *rcmenu.h* and the CMENU system header file *cmenu.h* (shared with the *cmenu* program).

The *rmenu* specific header file, *rcmenu.h* (Listing 8.7) defines all configuration options and data structures for the program. The data structures build upon the elementary *MENU* and *ITEM* types defined in *cmenu.h*. Both header files rely upon the specification of the target operating system, supplied on the C compiler command line through use of the *-D* compiler option. This is handled automatically by the *makefile*.

rmenu1.c contains the *main()* function, several utility functions, and the code to load a compiled menu file into memory for interpretation. Most of the code to handle the user interface, including all the display logic and keyboard command processing, is found in *rmenu2.c*. *rmenu3.c* contains routines to execute a selected menu item. *rmenu4.c* is the file where as much as possible of *rmenu*'s system dependent code has been localized.

Configuration

The first several sections of *rcmenu.h* contain an abundance of customization options affecting screen layout and menu behavior.

While most terminals are laid out in a 24 row by 80 column format, other screen configurations are easily supported by changing the symbolic constant values in lines 66 through 86 (Listing 8.7).

MAX_IROWS controls the size of the menu item block, telling how many physical screen lines are to be used for menu items alone. The value I used is eighteen, supporting either nine double spaced menu items or eighteen single spaced ones. The value of *MAX_IROWS* should always be even, so the screen placement algorithms do not get confused by double spacing.

The *HOME_X* and *HOME_Y* symbols specify the upper left hand corner of the menu item block. *SCREEN_COLS* should give the physical number of columns on the screen. Note that the last column is never used (to avoid wrap-around problems). The last five constants in this section (lines 71-75) specify row and column values for several key features of the menu system, and are self documenting.

Lines 22-46 allow *rmenu* to work with both new and older variations of the UNIX Curses library. Older versions of Curses did not contain predefined mappings for the cursor motion keys, among other minor differences. To test which flavor of Curses is available, the conditional preprocessor statement in line 28 tests to see if a symbol named *KEY_UP* has been defined. If so, we're running under a newer Curses library, if not, it's an old one. For old Curses, EMACS movement controls are used to define the cursor motion keys. This is an arbitrary choice; any four key code values may be substituted.

The number of lines usually available on the screen is another issue. Under DOS, there are twenty-five lines available; serial terminals under UNIX typically support twenty-four lines. The *LAST_ROW* symbol is set accordingly.

Lines 95-100 define the appearance of various portions of *rmenu*'s general command prompt string. Depending on whether shell escapes are enabled at any particular time during the interpretation of a menu system, the prompt string seen by the user may or may not mention the availability of the shell escape (*!*) command.

When shell escapes are enabled and the user selects to exercise that option, another compile time option comes into play. If the *SHELL_PROMPT* symbol (defined in line 53) has a value of *TRUE*, then the prompt string represented by the *SH_PROMPT_STR* symbol is shown, giving the user the opportunity to abort the shell escape. This feature is provided for users who do not know how to handle an accidental foray into "shell-land" under DOS.

The system command to invoke a subordinate shell is defined in lines 102-107. For UNIX, a special system prompt is constructed to remind the user that the menu system is still active. This prompt is then active during the lifespan of the subordinate shell.

Data Structures

To support recursive menu interpretation, *rmenu*'s data structures begin with *LMenus*, an array of structures of type *levels*. Each structure of type *levels* completely describes an active *.mnc* file. Within it are a number of substructures of type *menu2*. Each of these substructures describes a single menu definition from the parent *.mnc* file. Going one level deeper, the contents of each *menu2* structure includes a copy of the *MENU* header structure (named *Menu*), and an array (named *Items*) containing pointers to all the *ITEM* structures in the current menu. Additional information controlling the display of those individual menu items on the screen is included in an array of structures named *coords*.

The placement information in *coords* is computed at the time the *.mnc* file is first loaded into memory and remains constant throughout the period of that menu file's interpretation (i.e., until the user exits from the top level menu in the file). This information includes the item's position on the screen, and the quantity of filler characters (spaces) needed to clear the trailing portion of the item text field when the text length is less than the maximum field width. Figuring all those values for each menu item is a computationally intensive task; it is done just once for each menu invocation at the time the menu is loaded into memory. The reason it is done by *rmenu* at all, rather than at compile time, is to support the ability to use the same compiled *.mnc* file under different terminal configurations. In other words, the *.mnu* source to a particular menu system would not require recompilation if some characteristic of the user terminals, such as number of lines, ever changes. Only *rmenu* would need to be recompiled.

To shorten definitions and declarations of pointers to these varying structure types, I've created *typedef* aliases for them in lines 147-149.

Memory Allocation Strategy

The memory blocks for storage of *MENU2* structures are allocated dynamically, as is the storage for each *ITEM* structure to be represented within them.

One possible way to implement memory management for recursive menu files would be to allocate storage for each of an *.mnc* file's *MENU2* and *ITEM* structures when the file is opened, and to later free all that storage when the user exits the top level menu. If, however, the menu system spans several files, then each transition across compiled units would generate a number of *alloc()* and *free()* calls, proportional to the number of menus and items involved.

Rather than having *rmenu* fully allocate and release these blocks of memory on every external submenu call, I chose to add a bit of complexity to the allocation scheme in the interests of efficiency. First, note that every *MENU2* structure takes up exactly the same amount of storage. The same consistency applies to *ITEM* structures. Since *Menus* and *Items* are arrays of pointers each already dimensioned to the largest possible number of elements, there is no reason why storage allocated for one set of menus cannot be reused for every subsequent set that might need it. New blocks would only have to be allocated when the previous maximum number of menus or items in a menu is exceeded, and then only the incremental memory blocks would need to be allocated. In addition, none of the memory would ever have to be freed until the *rmenu* program terminates. At that point, all the memory could be freed at once.

That is the strategy employed in *rmenu*. In each nesting level, represented by a *LEVELS* structure in the *LMenus* array, an integer counter named *max_menus* keeps track of the largest number of menus in any single *.mnc* file loaded into that nesting (recursion) level during the current *rmenu* session.

Then, within each of the *MENU2* structures of each nesting level, a counter named *most_items* tracks the most *ITEM* structures loaded into the *Items* array during the entire *rmenu* session.

In a later section, we'll look at how the *ld_menu()* function maintains these counters during the process of loading a menu file into memory.

Other Shared Data

Most menu information is maintained in the large data structures described above. To support seamless recursion, a few items of data are made available globally for convenience.

The *nestlev* variable indicates the current nesting, or recursion, level of the menu system. Level 0 indicates the master *.mnc* file is active, in *LMenus[0]*; the first execution of the *emenu* action bumps the nesting level to 1 and loads the specified external *.mnc* file into *LMenus[1]*, and so on. Maintaining this value as a global eliminates the need to keep passing it up and down through the recursive *sub_menu()* calls.

The only other global data are some state variables used with the Curses functions to save the screen coordinates of the user input echo area (line 152).

A Menu is Run

When *rmenu* is invoked to interpret a menu system, there are three major subsystems, or categories of functionality:

1) screen display management (via the Curses library)
2) menu nesting management (memory allocation, data management and path construction, all supporting recursive submenus)
3) user input processing (responding to keyboard commands).

These subsystems are distributed so that not every function in the program necessarily belongs to one specific subsystem, although many functions can be classified in one or another of the categories. To explain how *rmenu* works, I'll focus first on each conceptual subsystem individually then show how they all interact.

Screen Management

One very powerful feature of the Curses library is delayed screen refresh. This means that updates made to an internal screen image do not show up on the user's terminal automatically. One of several special functions (e.g., *refresh()*) must be called to update the screen to match the internal memory image.

The benefits of such a scheme are many. Curses can optimize the refresh process to require as few I/O operations as possible to update the screen image. For example, a program deletes some portion of text from the memory image, then later restores it to the original form before ever calling the refresh function. If the refresh were then immediately performed, nothing would be written to that portion of the screen at all. A side effect of this mechanism is that there is no need to worry about the order in which a set of related screen updates is performed. During the refresh, a set of chaotic updates becomes a smoothly executed repaint.

There is one aspect of delayed refresh that takes some getting used to: you need to remember to call the refresh function. As I began to debug *rmenu* (my first project using Curses), I kept trying to figure out why some of my screen updates weren't happening. They were done with Curses calls, but I had forgotten to refresh the screen..

Curses requires initialization at the beginning of a session and some housecleaning at the session's end. If the screen is ever to be manipulated by software other than the Curses library while a Curses session is in progress (for example, when a user requests a system shell escape during an *rmenu* session), special calls must then be made to switch the user's keyboard and screen characteristics between Curses mode and normal interactive mode, as necessary. For example, the Curses library uses "raw" tty mode under UNIX, while normal shell interaction requires the tty mode be set to "cooked."

Unfortunately, I have not been able to find any single, universally portable set of system calls that switch back and forth between these terminal modes correctly under both XENIX Curses and PC Curses for DOS. The closest I've come is to write a pair of functions, named *tty_shell()* and *tty_Curses()*, employing one conditional compilation directive in the *tty_shell()* function. The functions work as written for both DOS and XENIX, but I haven't tried them elsewhere. XENIX's Curses is purported to be nonstandard. My guess is that a little bit of tweaking will be necessary for other kinds of UNIX systems. Such nonportable tweaking, however, should not be required outside of these two functions, since all the other Curses calls I use are supposed to be portable.

Menu Memory Management

The trickiest parts of maintaining a recursive menu structure have been described above. Look at some key entry points in the menu perusal process to get a sharper picture of how recursion is implemented.

In *rmenu1.c* (Listing 8.8), the top level menu processing function *do_menu()* begins on line 98. The *main()* function calls *do_menu()* just once per *rmenu* session, to process the menu file named on the command line (or *menu.mnc* if a menu name was omitted). *do_menu()* is also used to process *emenu* (external menu) action statements. *do_menu()* takes two strings as function parameters, representing the path and filename of the *.mnc* file to be run. Lines 110-117 construct the full pathname and attempt to load the file into memory with the *ld_menu()* function. If *ld_menu()* experiences an error in opening the file, then *do_menu()* returns the *EXITALL* value to its calling function, signalling a fatal error condition and forcing the program to unravel all recursive calls and terminate.

If *ld_menu()* loads the *.mnc* file successfully, then the *sub_menu()* function (top of *rmenu2.c*, Listing 8.9) is called to run the main menu of the new file. *sub_menu()* calls always run a menu at the current menu file nesting level (i.e., within the active *.mnc* file). Since all menus in a single *.mnc* file are loaded at once when the file is opened, calls to *sub_menu()* never require any memory management services (except, of course, for the normal stack operations always generated automatically by the C compiler as part of the standard function calling sequence).

sub_menu() is the function that interprets user keyboard commands. *sub_menu()* takes two parameters: the index number of a local menu to be executed, and the current default path specification. When the user selects an item for execution, a call is placed to the *do_item()* function in *rmenu3.c* (top of Listing 8.10) for execution of the item's action clause.

In *do_item()*, we finally see recursion in action. The first case occurs when an *lmenu* clause is encountered. In line 36 of *rmenu3.c* (Listing 8.10), *do_item()* places a direct call back to the *sub_menu()* function to run the local menu that was specified in the *lmenu* clause.

The next case of recursion involves the *emenu* action clause. In line 41 of the same listing, a special function named *do_emenu()* (line 102) is called to set up the external menu call, and *do_emenu()* in turn calls *do_menu()*—the function that started it all.

I've skipped the nitty-gritty details of these key functions so far, to highlight the design's recursive flow. These functions will be presented in more detail later.

Command Processing

Most of the user interface code appears in *rmenu2.c* (Listing 8.9), divided between the *sub_menu()* and *get_cmd()* functions. The *get_cmd()* function accepts keystroke commands and maps them onto a standard *K_* code (as defined in the *rcmenu.h* header file). *sub_menu()* acts upon those command codes. Some additional user interface code appears in the *do_cmnd()* function (Listing 8.10, line 49) when a prompt is required after an item's execution, but before control is returned to the menu navigation functions.

Loading a Menu File

The *ld_menu()* function (Listing 8.8, line 123) reads an *.mnc* file in from disk, allocating memory as necessary to hold the menu data and determines the precise way each menu item shall be positioned on the screen. All this is performed during one pass through the disk file.

The first thing *ld_menu()* does is initialize a convenience pointer named *Levp* (line 136) to simplify access to the *LMenus* structure representing the current nesting level. All operations performed by this instance of *ld_menu()* will be confined to the current nesting level. There is no reason to require the repetitive evaluation of a base expression such as

```
LMenus[nestlev]
```

when it can be evaluated once and assigned to a pointer. All the other pointers defined at the top of *ld_menu()* serve a similar purpose later in the function.

After the input file has been opened successfully, *ld_menu()* is ready to read in the data. First, the integer value telling the number of menus present in the file is read from the beginning of the file (lines 147-149). For portability reasons, the *sizeof* operator is used to determine the size of an integer variable.

The main loop (lines 151-222) executes once for each menu in the file. If the memory for the new menu's index position in the *LMenus* array has already been allocated, then the *M2p* pointer is simply assigned to point to that memory. If not, lines 156-161 perform the necessary memory allocation, and initialize the memory tracking variables *max_menus* (in the *LMenus* structure) and *most_items* (in the *Menus* structure for the new menu). These two variables track, respectively, the maximum number of menus loaded into a nesting level and the maximum number of items loaded into a particular menu. They retain their values as menus and items come and go dynamically.

When menu memory allocation issues have been settled, the *MENU* header structure for the current menu is loaded in lines 166-167. The menu item placement strategy is then computed.

Laying It All Out

The algorithm to calculate item positioning is complex, because of the number of variables involved. These variables include:

1) screen dimensions currently specified by symbolic constants, but could as easily be specified by a set of variables, (see the exercises for some ideas along this line);
2) explicit *columns* and *spacing* instructions appearing in the menu specification file;
3) the number of items in the menu;
4) an arbitrary default heuristic for arranging the items in the absence of explicit *columns* or *spacing* specifications.

The *placement()* function starts the process by examining the general characteristics of the entire menu and adjusting the values of the *columns* and *spacing* variables accordingly. Because *cmenu* provides the length of the menu's widest line of item text (in the *MENU* element named, appropriately, *widest*), *placement()* has all the information it needs in the *MENU* header and does not need to examine the individual items to establish the overall placement strategy.

The *MENU* elements *placement()* examines are: *spacing*, *columns*, *nitems*, and *widest*. Because the first three of these elements are examined repeatedly in *placement()*, I've assigned their values to namesake local variables (lines 237-239) to make the code easier to follow.

The first step of the placement algorithm is to fill in any missing values for *spacing* and *columns*. There is one case when neither are specified, one case when only *spacing* is specified, and one case when only *columns* is specified. Each of the three cases is handled individually.

When neither value is specified, the placement is based on the relationship between the number of items in the menu and the number of lines available on the screen for menu items. If the number of items is less than half the number of lines, we are free to use double spacing to fill up the screen, putting a blank line between each item line for enhanced readability.

If the number of items is greater than half, but less than or equal to the number of rows available, then we examine the length of the longest item to see if it would fit in half a screen width. If so, then we go to a two column format to allow double spacing. If the longest item is too long for a two column format, we stick with one column and go to single spacing.

If the number of items is greater than the number of rows, then single spacing is forced and the number of columns is set to whatever it takes to make room for all the items. If that means some of the item text might be truncated, well, too bad. You can always put additional information for any item into its *help* clause, which is guaranteed never to be truncated (since there is always a full line available for each item's *help* text).

If only an explicit *columns* value is given, then lines 263-264 calculate the spacing appropriate for that number of columns (either single or double).

If only an explicit *spacing* value is given, then lines 266-269 figure the best number of columns for that spacing value. No adjustment is made for items that might be truncated when double spacing is specified and more items exist than would fit in a single column. If the menu designer really wants double spacing, why should *rmenu* second-guess?

After the *spacing* and *columns* values are filled in, one more step is needed to guard against the case where an impossible configuration was specified (such as a *column* value of one, with a hundred items following). If necessary, the code in lines 273-277 reduces the spacing and increases the number of columns (in that order) until a proper fit is achieved. Control then returns to *ld_menu()*.

Back in *ld_menu()* (line 173), it is now time to read in the individual *ITEM* structures from the disk file. Armed with reasonable values for *spacing* and *columns*, the length of the uniform item fields is calculated and stored in the variable named *field_len*. This helps optimize screen refreshing speed. If the longest actual item text is shorter than the available space for each item, there is never any need to write into the region between the end of the item and the start of the next item to the right of it (or the end of the screen, if we're dealing with only one column).

Each pass through the loop in lines 179-221 reads in one menu item. Again, an incremental memory allocation strategy is employed. The code to perform the memory allocation is similar to that used to obtain memory for the *MENU* structures (lines 153-162), except for the names involved (and one less initialization).

The *ITEM* structure itself is loaded in line 191. Then, the item text is truncated to fit the available display field length.

The next section of code is a bit tricky. I thought it would be useful if menu items that select other menus were clearly marked as such. The description text for those items wouldn't need to state that the selection is a menu. The way I chose to implement this feature was to have *rmenu* insert the text "*(MENU)*" at the end of each line of item text that identifies a submenu (local or external). Additionally, all such identifiers are inserted at the same column position relative to the start of the item text. Thus, screen items keep an orderly appearance.

Where there isn't enough room left in an item's text description buffer for the six characters of additional text, no action is taken. Nothing inherent to the display algorithm will distinguish that particular item as a submenu selection (although the item's description or help text can impart that information).

The bulky *if* expression in lines 196-198 checks if the current item specifies a submenu, and if there is enough room for the additional text. If so, lines 200-207 insert the appropriate number of spaces after the end of the item text, then append the "*(MENU)*" text after the spaces. Note the assignment of the horizontal position to the variable *limit* in lines 202-203. The expression

```
M2p -> field_len - 7
```

represents the furthest to the right that the menu identifier could go to keep the combined text length within the established field width. It may not look good all the way to the right, however, if all the description texts are short. The *limit* value, therefore, is calculated as the minimum of the expression above and the length of the widest item plus two (to leave some breathing room). Care also must be taken not to write past the end of the *char* array that holds the description text; a condition to test for such an overflow is added to the loop that inserts the space characters into the text (line 205). I warned you this would be tricky.

The final calculation required for each item is to establish:

1) its text description's screen coordinates, and

2) the number of spaces needed to pad its text out to the uniform field length.

All these values are then stored in the *coords* array position for the item. The screen coordinates are calculated in lines 210-216 based on the spacing (single or double), the number of physical screen rows devoted to item descriptions (*MAX_IROWS*), the physical number of columns on the screen (*SCREEN_COLS*), and the coordinates of the top-left corner of the item description block (*HOME_Y, HOME_X*).

The number of spaces needed to fill out the text is calculated by the hairy expression in lines 218-220. These calculations are complex but they are only made once. After that, the resulting values are all stored directly in the 33*coords* data structure for rapid access during the screen refresh process.

Realtime Menu Processing

After all the preliminary steps have been completed, the *sub_menu()* function (Listing 8.9) is finally given the chance to run a menu for the user.

There are some state variables that *sub_menu()* maintains:

cur_item holds the index value of the currently highlighted menu item. It is initialized to zero for the first item in the menu. The index value of an item is always one less than the reference number displayed on the screen for that item. C programs like to count from zero, but most people prefer enumeration to begin with one.

sel_val represents the latest direct numeric item selection value entered by the user via the digit keys. It is directly set by the *get_cmd()* function whenever the user enters a numeric selection value, indicated by a return value of *K_DIRECT* from *get_cmd()* calls.

To display the menu on the user's screen, *sub_menu()* calls the *draw_menu()* function (Listing 8.9, line 165).

draw_menu() begins by centering the menu title text on screen line *TITLE_ROW* (lines 182-183). This represents our first glimpse of a Curses display sequence. The *move()* function positions the logical cursor to the specified row and column, and *addstr()* inserts a given text string at the current cursor position. The text does not appear on the screen yet, because the *refresh()* function hasn't been called yet.

The Curses library supports multiple windows. When the library is first initialized via a call to the *init_win()* function, one default window corresponding to the regular terminal screen is automatically opened. Most of the more common functions in the Curses library have two variations: one always acts upon the "default window," and one takes an additional parameter specifying a particular window on which to operate. Because we will always be dealing with the default window for this application, the shorter forms are used whenever available. (Actually, the shorter forms are implemented as macro definitions that expand to call the long form functions. They are not separate functions themselves. For the purpose of writing programs, however, they may be treated as shorter function calls.)

Drawing the Menu and its Items

The loop in lines 185-189 calls the *draw_item()* function (lines 204-254) to write each individual item to the default window. The currently selected item is written with instructions to use reverse video and display any optional associated help text in the help line area of the screen. All other items are written in normal video mode with help text suppressed.

After all items have been written, the prompt line is constructed on row *PROMPT_ROW*. It is constructed because it takes on one of two different appearances, depending upon the current value of the *escape* flag in the current menu's header. This flag tells whether the user is permitted to use the *!* command to invoke a command processor (shell) directly from within the current menu. If shell escapes are allowed, then the fragment of text that documents the option is included in the prompt string; if not, it is not included.

The last thing *draw_menu()* does is call *refresh()* to cause Curses to update the screen with all the changes.

The *draw_item()* function begins by moving the logical cursor to the location stored in the *coords* structure for the current item (line 220) and writing the item number there using the Curses function *printw()* (the item number is always written in normal video mode). If the *vid_mode* parameter specifies to use reverse video, then the Curses function *standout()* is called to switch screen writes into the standout video mode. The precise effect of calling *standout()* may vary from system to system and terminal to terminal (at least in the UNIX versions), because the sequences used are terminal dependent. On most terminals, however, you can expect *standout()* to enter reverse video mode.

The item text is then written to the logical screen (line 226), along with the appropriate number of spaces needed to fill out the total length of the item field. If standout mode was requested, then the *standend()* function is called to return to normal video mode.

If the *dohelp* parameter was specified (i.e., has a nonzero value), and the current item has help text associated with it, then that help text is displayed (lines 240-244). If there is no help text, then the help area is cleared.

Back to *sub_menu()*

Upon return from the *draw_menu()* call, *sub_menu()* constructs the new default incremental path via a call to the *make_path()* function and stores the returned result in the *newpath* string. (I'll describe *make_path()* more fully in a later section.)

The main user interface loop (lines 36-161) takes up the rest of the *sub_menu()* function. *get_cmd()* is called at the top of the loop to read a keyboard command from the user. The return value from *get_cmd()* indicates the nature of that command. All commands except direct item selection (by number) are entirely defined by the value of the command code returned. For direct item selections, the return value of *K_DIRECT* indicates that such a selection has been made. The number of the selected item is stored in the *sel_val* variable.

All the simple highlight bar movement commands are processed in lines 40-82. The up-arrow and down-arrow commands (and the space bar command, which is equivalent to down-arrow) are the easiest to process. The currently highlighted item is redrawn in normal video, the new item is selected by either incrementing or decrementing the *cur_item* variable (with wrap-around), and the new current item is redrawn in standout mode. Processing the direct item addressing command is just as easy (lines 113-120), except a test is thrown in that skips the redraw operations if the item selected is already the current item.

The left-arrow and right-arrow keys are trickier, because the index number of the new item must be calculated based on the physical arrangement of items on the screen. For example, when the right-arrow key is pressed, there may or may not be an item in the column to the right (there also might not be a column to the right).

Lines 60-64 and 74-79 compute the next item index in response to a left-arrow and right-arrow command, respectively. To achieve this feat, the algorithm considers the total number rows in the item display area (*MAX_IROWS*), the current spacing value, the total number of items in the menu, and the index value of the current item. In trying to get these few lines of code to work correctly, I experienced almost as much frustration as I did on the rest of the entire CMENU system. I finally realized that the key was knowing the maximum number of items that can fit into a single column (a value I called the "factor"), and testing for overflow by adding or subtracting that factor from the current item's index value.

When moving to the right, the new index is computed by adding the factor to the current item index. Either the resulting index is within the range of menu items (the case when an item to the right exists) or it is out of range (then the index corresponding to the item on the same row in the first column is calculated by computing the modulus of the original index and the factor).

When moving to the left, starting anywhere other than in the first column, the new item is simply in the column to the left. When starting in the first column, however, a loop is executed to find the index of the item in the right most column of the same row.

When *get_cmd()* returns *K_RUN*, then the action associated with the current item is executed. If the action code value is *ACT_EXIT*, *sub_menu()* is finished and returns with a value of *OK* to indicate no problem.

Any other type of action is passed to *do_item()* for processing. *do_item()* is discussed in a later section. For the time being, note that a fatal error might be encountered during the *do_item()* call. *do_item()* indicates a fatal error condition by returning a value of *EXITALL*, causing *sub_menu()* to immediately return to its caller with *EXITALL* as its return value.

If the *do_item()* call went smoothly, lines 90-108 determine the next menu item to be highlighted, according to the options specified in the menu source. The menu is then rewritten and control returns to the top of the main command loop.

Lines 122-144 process the shell escape command. If shell escapes are currently disabled, the *put_msg()* function is called to display an error message and wait for the user to press a key to return to normal menu processing.

If shell escapes are enabled, then there are two possible methods of dealing with the request, controlled by the symbolic constant *SHELL_PROMPT*.

If *SHELL_PROMPT* is true, then a special prompt string (*SH_PROMPT_STR*) is displayed, again employing the *put_msg()* function to show the message and wait for a keystroke. If the user presses the ESC key in response to this prompt, then the shell escape request is aborted. If any other key is pressed, the shell escape is performed.

If *SHELL_PROMPT* is false, no prompt string is displayed, and the shell escape is performed immediately. This may be thought of as expert mode, when there is no danger of confusing the user if the shell escape command key is pressed accidentally.

Lines 136-138 invoke the subordinate shell. A pair of functions, *pre_shell()* and *post_shell()*, together handle certain housekeeping tasks attendant to launching a subordinate command interpreter from within the Curses environment. The *system()* call invoking the shell is sandwiched between these two functions.

The last three functions in *sub_menu()* handle various forms of the exit command, or make a rude noise when an unrecognized key is pressed.

Keystroke Processing

At the lowest level of the user command processing loop, *get_cmd()* reads user keystrokes (lines 257-367). *get_cmd()* translates raw keystrokes into a set of standard command symbols and returns those command symbols. For most commands this involves a simple one-to-one mapping of keys to symbols.

get_cmd() also performs another somewhat trickier task. It processes any direct menu item numbers entered by the user, and manages the contents of the item number echo area at the far right portion of the prompt line where digits are echoed during direct item number entry.

Two parameters are passed to *get_cmd()*: *nitems* tells how many items there are in the current menu, and *curr* is the index of the currently highlighted item.

get_cmd() maintains a static Boolean variable named *digits* that tells if a string of digits (presumably representing a direct item number) are currently being entered. Since each keystroke is an individual command, the entry of a multiple digit item number must necessarily span several calls to *get_cmd()*.

The first thing *get_cmd()* does is to display the item number of the currently highlighted item in the echo area (lines 279-280). The item number is one greater than the item's index value, because item numbering begins with 1 from the user's point of view. Any characters left on the echo area from a previous call are cleared away. The cursor remains at the character position immediately to the right of the item number just displayed (lines 281-283), to give the user a sense of continuity when entering a multiple digit item number.

The loop in lines 286-366 processes a keystroke. It runs only once, except in the special case when either the ESC key or an illegal digit is pressed (see below).

A keystroke is fetched via the *getch()* function in line 288, and the ***digits*** flag is cleared if the key is not a decimal digit. Lines 293-335 then handle all the direct command mappings.

Lines 341-364 process the digit keys. Once a digit key is recognized, does the decimal value formed by the concatenation of this new key onto the decimal total of previous contiguous keystrokes yield a new item number within legal range for the current menu? The conditional test in lines 341-343 asks this question. If the answer is yes, then the integer pointed to by ***sel_val*** is set to the value of the new item number and *get_cmd()* returns *K_DIRECT* to indicate a new item has been directly selected.

If the answer to the above question is no, then the digit is still construed as legal if it alone represents a legal item number. Line 350 checks for that possibility. If true, then the echo area is cleared and the new item number is displayed there; again the selection value is assigned through the ***sel_val*** pointer and *get_cmd()* returns the value *K_DIRECT*.

Any digit that fails both of the above criteria for legality generates a warning bell (line 363) and is totally ignored.

The ESC key is interpreted by *get_cmd()* as a special command meaning "clear the digit echo area." If this command were not available, aborting a direct item number entry sequence could get confusing because of the cumulative handling of digit strings. For example, consider a menu containing thirty items, and a user mistakenly presses the digit 1 when meaning to select item 2. If the next keystroke is the digit 2, item twelve would be selected. If 2 is pressed again, item 2 would be selected (because there is no item 122). The ESC key could have cleared the numeric selection after the initial digit 1 keystroke, and let the user press 2 to select item 2.

Running an Item

Moving on to *rmenu3.c* (Listing 8.10), we arrive at the point where a menu item selected by the user is submitted for execution. The function *do_item()* takes parameters specifying the item to be executed and the current default path. It then constructs the new incremental path from that information, and dispatches control to one of several secondary functions, depending upon the type of action required: *do_cmnd()* to execute a system command action, *do_emenu()* to run an external menu, or *sub_menu()* (covered earlier) to run a local menu.

do_item() supplies *do_cmnd()* with pointers to an *ITEM* structure and the new incremental path. The system command that executes the specified action is constructed by the call to *make_cmd()* in line 61.

Constructing the System Command

make_cmd() contains system dependent code, so it has been placed in *rmenu4.c* (Listing 8.11, lines 150-183).

make_cmd() takes two string parameters, *path* and *action*. Under DOS, any forward slash characters (/) in the *path* string are converted into backslash (\) characters, for compatibility with the standard DOS command processor. A static character array named *cmd_line* will contain the constructed command string.

If the supplied path is non-null, then a *cd* command with the given path as the argument is written to the beginning of *cmd_line*. If running under DOS, a drive selection command is then appended (lines 170-176) to make sure the drive specified in the path string is selected as the current drive. This step is unnecessary under UNIX, since UNIX does not have current drives the way DOS does. After selecting the new current path, the last thing appended onto *cmd_line()* is the action text itself (line 177).

When the supplied path is null, then the action text is directly copied to *cmd_line* with no further processing.

Back at *do_cmnd()* (Listing 8.10, line 63), it is now time to prepare for executing the new command string. First the *pre_clear* flag is examined to see if the screen needs to be cleared before running the command. There are two conditions under which the screen gets cleared. Either *pre_clear* has been explicitly set by a *preclear* in the item specification, or there were no explicit instructions given about clearing the screen and the default action is to clear it (if *DEF_PRECLEAR* is *YES*).

The screen cursor is then moved to the home position and the screen is refreshed. Before executing the system command, the *pre_shell()* function is called to prepare for the excursion. *pre_shell()* (lines 126-137) calls *push_path()* to save the current path (significant only under DOS) and calls *tty_shell()* to set the terminal to a normal interactive mode (significant under all systems).

Finally, in line 74, the *system0()* function is called to execute the constructed command string.

Running the System Command

system0() is another system dependent function. Flip over to Listing 8.11 again (line 186) to examine it.

First, note there are two versions of this function. The UNIX/XENIX version is so trivial that I wrote it out separately to keep from cluttering the DOS version with conditional directives. All normal command processors under UNIX/XENIX (sh, csh, etc.,) already directly support multiple commands and preservation of the parent's current directory. All that's necessary is to pass the command string directly to the active command processor via the *system()* function.

Under DOS, these mechanisms must be simulated. The current path has already been saved by *pre_shell()*'s call to *push_path()*. All that remains is to detect the presence of multiple commands, and to feed each individual command in sequence to DOS's command processor.

The way I did it is cheap and effective. First, the original command string is copied (to not butcher the original) and the pointer *cp* is set to point to the beginning of the copy. In the main loop, any leading semicolons are first skipped over (lines 218-219) and the pointer *cmdp* is set to the start of the next command. Then *cp* is advanced to the end of that command by scanning for one of two possible terminating characters: either a semicolon or a null. When one of these is found, its value is saved in *lastc* and then its character position is forced to a null. Now *cmdp* points to a single system command, and in line 225 that command is finally passed to the DOS command processor.

Upon return, the original terminating character is restored and the loop continues on to process the next command (if any).

The value returned by *system0()* is the return value of the last *system()* call. This value cannot be trusted under DOS, however, since many DOS programs do not return any meaningful value for the command processor to pass back.

Running an External Menu

When *do_item()* encounters an external menu, it calls upon the *do_emenu()* function (Listing 8.10, line 106) to process that external menu. *do_emenu()* checks if we're already at the maximum level of external menu nesting; if so, it aborts with a fatal error.

If not already at the maximum level of external menu nesting, the current default path and the action text are combined by a *make_path()* call into the complete pathname for the new external menu, and that pathname is stored in *filename* (line 116). The global nesting level variable *nestlev* is then incremented, and *do_menu()* is called, recursively, to begin processing the external menu.

After the *do_menu()* call, the nesting level is decremented and the value returned by *do_menu()* is relayed back by *do_emenu()*.

The Path Stack

The source file *rmenu4.c* (Listing 8.11) contains most of the *rmenu* code that is system dependent.

The first two functions, *push_path()* and *pop_path()*, maintain a path stack when running under DOS.

Before doing a shell escape or executing any action command, *rmenu* always calls the *push_path()* function. Under UNIX based systems, this function is a no-op, because there is no way for any child process to alter the parent's current directory.

Under DOS there is no such security. While shelled out to a command processor like COMMAND.COM, a user may select a different disk drive or path. Upon return from the shell session that drive and path will remain selected, potentially confusing the parent program's idea of what the current directory really is. To guard against that possibility, the *push_path()* function saves the current drive and path in an internal path stack before any system call that might potentially change them. The *pop_path()* function restores the drive and path saved in the last call to *push_path()*.

Each time *push_path()* is called, the currently logged drive and current working directory are pushed on the stack represented by the static structure array named *path_stack*, and stack pointer *path_stackp*. The current drive and directory are obtained via calls to the DOS standard library functions *getdisk()* and *getcwd()*.

pop_path() pops the last pushed drive and directory off the path stack, and calls the DOS standard library functions *setdisk()* and *chdir()* to restore the current drive and path.

Setting Curses Modes

The next two functions in *rmenu4.c* set the terminal mode for either Curses or non-Curses operation. *tty_shell()* sets the mode for interactive, non-Curses use by calling the Curses function *reset_tty()*. *tty_curses()* sets the mode for use with Curses by calling several Curses library functions to set things up as necessary. Since this program has not been tested under any operating systems except XENIX and DOS, I suspect that *tty_shell()* and *tty_curses()* will be the first functions to require some attention if *rmenu* is ported to any other UNIX variants.

Path Construction

The only function left to describe is *make_path()* (Listing 8.11, lines 114-147), used in the construction of incremental pathnames. *make_path()* takes two parameters: *old_path* represents the current default path, and *incr_path* is the new incremental path to be merged with the current path. (Under DOS, both strings are run through *trans_slash()* to convert forward slashes into backslashes.) The method of merging depends on the nature of *incr_path*: if *incr_path* is an absolute path (beginning with a slash character or, under DOS, with either a slash or a disk designator), then *make_path()* returns *incr_path* as the final new path specification.

If *incr_path* begins with anything other than a slash or drive designator, then it is treated as a relative path to be appended onto *old_path* to yield the new incremental path. This is done in lines 136-145.

First, *old_path* is copied into *newpath* (the buffer to hold the result). If both the relative path *incr_path* and the old path (now stored in *newpath*) are non-null, a path delimiter character is appended onto *newpath*. Finally, the new relative path is appended onto *newpath* and the incremental path is complete.

Exercises

1) The symbolic constants having names beginning with *DEF_* control the default behavior of CMENU language options that are not explicitly controlled in an item definition. Make these default options, presently hardwired at compile time, into CMENU language options that may be specified as part of a menu specification's option section (that is, at the same level as the *title* and *spacing* options).

2) A bit tougher: extend the default scope of the default specifications created in 1) above, as well as the *escape/noescape* permission status, to any and all submenus that may be invoked. Hint: you'll need to add parameters specifying the current state of all the affected options to the *sub_menu()* function's parameter list.

3) Extend the *rmenu* memory allocation strategy to include *COORDS* structure information as part of the dynamic *ITEM* allocation scheme (i.e., make it so that storage for the *COORDS* data is only allocated when necessary). After doing that, calculate how much memory is saved, and contrast the value of saving that memory with the price of the added complexity necessary to support the savings. Was it worth it? The answer probably will depend on how neatly the mechanism has been incorporated into the existing framework.

4) Remove the hardwired aspect of the screen characteristic definitions, so that *rmenu* does not have to be recompiled to support different terminal sizes. There are at least two ways to accomplish this: a) extend the CMENU language to allow screen dimensions to be written into menu specification files (this approach will most likely require major changes to all portions of the

system); b) allow some or all of the screen characteristics to be specified at *rmenu* run time. This may be implemented in terms of individual command line options to *rmenu*, or perhaps just one option that gives the name of a special ASCII initialization file that *rmenu* can read at the beginning of a session to determine what screen characteristics to use.

5) Under DOS, any semicolon characters found in action strings are treated as delimiters between multiple commands. Thus, the semicolon character is precluded from being part of any actual system command. Extend the *system0()* function to support a method for escaping semicolons.

6) Add a command to the *rmenu* user interface to show the exact sequence of commands that would be submitted to the system's command processor to execute any highlighted action item. Hint: most of the work can be done by cloning the *do_item()* and *do_cmnd()* functions, and using *put_msg()* to display the information on the screen.

LISTING 8.1 cmenu.h

```
/*************************************************************
 *  Program:    CMENU/RMENU Menu Compiler
 *  Written by: Leor Zolman, 11/90
 *
 *  Module: cmenu.h -- master header file
 *
 *  This include file contains definitions common to both
 *  the cmenu and rmenu programs.
 *************************************************************/

#include <stdio.h>

#define VERSION     "1.2 (10/7/91)"

/************** System-dependent stuff: *********************/

#if __STDC__ || XENIX
#   define Void void
#else
#   define Void int
#endif

/******************** Maximum sizes/lengths: ****************/

#define MAX_PATH    30
#define MAX_MENUS   25
#define MAX_NEST    3
#define MAX_TXTWID  60
#define MAX_ITEMS   36
#define MAX_CMD     130
#define MAX_HELP    79
#define MAX_NAME    20

/****************** Magic constants: ************************/

#define DEFAULT     0
#define YES         1
#define NO          2

#define ERROR       (-1)

/******************* Nextitem types: ***********************/

#define NXT_FIRST   1
#define NXT_LAST    2
#define NXT_NEXT    3
#define NXT_DIRECT  4

```

LISTING 8.1 cmenu.h *continued*

```
/*********************** Action types: ***********************/

#define ACT_NONE    0
#define ACT_CMND    1
#define ACT_LMENU   2
#define ACT_EMENU   3
#define ACT_EXIT    4

/************************ typedefs: **************************/

typedef char    BOOL;

typedef struct menu {
    char    title[MAX_TXTWID];
    char    path[MAX_PATH];
    int     nitems;
    char    align;
    int     columns;
    int     spacing;
    int     widest;
    char    escape;
} MENU;

typedef struct item {
    char    text[MAX_TXTWID];
    char    path[MAX_PATH];
    char    action[MAX_CMD];
    char    help[MAX_HELP];
    char    pre_clear,
            post_clear,
            prompt;
    char    acttyp;
    int     lmenunum;
    char    nextcode;
    int     nextitem;
} ITEM;
```

LISTING 8.2 ccmenu.h

```
/*************************************************************
 *  Program: CMENU Menu Compiler
 *  Module: ccmenu.h -- Compiler Module header file
 *  Written by: Leor Zolman, 11/90
 *************************************************************/

/********************* Misc. constants **********************/

#define TRUE    1
#define FALSE   0
#define OK      0

#define UNDEF_FWD (-1)           /* undefined forward reference flag */


/********************** extern control **********************/

#ifndef MASTER
#   define Extern extern                /* external declarations    */
#else
#   define Extern                       /* one-time definitions     */
#endif


/********************* Type Definitions *********************/

typedef struct {
    char Name[MAX_NAME];
    ITEM Item;
} IINFO;

typedef struct {
    char Name[MAX_NAME];
    BOOL Processed;
    MENU Menu;
    IINFO *Items[MAX_ITEMS];
} MINFO;

/********************** Token codes: ***********************/

#if __STDC__

enum {
    T_NULL,                                     /* special code */
    T_MENU, T_TITLE, T_PATH,
    T_SPACING, T_COLUMNS, T_ENDMENU,
    T_ITEM, T_TEXT,
    T_ALIGN, T_LEFT, T_CENTER, T_RIGHT,
    T_NEXTITEM, T_FIRST, T_LAST, T_NEXT,
    T_EMENU, T_LMENU, T_ACTION,
    T_HELP,
    T_PROMPT, T_PAUSE,                              /* synonyms */
    T_NOPROMPT, T_NOPAUSE,                          /* synonyms */
    T_PRECLEAR, T_NOPRECLEAR, T_POSTCLEAR, T_NOPOSTCLEAR,
```

LISTING 8.2 ccmenu.h *continued*

```
    T_EXIT,
    T_ESCAPE, T_NOESCAPE,
    T_STRING, T_VALUE, T_COLON, T_EOF                 /* special tokens */
};

#else                                                 /* __STDC__ */

#define T_NULL      0                                 /* special code */
#define T_MENU      1
#define T_TITLE     2
#define T_PATH      3
#define T_SPACING   4
#define T_COLUMNS   5
#define T_ENDMENU   6
#define T_ITEM      7
#define T_TEXT      8
#define T_ALIGN     9
#define T_LEFT      10
#define T_CENTER    11
#define T_RIGHT     12
#define T_NEXTITEM  13
#define T_FIRST     14
#define T_LAST      15
#define T_NEXT      16
#define T_EMENU     17
#define T_LMENU     18
#define T_ACTION    19
#define T_HELP      20
#define T_PROMPT    21                                /* synonyms */
#define T_PAUSE     22
#define T_NOPROMPT  23                                /* synonyms */
#define T_NOPAUSE   24
#define T_PRECLEAR  25
#define T_NOPRECLEAR    26
#define T_POSTCLEAR     27
#define T_NOPOSTCLEAR   28
#define T_EXIT      29
#define T_ESCAPE    30
#define T_NOESCAPE  31
#define T_STRING    32                                /* special tokens */
#define T_VALUE     33
#define T_COLON     34
#define T_EOF       35

#endif                                                /* __STDC__ */

/********************** Prototypes: *************************/

#if __STDC__ || XENIX                                 /* ANSI Prototypes: */

int write_file(void);
int dofile(char *);

void itemcheck(void);
```

LISTING 8.2 ccmenu.h *continued*

```
int gettok();
int error(char *, ...);
int fatalerr(char *, ...);
MINFO create_menu(char *);
IINFO *create_item(char *);
MINFO *find_menu(char *);
IINFO *find_item(char *);
int do_menu(void);
int do_title(void);
int do_path(void);
int do_spacing(void);
int do_columns(void);
int do_item(void);
int do_endmenu(void);
int do_align(void);
int do_text(void);
int do_text2(void);
int do_nextitem(void);
int do_action(void);
int do_help(void);
int do_prompt(void);
int do_clear(void);
int do_err(void);
int do_escape();
int do_opts(void);
#else                                          /* K&R Prototypes: */
int write_file();
int dofile();
Void itemcheck();
int gettok();
int error();
int fatalerr();
MINFO create_menu();
IINFO *create_item();
MINFO *find_menu();
IINFO *find_item();
int do_menu();
int do_title();
int do_path();
int do_spacing();
int do_columns();
int do_item();
int do_endmenu();
int do_align();
int do_text();
```

LISTING 8.2 ccmenu.h *continued*

```
int do_text2();
int do_nextitem();
int do_action();
int do_help();
int do_prompt();
int do_clear();
int do_err();
int do_escape();
int do_opts();

#endif

#ifdef NEEDSTR
char *strstr();
#endif


/************ Keyword / function dispatch table *************/

struct keywd {
    char *keyword;
    int (*t_func)();
};

extern struct keywd keywords[];

#ifdef MASTER
struct keywd keywords[] = {
    "(null)", do_err,                                /* for db only  */
    "menu", do_menu,
    "title", do_title,
    "path", do_path,
    "spacing", do_spacing,
    "columns", do_columns,
    "endmenu", do_endmenu,
    "item", do_item,
    "text", do_text,
    "align", do_align,
        "left", do_err,
        "center", do_err,
        "right", do_err,
    "nextitem", do_nextitem,
        "first",  do_err,
        "last", do_err,
        "next", do_err,
    "emenu", do_action,
    "lmenu", do_action,
    "action", do_action,
    "help", do_help,
    "prompt", do_opts,
    "pause", do_opts,
    "noprompt", do_opts,
    "nopause", do_opts,
    "preclear", do_opts,
```

LISTING 8.2 ccmenu.h *continued*

```
    "nopreclear", do_opts,
    "postclear", do_opts,
    "nopostclear", do_opts,
    "exit", do_action,
    "escape", do_escape,
    "noescape", do_escape,
    "(!string)", do_err,                              /* for db only  */
    "(!value)", do_err,                               /* for db only  */
    "(!colon)", do_err,                               /* for db only  */
    "(!EOF)", do_err                                  /* for db only  */
};
#endif

#define N_KEYWORDS  (sizeof keywords / sizeof (struct keywd))


/*************** Other Data structures *********************/

Extern  MINFO MInfo[MAX_MENUS], *MIp;
Extern  IINFO *IIp;

Extern  MENU *Mp, *CMp;           /* General, Current Menu Pointers   */
Extern  ITEM *Ip, *CIp;           /* General, Current Item Pointers   */

Extern  struct {                  /* Item Forward Reference Table     */
    char iname[MAX_NAME];         /* Item name                        */
    int *refp;                    /* Pointer to reference location    */
    int lineno;                   /* source line number of reference  */
} fwd_refs[MAX_ITEMS];

Extern  int n_refs;                   /* Number of forward references */

/************** Miscellaneous data items ********************/

Extern  FILE    *fp;
Extern  int     token, token2;              /* token codes          */
Extern  char    tparam[MAX_CMD];            /* text parameter       */
Extern  int     vparam;                     /* value parameter      */
Extern  int     lineno;                     /* current line number  */
Extern  int     n_menus,
                n_items;
Extern  BOOL    in_menu,
                in_item;
Extern  BOOL    err_flag,
                fatal;
Extern  int     item_num,
                menu_num;

Extern  char    src_name[MAX_PATH];
Extern  char    obj_name[MAX_PATH];
```

LISTING 8.3 cmenu1.c

```
/*************************************************************
 *  Program: CMENU Menu Compiler
 *  Module: cmenu1.c
 *       Menu Compiler:
 *       Main and Utility Functions
 *  Written by: Leor Zolman, 7/91
 *************************************************************/

#define MASTER
#include "cmenu.h"
#include "ccmenu.h"

#include <string.h>

#if __STDC__
#   include <stdarg.h>
#else
#   include <varargs.h>
#endif

int main(argc,argv)
int argc;
char **argv;
{
    register i;

    printf("CMENU Menu Compiler v%s\n", VERSION);
    if (argc < 2)
    {
        puts("usage: cmenu <menu-source-file(s)>\n");
        return 0;
    }

    for (i = 1; i < argc; i++)
        if (dofile(argv[i]) == ERROR)          /* process source files */
            return 1;
    return 0;
}

/*************************************************************
 * dofile():
 *  Process a single .mnu source file
 *************************************************************/

int dofile(name)
char *name;
{
    register i;
    char *cp;

    if ((cp = strstr(name, ".mnu")) ||
       (cp = strstr(name, ".MNU")))
                *cp = '\0';

```

LISTING 8.3 cmenu1.c *continued*

```
    strcpy(src_name, name);
    strcat(src_name, ".mnu");
    strcpy(obj_name, name);

    if ((fp = fopen(src_name, "r")) == NULL)
        return fprintf(stderr, "Can't open %s\n", src_name);

    n_menus = 0;
    lineno = 1;
    in_menu = FALSE;
    fatal = FALSE;

    /*  Main processing loop. Read a token and process it,
     *  until end of file is reached:
     */

    while ((token = gettok(fp)) != T_EOF)
    {
        if (!in_menu && token != T_MENU)
        {
            error("Each menu must begin with the Menu keyword");
            break;
        }
        if ((*keywords[token].t_func)() == ERROR)
            if (fatal)                  /* If fatal error, exit loop    */
                break;
    }

    fclose(fp);

    if (!n_menus)
        return error("No menus defined");

    if (in_menu)
    {
        if (n_items)
            itemcheck();
        error("Menu definition missing \"Endmenu\" statement");
    }

    for (i = 0; i < n_menus; i++)               /* check for undefined  */
        if (!MInfo[i].Processed)                /* "lmenu" references   */
        {
            printf("Local Menu \"%s\" is undefined.\n",
                    MInfo[i].Name);
            err_flag = TRUE;
        }

    if (err_flag)
        return ERROR;
```

LISTING 8.3 cmenu1.c *continued*

```

    if (write_file() == ERROR)
        return ERROR;
    return OK;
}


/************************************************************
 * create_menu():
 *  Construct a new menu information structure and
 *  return it (by value).
 *  Set fatal to TRUE if can't create.
 ************************************************************/

MINFO create_menu(name)
char *name;
{
    MINFO mi;

    if (n_menus == MAX_MENUS)
        fatalerr("Maximum # of menus (%d) exceeded", MAX_MENUS);
    else
    {
        strcpy(mi.Name, name);
        mi.Processed = FALSE;
    }
    return mi;
}


/************************************************************
 * find_menu():
 *  Search the Menu Info table for a named local menu.
 *  If found:
 *      Return a pointer to the entry if found, and set
 *      global variable menu_num to the menu's index
 *  else:
 *      return NULL
 ************************************************************/

MINFO *find_menu(name)
char *name;
{
    int i;

    for (i = 0; i < n_menus; i++)
        if (!strcmp(MInfo[i].Name, name))
        {
            menu_num = i;
            return &MInfo[i];
        }
    return NULL;
}

```

LISTING 8.3 cmenu1.c *continued*

```

/************************************************************
 * create_item(): Allocate space for Item Info structure,
 *  Initialize it and return a pointer to the structure
 *  Return NULL if there was a creation error.
 ************************************************************/

IINFO *create_item(name)
char *name;
{
    IINFO *IIp;
    ITEM *Ip;

    if (n_items == MAX_ITEMS)
    {
        fatalerr("Max. # of items (%d) exceeded", MAX_ITEMS);
        return NULL;
    }

    if ((IIp = (IINFO *) malloc(sizeof(IINFO))) == NULL)
    {
        fatalerr("Out of memory");
        return NULL;
    }

    strcpy(IIp->Name, name);
    Ip = &IIp->Item;
    Ip->acttyp = ACT_NONE;
    Ip->pre_clear = Ip->post_clear = Ip->prompt = DEFAULT;
    Ip->nextcode = DEFAULT;
    Ip->nextitem = Ip->lmenunum = 0;
    *Ip->text = *Ip->path = *Ip->action = *Ip->help = '\0';
    return IIp;
}


/************************************************************
 * find_item():
 *  Search the Item Info table for a named item in the
 *  currently active menu definition.
 *  If item name found:
 *      Set item_num to the index value of the Item,
 *      Return a pointer to the entry
 *  else:
 *      return NULL
 ************************************************************/

IINFO *find_item(name)
char *name;
{
    int i;

    for (i = 0; i < n_items; i++)
        if (!strcmp(MIp->Items[i]->Name, name))
```

LISTING 8.3 cmenu1.c *continued*

```
        {
            item_num = i;
            return MIp->Items[i];
        }
    return NULL;
}


/*************************************************************
 * itemcheck():
 *  Check the currently active item to make sure
 *  both a Text and an Action clause have been
 *  explicitly given.
 *************************************************************/

Void itemcheck()
{
    if (!*Ip->text)
        error("No TEXT clause found for current item");
    if (Ip->acttyp == ACT_NONE)
        error("No ACTION clause found for current item");
}


/*************************************************************
 * write_file():
 *      Write menu object file to disk, ready for
 *      execution via rmenu.
 *          Menu object file format:
 *      --------------------------------
 *      <count>         (integer count of # of menus in file)
 *      MENU 1          (MENU structure for 1st Menu)
 *          ITEM 1
 *          ITEM 2
 *          ...
 *          ITEM n_items
 *      MENU 2          (MENU structure for 2nd Menu)
 *          ...
 *      .
 *      .
 *      .
 *      MENU <count>    (MENU structure for final Menu)
 *          ...
 *      --------------------------------
 *
 **************************************************************/

int write_file()
{
    int i,j;

    strcat(obj_name, ".mnc");

    if ((fp = fopen(obj_name, "wb")) == NULL)
```

LISTING 8.3 cmenu1.c *continued*

```
    {
        fprintf(stderr,
            "Cannot open %s for writing.\n", obj_name);
        return ERROR;
    }

    if (fwrite((Void *)&n_menus, sizeof n_menus, 1, fp) != 1)
    {
        fprintf(stderr,
            "Error writing menu count to %s\n", obj_name);
        return ERROR;
    }

    for (i = 0; i < n_menus; i++)
    {
        Mp = &MInfo[i].Menu;
        if (fwrite((Void *) Mp, sizeof (MENU), 1, fp) != 1)
        {
            fprintf(stderr,
                "Error writing to %s\n", obj_name);
            return ERROR;
        }

        for (j = 0; j < Mp->nitems; j++)
        {
            if (fwrite((Void *) &MInfo[i].Items[j]->Item,
                    sizeof (ITEM), 1, fp) != 1)
            {
                fprintf(stderr,
                    "Error writing to %s\n", obj_name);
                return ERROR;
            }
            free(MInfo[i].Items[j]);
        }
    }
    printf("Menu object file %s written.\n", obj_name);
    return OK;
}


/*************************************************************
 * warning():
 *  Display a warning message, preceded by source
 *  file name and line number, supporting format
 *  conversions.
 *************************************************************/

#if __STDC__
  int warning(char *text, ...)
#else
  int warning(text)
  char *text;
#endif
```

LISTING 8.3 cmenu1.c *continued*

```
{
    char **textp = &text;
    fprintf(stderr, "%s (%d): ", src_name, lineno);
    fprintf(stderr, text, *++textp, *++textp);
    fprintf(stderr, "\n");
    return OK;
}


/************************************************************
 * error():
 *  Display an error message, preceded by source
 *  file name and line number, supporting format
 *  conversions.
 ************************************************************/

#if __STDC__                        /* ANSI variable-#-of-args method: */
int error(char *fmt, ...)
{
    va_list arglist;
    va_start(arglist, fmt);

#else                                         /* old "varargs" method: */
int error(fmt, va_alist)
char *fmt;
va_dcl
{
    va_list arglist;
    va_start(arglist);
#endif

                                /* the rest is the same, ANSI or varargs: */

    fprintf(stderr, "%s (%d): ", src_name, lineno);
    vfprintf(stderr, fmt, arglist);
    va_end(arglist);
    fprintf(stderr, "\n");
    err_flag = TRUE;
    return ERROR;
}


/************************************************************
 * fatalerr():
 *  Like error, except global flag "fatal" is set.
 ************************************************************/

#if __STDC__                        /* start function the ANSI way... */
int fatalerr(char *fmt, ...)
{
    va_list arglist;

    va_start(arglist, fmt);
```

LISTING 8.3 cmenu1.c *continued*

```
#else                                /* or the old "varargs" way... */
int fatalerr(fmt, va_alist)
char *fmt;
va_dcl
{
    va_list arglist;

    va_start(arglist);
#endif

    error(fmt, arglist);         /* the rest is same, ANSI or varargs */
    va_end(arglist);
    fatal = TRUE;
    return ERROR;
}


/************************************************************
 * matchkey():
 *  Test if given string is a reserved word. Return the token
 *  value of the matching token if so; else return NULL.
 ************************************************************/

int matchkey(str)
char *str;
{
    char str2[MAX_CMD], *cp;
    int i;

    strcpy(str2, str);
    for (cp = str2; *cp; cp++)
        *cp = tolower(*cp);

    for (i = 0; i < (int) N_KEYWORDS; i++)
        if (!strcmp(keywords[i].keyword, str2))
            return i;

    return NULL;
}


#ifdef NEEDSTR
/*
 * Search for first occurence of substring s2 in s1:
 *  (provided for Xenix only; this function is in
 *   most modern standard distribution libraries)
 */

char *strstr(s1, s2)
char *s1, *s2;
{
    int i, j, nposs;
    int len1 = strlen(s1);

```

LISTING 8.3 cmenu1.c *continued*

```
    int len2 = strlen(s2);
    char *p1;


    if (len1 < len2)
        return NULL;

    nposs = len1 - len2;

    for (i = 0; i <= nposs; i++)
    {
        for (j = 0, p1 = &s1[i]; j < len2;  j++)
            if (*p1++ != s2[j])
                break;
        if (j == len2)
            return &s1[i];
    }
    return NULL;
}
#endif
```

LISTING 8.4 cmenu2.c

```
/*************************************************************
 *  Program: CMENU Menu Compiler
 *  Module: cmenu2.c
 *      Menu Compiler:
 *      Menu/Item Token Processing Functions
 *  Written by: Leor Zolman, 7/91
 *************************************************************/

#include "cmenu.h"
#include "ccmenu.h"

#include <ctype.h>


/*************************************************************
 * do_menu():
 *  Process the MENU keyword
 *************************************************************/

int do_menu()
{
    int tok;

    if (in_menu)                /* Are we currently processing a menu?  */
    {                           /* yes.                                 */
        warning("Endmenu missing from previous menu");
        do_endmenu();           /* give them the benefit of the doubt   */
    }

    if ((tok = gettok()) != T_STRING)
    {
        if (n_menus)
            error("Menu name missing; menu unreachable");
        sprintf(tparam, "menu%d", n_menus + 1);    /* force a name      */
        ungettok(tok);
    }

    if (strlen(tparam) > MAX_NAME)
    {
        error("The name '%s' is too long (%d chars max)",
                tparam, MAX_NAME);
        tparam[MAX_NAME] = '\0';                   /* truncate name     */
    }

    if ((MIp = find_menu(tparam)) == NULL)         /* menu exist?       */
    {
        MInfo[n_menus] = create_menu(tparam);      /* no.               */
        if (fatal)
            return ERROR;                          /* creation error    */
        else
            MIp = &MInfo[n_menus++];               /* OK, bump count    */
    }
```

LISTING 8.4 cmenu2.c *continued*

```
    else
        if (MIp -> Processed)                           /* redefinition?    */
            return fatalerr("Duplicate Menu definition");    /* yes.     */

    Mp = &MIp -> Menu;
    *Mp->title = *Mp->path = '\0';
    Mp->nitems = Mp->widest = 0;
    Mp->spacing = Mp->columns = Mp->escape = DEFAULT;
    Mp->align = DEFAULT;

    in_item = FALSE;                /* state variables describing the    */
    in_menu = TRUE;                 /* current menu being processed      */
    n_items = 0;
    n_refs = 0;                     /* no forward item references yet    */

    if ((tok = gettok()) != T_COLON)                /* optional colon    */
        ungettok(tok);

    return OK;
}


/****************************************************************
 * do_title():
 *  Process the TITLE clause for a menu.
 ****************************************************************/

int do_title()
{
    int tok;

    if ((tok = gettok()) != T_STRING)
    {
        error("Title text missing");
        ungettok(tok);
    }

    if (!in_item)                               /* Before all items?     */
    {                                           /* yes.                  */
        if (*Mp->title)
            return error("A Menu Title has already been specified");
        strcpy(Mp->title, tparam);
    }
    else
        return error("The Menu Title must precede all Menu Items.");

    return OK;
}

```

LISTING 8.4 cmenu2.c *continued*

```

/************************************************************
 * do_path():
 *  Process the PATH option.
 *  Note that the PATH option may apply to an entire
 *  menu or just to a single menu item (determined
 *  by context.)
 ************************************************************/

int do_path()
{
    int tok;
    char *cp;

    if ((tok = gettok()) != T_STRING)
    {
        error("Path text missing");
        ungettok(tok);
    }

    if (tparam[strlen(tparam) - 1] == '/' ||
                tparam[strlen(tparam) - 1] == '\\')        /* delete */
        tparam[strlen(tparam) - 1] = '\0';          /* trailing slash  */

    if (!in_item)                           /* Referring to the menu?   */
    {                                       /* yes.                     */
        if (*Mp->path)
            return error("A Menu Path has already been specified");
        strcpy(Mp->path, tparam);
    }
    else
    {                                       /* Must be for the item.    */
        if (*Ip->path)
            return error("An Item Path has already been specified");
        strcpy(Ip->path, tparam);
    }
    return OK;
}


/************************************************************
 * do_align():
 *  Process text alignment option.
 *  Note: this option is a no-op. I decided there wasn't
 *  any real need for any other than left-justified item
 *  alignment. But, in case anyone thinks of a use for it,
 *  I'm leaving in the ability to process the option.
 ************************************************************/

int do_align()
{
    int tok;

    if (in_item)
```

LISTING 8.4 cmenu2.c *continued*

```
        return error("The Align clause must precede all Menu Items.");

    if (Mp->align)
        return error("Align option already specified for this menu");

    switch (tok = gettok())
    {
        case T_LEFT:
            Mp->align = 'L';
            break;

        case T_RIGHT:
            Mp->align = 'R';
            break;

        case T_CENTER:
            Mp->align = 'C';
            break;

        default:
            ungettok(tok);
            return error("Align missing valid modifier");
    }
    return OK;
}


/*************************************************************
 * do_spacing():
 *  Process the SPACING option (applies
 *  to menus only.)
 *************************************************************/

int do_spacing()
{
    int tok;

    if ((tok = gettok()) != T_VALUE)
    {
        error("Spacing value missing");
        ungettok(tok);
    }

    if (in_item)
        return error("Spacing option must precede all menu items");

    if (Mp->spacing)
        return error("Spacing option already specified");

                    /* only single and double spacing supported    */
    if (vparam != 1 && vparam != 2)
```

LISTING 8.4 cmenu2.c *continued*

```
            return error("Spacing value must be either 1 or 2");

    Mp->spacing = vparam;
    return OK;
}


/************************************************************
 * do_columns():
 *  Process the COLUMNS option
 ************************************************************/

int do_columns()
{
    int tok;

    if ((tok = gettok()) != T_VALUE)
    {
        error("Columns value missing");
        ungettok(tok);
    }

    if (in_item)
        return error("Columns option must precede all menu items");

    if (Mp->columns)
        return error("Columns option already specified");

    if (vparam < 1 || vparam > 6)        /*  6 seems a reasonable max. */
        return error("Columns value must be between 1 and 6");
    Mp->columns = vparam;
    return OK;
}


/************************************************************
 * do_escape():
 *  Process "escape" and "noescape" menu options
 ************************************************************/

int do_escape()
{
    if (in_item)
        return error("\"%s\" must appear before all menu items",
            keywords[token].keyword);

    if (Mp->escape)
        return error("Escape option already specified");
    Mp->escape = (token == T_ESCAPE) ? YES : NO;

    return OK;
```

LISTING 8.4 cmenu2.c *continued*

```
}


/************************************************************
 * do_endmenu():
 *  Process ENDMENU keyword
 ************************************************************/

int do_endmenu()
{
    int i;

    if (!n_items)
        error("No menu items specified for this menu");

    for (i = 0; i < n_refs; i++)            /* check for unresolved     */
    {                                       /* forward Item references  */
        if (*fwd_refs[i].refp == UNDEF_FWD)
        {
            int save_lineno = lineno;
            lineno = fwd_refs[i].lineno;
            error("Unresolved reference to Item \"%s\"",
                fwd_refs[i].iname);
            lineno = save_lineno;
        }
    }

    in_menu = in_item = FALSE;              /* done with current menu   */
    MIp -> Processed = TRUE;                /* it is now processed      */
    Mp -> nitems = n_items;
    return OK;
}


/************************************************************
 * do_item():
 *  Process the ITEM clause. Create a new ite
 *  and fill in any existing forward references to it.
 ************************************************************/

int do_item()
{
    int tok, i;
    char *cp, c;

    if (n_items)
        itemcheck();            /* check for previous item's completion */

    if ((tok = gettok()) != T_STRING)           /* label specified?     */
    {                                           /* If not, stuff unique */
        sprintf(tparam,"dummy!%d", n_items);          /* dummy name in   */
            ungettok(tok);
```

LISTING 8.4 cmenu2.c *continued*

```
    }
    else
    {
        if (strlen(tparam) > MAX_NAME)
        {
            error("Item name \"%s\" too long. Max %d chars.",
                        tparam, MAX_NAME);
            tparam[MAX_NAME] = '\0';
        }
        else for (cp = tparam; c = *cp; cp++)
            if (!(isalpha(c) || isdigit(c) || c == '_'))
            {
                error("Invalid char in identifier name: \"%s\"",
                            tparam);
                *cp = '\0';
                break;
            }
    }

    if ((IIp = find_item(tparam)) != NULL)          /* Item name found? */
        return error("Item name previously used.");

    if ((MIp->Items[n_items] = IIp = create_item(tparam))
                == NULL)
        return ERROR;

    in_item = TRUE;
    Ip = &IIp->Item;

    for (i = 0; i < n_refs; i++)                /* check for fwd refs   */
        if (!strcmp(fwd_refs[i].iname, tparam))
            *fwd_refs[i].refp = n_items;        /* fill in with item # */

    n_items++;                                  /* bump item count      */

    if ((token = gettok()) != T_COLON)          /* optional colon?      */
    {
        ungettok(token);                        /* if not, all done     */
        return OK;
    }

    if ((token = gettok()) == T_STRING)         /* short-form text?     */
        return do_text2();                      /* if so, go process    */
    else
    {
        ungettok(token);                        /* else all done        */
        return OK;
    }
}
```

LISTING 8.4 cmenu2.c *continued*

```
/************************************************************
 * do_opts():
 *  Process simple "binary" options for prompt,
 *  pre- and post-clear specifications.
 *  Note: upon entry, global "token" contains the
 *  value of the token to be processed.
 ************************************************************/

int do_opts()
{
    if (!in_item)
        return error("\"%s\" only valid within an item",
            keywords[token].keyword);

    switch(token)
    {
        case T_PROMPT: case T_PAUSE:
        case T_NOPROMPT: case T_NOPAUSE:
            if (Ip->prompt != DEFAULT)
                return error("Prompt option already specified");
            Ip->prompt= (token==T_PROMPT || token==T_PAUSE)? YES :NO;
            break;

        case T_POSTCLEAR:               /* these are actually no-ops,   */
        case T_NOPOSTCLEAR:             /* but again, I've left them in */
            if (Ip->post_clear != DEFAULT)
                return error("Postclear option already specified");
            Ip->post_clear = (token == T_POSTCLEAR) ? YES : NO;
            break;

        case T_PRECLEAR:
        case T_NOPRECLEAR:
            if (Ip->pre_clear != DEFAULT)
                return error("Preclear option already specified");
            Ip->pre_clear = (token == T_PRECLEAR) ? YES : NO;
            break;
    }
    return OK;
}


/************************************************************
 * do_nextitem():
 *  Process NEXTIEM option.
 ************************************************************/

int do_nextitem()
{
    int tok;

    if (Ip->nextcode != DEFAULT)
        error("Nextitem option already specified");
```

LISTING 8.4 cmenu2.c *continued*

```

    switch (tok = gettok())
    {
        case T_FIRST:
            Ip->nextcode = NXT_FIRST;
            break;

        case T_LAST:
            Ip->nextcode = NXT_LAST;
            break;

        case T_NEXT:
            Ip->nextcode = NXT_NEXT;
            break;

        case T_STRING:
            Ip->nextcode = NXT_DIRECT;
            if (find_item(tparam))
                Ip->nextitem = item_num;
            else
            {                         /* record forward item reference */
                strcpy(fwd_refs[n_refs].iname, tparam);
                fwd_refs[n_refs].refp = &Ip->nextitem;
                fwd_refs[n_refs++].lineno = lineno;
                Ip->nextitem = UNDEF_FWD;
            }
            break;

        default:
            ungettok(tok);
            return error("Bad Nextitem specification");
    }
    return OK;
}


/************************************************************
 * do_text():
 *  Process Text parameter
 ************************************************************/

int do_text()
{
    int tok;

    if (!in_item)
        return error("Text clause must be within an item");
    if (*Ip->text)
        return error("Text clause already specified for this item");
```

LISTING 8.4 cmenu2.c *continued*

```

    if ((tok = gettok()) != T_STRING)
    {
        ungettok(tok);
        return error("Text clause specified without the text.");
    }

    return do_text2();
}


/************************************************************
 * do_text():
 *  Continued TEXT clause processing, shared between
 *  do_text() and do_item().
 ************************************************************/

int do_text2()
{
    if (strlen(tparam) > MAX_TXTWID)
    {
        *Ip->text = 'x';              /* to avoid "missing text" error */
        return error("Text is too long; maximum %d chars",
            MAX_TXTWID);
    }
    else
        strcpy(Ip->text, tparam);

    if (strlen(tparam) > Mp -> widest)
        Mp -> widest = strlen(tparam);

    return OK;
}


/************************************************************
 * do_action():
 *  Process standard action, Exit, Lmenu or Emenu clause
 ************************************************************/

int do_action()
{
    int tok;
    int old_acttyp = Ip->acttyp;

    if (!in_item)
        return error("%s clause only valid within an item",
            keywords[token].keyword);

    if (token == T_EXIT || (tok = gettok()) == T_EXIT)
        Ip->acttyp = ACT_EXIT;
```

LISTING 8.4 cmenu2.c *continued*

```
    else
        if (tok != T_STRING)
        {
            ungettok(tok);
            error("Incomplete %s specification",
            keywords[token].keyword);
        }
    else
        if (strlen(tparam) > MAX_CMD)
            error("%s parameter too long (max %d chars)",
                keywords[token].keyword, MAX_CMD);
    else
        switch(token)
        {
          case T_ACTION:
            strcpy(Ip->action, tparam);
            Ip->acttyp = ACT_CMND;
            break;

          case T_LMENU:
            if (find_menu(tparam) != NULL)     /* named menu defined?  */
                Ip->lmenunum = menu_num;       /* yes.                 */
            else
            {                                  /* no. create entry     */
                MInfo[n_menus] = create_menu(tparam);
                if (fatal)
                    return ERROR;              /* creation error       */
                else
                    Ip->lmenunum = n_menus++;      /* OK; assign.      */
            }

            Ip->acttyp = ACT_LMENU;
            break;

          case T_EMENU:
            strcpy(Ip->action, tparam);
            Ip->acttyp = ACT_EMENU;
            break;
        }

    if (old_acttyp)
        return error("Only one Action clause allowed per item");

    return OK;
}
```

LISTING 8.4 cmenu2.c *continued*

```

/************************************************************
 * do_help():
 *  Process help clause.
 ************************************************************/

int do_help()
{
    int tok;

    if (!in_item)
        return error("Help clause only valid within an item");

    if ((tok = gettok()) != T_STRING)
    {
        ungettok(tok);
        return error("No Help text specified");
    }

    if (strlen(tparam) > MAX_HELP)
        return error("Help text too long (max %d chars)",
            MAX_HELP);

    if (*Ip->help)
        return error("Only one help line allowed per item");

    strcpy(Ip->help, tparam);
    return OK;
}


/************************************************************
 * do_err():
 *  Diagnose hopelessly bad syntax (i.e., encountering a
 *  totally unexpected keyword)
 ************************************************************/

int do_err()
{
    return fatalerr("Unrecoverable Syntax error.");
}

```

LISTING 8.5 cmenu3.c

```
/*************************************************************
 *  Program: CMENU Menu Compiler
 *  Module: cmenu3.c
 *      Menu Compiler:
 *      Token Processing Functions
 *  Written by: Leor Zolman, 7/91
 *************************************************************/

#include "cmenu.h"
#include "ccmenu.h"

#include <ctype.h>

static int unget_flag = FALSE;
static int unget_token;
static char unget_tparam[MAX_CMD];
static int unget_vparam;

static int quoted_text;

#if __STDC__
char *getword(void);
int matchkey(char *);
#else
char *getword();
int matchkey();
#endif

/************************************************************
 * ungettok():
 *  Push a token back into the input stream, to
 *  be returned by the following call to gettok().
 *  Only one level of push-back is supported; any attempt to
 *  push back a token when there is already one pushed back
 *  draws an "internal error" diagnostic.
 ************************************************************/

Void ungettok(tok)
int tok;
{
    if (unget_flag)                 /* can't "unget" more than 1 item! */
        fatalerr("internal error: ungettok() overflow");

    unget_flag = TRUE;
    unget_token = tok;
    unget_vparam = vparam;
    strcpy(unget_tparam, tparam);
    return;
}

```

LISTING 8.5 cmenu3.c *continued*

```

/*************************************************************
 * gettok():
 *  Read a token from the source input stream.
 *  If the token is a reserved word, the appropriate token
 *      value is returned.
 *  If the token is a string, the global "tparam" is set
 *      to the text of the string. White space within the
 *      string is only recognized if double quote ("...")
 *      characters are used to delimit the string.
 *      T_STRING is returned.
 *  If the token is a numeric value, the global "vparam"
 *      is set to the integer value specified, and
 *      T_VALUE is returned.
 *  Returns T_EOF on end-of-file.
 *************************************************************/

int gettok()
{
    register c;
    char nexttok[MAX_CMD];
    char *wordp;

    if (unget_flag)                    /* was a token "pushed back"?   */
    {                          /* yes. set the pushed-back values and  */
        vparam = unget_vparam;                         /* attributes    */
        strcpy(tparam, unget_tparam);                  /* clear the     */
        unget_flag = FALSE;                            /* flag          */
        return unget_token;                    /* return pushed token   */
    }

    *tparam = '\0';                                /* clear parameter   */
    vparam = 0;                                    /* value registers   */

    if (!*(wordp = getword()))                     /* get a token.      */
        return token = T_EOF;                      /* End of file       */

    if (quoted_text)                               /* string enclosed   */
    {                                              /* in quotes?        */
        strcpy(tparam, wordp);
        return T_STRING;
    }

    if (!strcmp(wordp, ":"))                       /* colon is special */
        return T_COLON;                            /* (non-alphabetic) */

    if (c = matchkey(wordp))                       /* reserved word?   */
        return c;                                  /* yes, just return */

    if (isdigit(*wordp))                   /* handle numeric value */
    {
        vparam = atoi(wordp);
        return T_VALUE;
    }
```

LISTING 8.5 cmenu3.c *continued*

```
    else
    {
        strcpy(tparam, wordp);
        return T_STRING;
    }
}


/**************************************************************
 * getword():
 *  Read the next syntactic object from the input stream,
 *  and return a pointer to it.
 *  Return pointer to a null string on EOF.
 *  If object is a quoted string, drop the quotes and
 *      set the quoted_text flag (preserve whitespace).
 *  Otherwise strip all whitespace, commas and comments,
 *      return pointer to next word/number.
 *  Track current line number by incrementing lineno
 *      on each newline encountered.
 *************************************************************/

char *getword()
{
    static char tok[MAX_CMD];
    char quote_char;
    register c,i;

    quoted_text = FALSE;
    *tok = '\0';

    while ((c = getc(fp)) != EOF)
    {
        if (c == '\n')                          /* bump line number if  */
            lineno++;                           /* newline encountered  */

        if (isspace(c))                         /* skip all whitespace  */
            continue;

        if (c == ',' || c == ';')               /* legal separators: ,; */
            continue;

        if (c == ':')                           /* special case: colon  */
            return ":";

        if (c == '#')                           /* process comment      */
        {                                   /* wait for newline or EOF  */
            while(c = getc(fp))
            {
                if (c == EOF)
                    break;
```

LISTING 8.5 cmenu3.c *continued*

```
            if (c == '\n')
            {
                lineno++;
                break;
            }
        }
        continue;                           /* then get next token  */
    }

    if (c == '"' || c == '\'')              /* quoted string?       */
    {
        quoted_text = TRUE;
        quote_char = c;
        for (i = 0; ;i++)
        {
            switch (c = getc(fp))
            {
                case '\n':
                    fatalerr("Unterminated string");
                    return NULL;

                case EOF:
                    fatalerr("Unterminated string (line %d)",
                            lineno);
                    return NULL;

                case '"':
                case '\'':
                    if (c == quote_char)
                    {
                        tok[i] = '\0';
                        return tok;
                    }

                default:
                    if (i == MAX_CMD)
                    {
                        tok[i - 1] = '\0';
                        fatalerr("String too long (max %d chars)",
                            MAX_CMD);
                        return NULL;
                    }
                    tok[i] = c;
            }
        }
    }

    tok[0] = c;
    for (i = 1; (c = getc(fp)) != EOF; i++)
        if (isspace(c) || c == ';' || c == ','
                || c == ':')
            break;
```

LISTING 8.5 cmenu3.c *continued*

```
            else
                tok[i] = tolower(c);
        tok[i] = '\0';
        ungetc(c, fp);
        break;
    }
    return tok;
}
```

LISTING 8.6 dmenu.c

```
/*************************************************************
 *  Program:    DMENU Menu Object File Analyzer
 *  Module:     dmenu.c
 *  dmenu.c:    Reads a menu object file, for debuging menu
 *              compiler
 *
 *  Written by: Leor Zolman, 7/91
 *
 *  Menu object file format:
 *  ----------------------------------------------------------
 *      <count>         (integer count of # of menus in file)
 *      MENU 1          (MENU structure for 1st Menu)
 *          ITEM 1
 *          ITEM 2
 *          ...
 *          ITEM n_items
 *      MENU 2          (MENU structure for 2nd Menu)
 *          ...
 *      .
 *      .
 *      .
 *      MENU <count>    (MENU structure for final Menu)
 *          ...
 *
 *  ----------------------------------------------------------
 *  Compile:
 *      Xenix:  cc dmenu.c -o dmenu
 *      DOS:    bcc dmenu.c     (Borland C++)
 *************************************************************/

#include <stdio.h>
#include "cmenu.h"

#define OK  0

MENU Menu;
ITEM Item, *ip = &Item;

char obj_name[MAX_CMD];
int n_menus;

int main(argc,argv)
int argc;
char **argv;
{
    register i, j;
    int count;
    FILE *fp;

    if (argc != 2)
        exit(puts("usage: dmenu <menu-object>\n"));

    strcpy(obj_name, argv[1]);
    strcat(obj_name, ".mnc");
```

LISTING 8.6 dmenu.c *continued*

```

    if ((fp = fopen(obj_name, "rb")) == NULL)
    {
        fprintf(stderr,
            "Cannot open %s for reading.\n", obj_name);
        return ERROR;
    }

    if (fread((Void *)&n_menus, sizeof n_menus, 1, fp) != 1)
    {
        fprintf(stderr,
            "Error reading menu count from %s\n", obj_name);
        return ERROR;
    }
    printf("Menu count = %d\n", n_menus);

    for (i = 0; i < n_menus; i++)
    {
        if (fread((Void *) &Menu, sizeof (MENU), 1, fp) != 1)
        {
            fprintf(stderr,
                "Error reading from %s\n", obj_name);
            return ERROR;
        }

        printf("******** Start of Menu #%d: *********\n", i+1);
        printf("\tTitle: %s\n", Menu.title);
        printf("\tPath:  %s\n", Menu.path);
        printf("\tContains %d items.\n", Menu.nitems);
        printf("\talign =  %c\n", Menu.align);
        printf("\tColumns = %d, ", Menu.columns);
        printf("Spacing = %d, Widest = %d\n",
                Menu.spacing, Menu.widest);
        printf("\tShell escapes are %sallowed",
                Menu.escape == YES ? "" : "NOT ");
        printf("\n");

        for (j = 0; j < Menu.nitems; j++)
        {
            if (fread((Void *) ip, sizeof (ITEM), 1, fp) != 1)
            {
                fprintf(stderr,
                    "Error reading from %s\n", obj_name);
                return ERROR;
            }
            printf("Item #%d:\n", j+1);
            printf("\tTEXT =   %s\n", ip->text);
            printf("\tPATH =   %s\n", ip->path);
            printf("\tACTION = %s\n", ip->action);
            printf("\tHELP =   %s\n", ip->help);
            printf("pre-clear =  %c\n", ip->pre_clear);
            printf("post-clear = %c\n", ip->post_clear);
            printf("prompt =     %c\n", ip->prompt);
            printf("acttyp =     %d\n", ip->acttyp);
```

LISTING 8.6 dmenu.c *continued*

```
            printf("lmenunum =   %d\n", ip->lmenunum);
            printf("nextcode =   %d\n", ip->nextcode);
            printf("nextitem =   %d\n", ip->nextitem);
            printf("\n");
        }
        printf("**** END OF MENU #%d ****\n", i+1);
    }
    return OK;
}
```

LISTING 8.7 rcmenu.h

```
/************************************************************
 *  Program: RMENU Menu Interpreter
 *  Module: rcmenu.h -- Interpreter Module header file
 *  Written by: Leor Zolman, 7/91
 ************************************************************/

#include <curses.h>

/********************** Extern control **********************/

#ifndef MASTER
#   define Extern extern
#else
#   define Extern
#endif

#define min(x,y) ((x) < (y) ? (x) : (y))


/********************* Curses Configuration ****************/

#ifndef KEY_UP
#   define  OLD_CURSES 1
#else
#   define  OLD_CURSES 0
#endif

#if OLD_CURSES
#   define  INIT_FAIL   ERR
#   ifdef CTRL
#       undef CTRL
#   endif
#   define CTRL(x)      ((x) & 037)
#   define  KEY_UP      CTRL('P')
#   define  KEY_DOWN    CTRL('N')
#   define  KEY_LEFT    CTRL('B')
#   define  KEY_RIGHT   CTRL('F')
#   define  beep()      write(1, "\007", 1);
#   define  keypad(a,b)
#else
#   define  INIT_FAIL   NULL
#endif

#if XENIX
#define resetty reset_tty
#endif


/*************** Default menu control options ***************/

#define ON_ERROR        50                  /* prompt option            */

#define SHELL_PROMPT    FALSE               /* Prompt for shell escape? */

```

LISTING 8.7 rcmenu.h *continued*

```
#define DEF_PRECLEAR    YES
#define DEF_POSTCLEAR   NO
#define DEF_PROMPT      ON_ERROR            /*  YES, NO or ON_ERROR   */
#define DEF_ESCAPE      YES

#define DEF_COLUMNS     1
#define DEF_SPACING     2


/************** Screen layout characteristics ***************/

#define MAX_IROWS   18                 /* # of item rows MUST BE EVEN) */
#define HOME_Y      2                  /* upper left y for 1st Item    */
#define HOME_X      1                  /* upper left x for 1st Item    */
#define SCREEN_COLS 80                 /* # of columns on the screen   */

#define TITLE_ROW   0                  /* row on screen for menu title */
#define HELP_ROWO   20                 /* row that "HELP" sign goes on */
#define HELP_COLO   36                 /* column that "HELP" sign goes */
#define HELP_ROW    21                 /* row on screen for HELP text  */
#define PROMPT_ROW  23                 /* row for prompt text          */

/** System/hardware-dependent Key codes and line numbers: ***/

#if DOS
#   define LAST_ROW       24               /* last row of screen       */
#   define MAX_PATH_STACK 5                /* maximum nested submenus  */
#else
#   define LAST_ROW     23                 /* last row of screen       */
#endif

#define ERR_ROW     (PROMPT_ROW - 1)


/************** Shell Escape Control Parameters *************/

#define SH_PROMPT_STR \
     " Press Enter for sub-shell, ESC to abort\
 ('exit' returns from shell): "

#define MENU_OPTS \
 " Space/arrows/item#=Choose  ENTER=Run\
  'e'=Previous  'x'=Exit "

#define MENU_SHELL  " !=shell "
#define MENU_PROMPT " -> "

#if DOS
#   define  SHELL_ESC   "command"
#else
#   define SHELL_ESC    "PS1=\"\n('exit' returns to\
 Menu)\n$ \"; export PS1; exec sh -"
#endif

```

LISTING 8.7 rcmenu.h *continued*

```

/********** Other Miscellaneous constants: *****************/

#define ESC         033                 /* ESC key                    */
#define EXITALL     2                   /* "super exit" code          */

#define KEY_RUN     '\r'                    /* raw-mode Enter key     */

#define K_DIRECT    (-2)                /* values returned by get_cmd() */
#define K_EXIT      (-3)
#define K_EXITALL   (-4)
#define K_SHELL     (-5)
#define K_UNKNOWN   (-6)
#define K_VERSION   (-7)                /* report version number      */

#define STANDOUT    1                   /* video mode codes passed to  */
#define NORMAL      2                   /* the draw_item() function    */


/********************** Global data *************************/

Extern struct levels {
    int n_menus;                                /* # currently active   */
    int max_menus;                              /* highest ever active  */
    struct menu2 {
        int most_items;                         /* most Items allocated */
        MENU Menu;                              /* the header structure */
        ITEM *Items[MAX_ITEMS];                 /* the actual items     */

        int field_len;                          /* length of item field */
        struct coord {                          /* coords of each item  */
            int ypos, xpos;
            int spaces_needed;                  /* # of spaces to fill  */
        } coords[MAX_ITEMS];

    } *Menus[MAX_MENUS];
} LMenus[MAX_NEST];

typedef struct levels LEVELS;
typedef struct menu2 MENU2;
typedef struct coord COORDS;

Extern  int     nestlev;                /* current nesting level       */
Extern  int     echox, echoy;           /* Location of item # echo area */
Extern  int     debug;                  /* true to display sys commands */

/********************** Prototypes: *************************/

#if __STDC__ || XENIX           /* Standard C, supporting prototypes: */

void    init_win(void);
void    close_win(void);
void    pre_shell(void);
void    post_shell(void);
```

LISTING 8.7 rcmenu.h *continued*

```
void    tty_curses(void);
void    tty_shell(void);
void    push_path(void);
void    pop_path(void);

int     ld_menu(char *);
void    placement(MENU *);
void    free_menus(void);
int     do_menu(char *, char *);
int     sub_menu(int, char *);
void    draw_menu(MENU2 *, int);
int     get_cmd(int, int, int *);
int     put_msg(int, char *, ...);
int     do_item(MENU2 *, int, char *);
void    draw_item(MENU2 *, int, int, int);
int     fatal(char *, ...);
void    do_cmnd(ITEM *, char *);
int     do_emenu(ITEM *, char *);
int     system0(char *);
char *  make_path( char *, char *);
char *  make_cmd( char *, char *);

#else                                   /* K&R C, minimal "prototypes:" */

int     init_win();
int     close_win();
int     pre_shell();
int     post_shell();
int     tty_curses();
int     tty_shell();
int     push_path();
int     pop_path();

int     ld_menu();
int     placement();
int     free_menus();
int     do_menu();
int     sub_menu();
int     draw_menu();
int     get_cmd();
int     put_msg();
int     do_item();
int     draw_item();
int     fatal();
int     do_cmnd();
int     do_emenu();
int     system0();
char *  make_path();
char *  make_cmd();

#endif
```

LISTING 8.8 rmenu1.c

```
/************************************************************
 *  Program: RMENU Menu Interpreter
 *  Module: rmenu1.c
 *      Main and Utility Functions
 *  Written by: Leor Zolman, 7/91
 ************************************************************/

#define MASTER
#include "cmenu.h"
#include "rcmenu.h"

#if __STDC__
#   include <stdarg.h>
#else
#   include <varargs.h>
#endif

/************************************************************
 * main():
 *  Initialize the program and run
 *  the master menu
 ************************************************************/

main(argc, argv)
int argc;
char **argv;
{
    char *mname = "menu";
    int i, j;

    debug = 0;                          /* No debugging by default      */

                                       /* Process command line options: */
    for (i = 1; i < argc; i++)
        if (argv[i][0] == '-')
        {
            switch (tolower(argv[i][1]))
            {
                case 'd':   debug = TRUE;
                            break;

                default:    fprintf(stderr, "Unknown option: '%s'\n",
                                        argv[i]);
                            exit(0);
            }
            for (j = i; j < argc - 1; j++)              /* compress */
                argv[j] = argv[j + 1];                  /* arg list */
            argc--;
            i--;
        }
```

LISTING 8.8 rmenu1.c *continued*

```
    init_win();                                     /* initialize curses */

    if (argc == 2)
        mname = argv[1];

    nestlev = 0;
    do_menu("", mname);
    free_menus();
    close_win();
    return OK;
}


/************************************************************
 * init_win():
 *  Initialize Curses system.
 ************************************************************/

Void init_win()
{
                           /* initialize screen, and check for failure */
    if (initscr() == INIT_FAIL)
    {
        printf("initscr failed!\n");
        exit(1);
    }

    tty_curses();                              /* set tty modes for curses */
    return;
}


/************************************************************
 * close_win():
 *  Terminate Curses system
 ************************************************************/

Void close_win()
{
    clear();
    noraw();
    refresh();                        /* This is so cursor shows back up  */
    endwin();
}

```

LISTING 8.8 rmenu1.c *continued*

```

/**************************************************************
 * do_menu():
 *  Run a compiled menu file, supporting recursive
 *  calls for nested external menus.
 *  Default command/menu path is supplied as "path".
 **************************************************************/

int do_menu(path, file)
char *path, *file;
{
    char pathname[MAX_PATH];

    strcpy(pathname, path);
    if (*path)
        strcat(pathname, "/");
    strcat(pathname, file);
    strcat(pathname, ".mnc");

    if (ld_menu(pathname) == ERROR)
        return EXITALL;

    return sub_menu(0, path);                /* run main menu in file */
}


/**************************************************************
 * ld_menu():
 *  Load a compiled menu object file from disk,
 *  into nesting level nestlev, allocating memory
 *  as required.
 *  For each menu in the menu file being loaded,
 *  compute screen placement as per spacing/columns
 *  specifications and the total number of items.
 **************************************************************/

int ld_menu(path)
char *path;
{
    LEVELS *Levp = &LMenus[nestlev];
    MENU *Mp;
    ITEM *Ip;
    MENU2 *M2p;

    FILE *fp;
    int i, j, k, l;

    if ((fp = fopen(path, "rb")) == NULL)
        return fatal("Can't open %s\n", path);

    if (fread((Void *) &Levp->n_menus, sizeof (int), 1, fp)
                != 1)
        return fatal("Error reading menu count from %s\n", path);

```

LISTING 8.8 rmenu1.c *continued*

```
    for (i = 0; i < Levp->n_menus; i++)
    {
        if (i < Levp -> max_menus)
            M2p = Levp -> Menus[i];
        else                                   /* allocate memory for Menu */
        {
            M2p = Levp -> Menus[i] = (MENU2 *) malloc(sizeof(MENU2));
            if (M2p == NULL)
                return fatal("Out of memory loading %s\n", path);
            Levp -> max_menus++;
            M2p -> most_items = 0;
        }

        Mp = &M2p -> Menu;

        if (fread((Void *) Mp, sizeof(MENU), 1, fp) != 1)
            return fatal("Error reading Menu data from %s\n", path);

                           /* Now determine screen placement strategy. */

        placement(Mp);

        M2p -> field_len = min(MAX_TXTWID,
                    (SCREEN_COLS / Mp -> columns) - 5);

               /* Read in each item, and assign screen coordinate info */
               /* to each on-the-fly as per spacing/column parameters  */

        for (j = 0; j < Mp -> nitems; j++)
        {
            if (j < M2p -> most_items)
                Ip = M2p -> Items[j];
            else
            {
                Ip = M2p -> Items[j] = (ITEM *) malloc(sizeof(ITEM));
                if (Ip == NULL)
                    fatal("Out of memory loading %s, menu #%d/item #%d",
                        path, i,j);
                M2p -> most_items++;
            }
            if (fread((Void *) Ip, sizeof(ITEM), 1, fp) != 1)
                return fatal("Error reading %s\n", path);

            Ip -> text[M2p -> field_len - 1] = '\0';        /* truncate */

            if ((Ip -> acttyp == ACT_LMENU ||
                 Ip -> acttyp == ACT_EMENU) &&
                strlen(Ip -> text) + 6 < M2p -> field_len)
            {
                int limit;

                limit = min (Mp -> widest + 2,
                        M2p -> field_len - 7);
                for (k = strlen(Ip -> text);
```

LISTING 8.8 rmenu1.c *continued*

```
                        k < limit && k < (MAX_TXTWID - 6); k++)
                    strcat(Ip -> text, " ");
                strcat(Ip -> text, "(MENU)");
            }

            M2p -> coords[j].ypos =
                    HOME_Y + (j % (MAX_IROWS / Mp -> spacing))
                                * Mp -> spacing;

            M2p -> coords[j].xpos =
                    HOME_X + (j / (MAX_IROWS / Mp -> spacing))
                            * (SCREEN_COLS / Mp -> columns);

            M2p -> coords[j].spaces_needed =
                    min(M2p -> field_len, Mp -> widest)
                            - strlen(Ip -> text);
        }
    }
    fclose(fp);
    return OK;
}


/*************************************************************
 * placement():
 *  Calculate values for columns and spacing
 *  for the given Menu:
 *************************************************************/

Void placement(Mp)
MENU *Mp;
{
    int columns = Mp -> columns;
    int spacing = Mp -> spacing;
    int nitems = Mp -> nitems;

                           /* Step 1: fill in real values if either    */
                           /*    columns or spacing was not specified: */

    if (spacing == DEFAULT && columns == DEFAULT)
    {
        if (nitems <= (MAX_IROWS / 2))
        {
            Mp -> columns = 1;
            Mp -> spacing = 2;
        }
        else if (nitems <= MAX_IROWS)
            if ((Mp -> widest * 2 + 5) <= SCREEN_COLS)
                Mp -> columns = Mp -> spacing = 2;
            else
                Mp -> columns = Mp -> spacing = 1;
        else
        {
            Mp -> spacing = 1;
```

LISTING 8.8 rmenu1.c *continued*

```
            Mp -> columns = (nitems - 1) / MAX_IROWS + 1;
        }
    }
    else if (spacing == DEFAULT)
        Mp -> spacing =
                (nitems <= (MAX_IROWS / 2)) ? 2 : 1;
    else if (columns == DEFAULT)
        if (Mp -> spacing == 1)
            Mp -> columns = (nitems - 1) / MAX_IROWS + 1;
        else
            Mp -> columns = (nitems - 1) / (MAX_IROWS / 2) + 1;

                                    /* Step 2: Adjust if out of range: */

    while (MAX_IROWS / Mp -> spacing * Mp -> columns < nitems)
        if (Mp -> spacing != 1)
            Mp -> spacing = 1;
        else
            Mp -> columns++;
    return;
}


/*************************************************************
 * free_menus():
 *  Free up memory allocated for ALL menu items:
 *************************************************************/

Void free_menus()
{
    int i, j, k;
    MENU2 *m2p;

    for (i = 0; i < MAX_NEST; i++)
        for (j = 0; j < LMenus[i].max_menus; j++)
        {
            m2p = LMenus[i].Menus[j];
            for (k = 0; k < m2p -> most_items; k++)
                free(m2p -> Items[k]);
            free(m2p);
        }
}

```

LISTING 8.8 rmenu1.c *continued*

```

/****************************************************************
 * fatal(): Complain and exit.
 ****************************************************************/

#if __STDC__                      /* use ANSI variable-#-of-args method   */

int fatal (char *fmt, ...)
{
    va_list arglist;

    va_start(arglist, fmt);

#else                             /* or old varargs method:               */

int fatal(fmt, va_alist)
char *fmt;
va_dcl
{
    va_list arglist;

    va_start(arglist);

#endif
                                  /* rest of function same, ANSI or not:  */
    pre_shell();
    beep();
    fprintf(stderr, "\n\nFatal error in rmenu: ");
    vfprintf(stderr, fmt, arglist);
    va_end(arglist);
    fprintf(stderr, "(Press any key to continue)");
    post_shell();
    (Void)getch();
    return ERROR;
}


/****************************************************************
 * put_msg(): Display a message on the menu screen
 *  Return the character typed to continue
 ****************************************************************/

#if __STDC__
  int put_msg (int bell, char *text, ...)
#else
  int put_msg(bell, text)
  int bell;
  char *text;
#endif
```

LISTING 8.8 rmenu1.c *continued*

```
{
    char **textp = &text;
    int c;

    move(ERR_ROW, 0);
    standout();

    if (bell)
        beep();

    printw(text, *(textp + 1), *(textp + 2));
    refresh();

    c = getch();

    move (ERR_ROW, 0);
    standend();
    clrtoeol();
    refresh();
    return c;
}
```

LISTING 8.9 rmenu2.c

```
/*************************************************************
 *  Program: RMENU Menu Interpreter
 *  Module: rmenu2.c
 *  Top-level menu processing
 *  Written by: Leor Zolman, 7/91
 *************************************************************/

#include "cmenu.h"
#include "rcmenu.h"

#include <ctype.h>


/*************************************************************
 * sub_menu():
 *  Run a local menu at the given nesting level
 *  Default command/menu path is supplied via "path".
 *************************************************************/

int sub_menu(mnum, path)
int mnum;
char *path;
{
    MENU2 *M2p = LMenus[nestlev].Menus[mnum];
    MENU *Mp = &M2p -> Menu;
    char newpath[MAX_PATH];

    int cur_item = 0;
    int sel_val = 0;
    int factor;

    draw_menu(M2p, cur_item);                  /* display the menu     */

    strcpy(newpath, make_path(path, Mp -> path));

    while (1)
    {
        switch (get_cmd(Mp -> nitems, cur_item, &sel_val))
        {
            case  KEY_UP:
                draw_item(M2p, cur_item, NORMAL, NO);
                cur_item = cur_item ? cur_item - 1 :
                        Mp -> nitems - 1;
                draw_item(M2p, cur_item, STANDOUT, YES);
                break;

            case KEY_DOWN:
                draw_item(M2p, cur_item, NORMAL, NO);
                cur_item = (cur_item == Mp -> nitems - 1) ? 0 :
                        cur_item + 1;
                draw_item(M2p, cur_item, STANDOUT, YES);
                break;
```

LISTING 8.9 rmenu2.c *continued*

```

            case KEY_RIGHT:
                if (Mp -> columns == 1)
                    break;

                draw_item(M2p, cur_item, NORMAL, NO);

                factor = MAX_IROWS / Mp -> spacing;
                if (cur_item + factor < Mp -> nitems)
                    cur_item += factor;
                else
                    cur_item %= factor;

                draw_item(M2p, cur_item, STANDOUT, YES);
                break;

            case KEY_LEFT:
                if (Mp -> columns == 1)
                    break;
                draw_item(M2p, cur_item, NORMAL, NO);

                factor = MAX_IROWS / Mp -> spacing;
                if (cur_item >= factor)
                    cur_item -= factor;
                else
                    while (cur_item + factor < Mp -> nitems)
                        cur_item += factor;

                draw_item(M2p, cur_item, STANDOUT, YES);
                break;

            case KEY_RUN:
                if (M2p -> Items[cur_item] -> acttyp == ACT_EXIT)
                    return OK;
                if (do_item(M2p, cur_item, newpath) == EXITALL)
                    return EXITALL;

                switch(M2p -> Items[cur_item] -> nextcode)
                {
                    case NXT_FIRST:
                        cur_item = 0;
                        break;

                    case NXT_LAST:
                        cur_item = M2p -> Menu.nitems - 1;
                        break;

                    case NXT_NEXT:
                        if (cur_item < M2p -> Menu.nitems - 1)
                            cur_item++;
                        break;

```

LISTING 8.9 rmenu2.c *continued*

```
                    case NXT_DIRECT:
                        cur_item = M2p -> Items[cur_item] -> nextitem;
                        break;
                }

                draw_menu(M2p, cur_item);                    /* redisplay menu */
                break;

            case K_DIRECT:
                if ((sel_val - 1) != cur_item)
                {
                    draw_item(M2p, cur_item, NORMAL, NO);
                    cur_item = sel_val - 1;
                    draw_item(M2p, cur_item, STANDOUT, YES);
                }
                break;

            case K_SHELL:
                if (M2p -> Menu.escape == YES ||
                  (M2p -> Menu.escape == DEFAULT && DEF_ESCAPE == YES))
                {
#if SHELL_PROMPT
                    if (put_msg(0, SH_PROMPT_STR) == ESC)
                        break;
#else
                    move(ERR_ROW, 0);
                    standout();
                    addstr("Invoking shell. . .");
                    standend();
#endif

                    pre_shell();          /* set up for shell call    */
                    system(SHELL_ESC);    /* run a shell              */
                    post_shell();         /* restore everything       */

                    draw_menu(M2p, cur_item);
                }
                else
                  put_msg(1, "Sorry, shell escapes are disabled.");
                break;

            case K_EXIT:
                return OK;

            case K_EXITALL:
                return EXITALL;

            case K_VERSION:
                put_msg(0, " RMENU Menu Interpreter v%s ",
                             VERSION);
                break;

```

LISTING 8.9 rmenu2.c *continued*

```
            case K_UNKNOWN:
                beep();
        }
        refresh();
    }
}


/*************************************************************
 * draw_menu():
 *  Display the entire menu, including all prompts,
 *  and titles and help text (if any) for current item
 *  on the screen.
 *************************************************************/

Void draw_menu(M2p, curr)
MENU2 *M2p;
int curr;
{
    MENU *Mp = &M2p -> Menu;
    int title_len = strlen(Mp -> title);
    int i, j;

    clear();

    move(TITLE_ROW, (SCREEN_COLS - title_len)/2);
    addstr(Mp -> title);                            /* Put up menu title */

    for (i = 0; i < Mp -> nitems; i++)
        if (i == curr)
            draw_item(M2p, i, STANDOUT, YES);
        else
            draw_item(M2p, i, NORMAL, NO);

    move(PROMPT_ROW, 0);
    addstr(MENU_OPTS);
    if (Mp -> escape == YES ||
            (Mp -> escape == DEFAULT && DEF_ESCAPE == YES))
        addstr(MENU_SHELL);
    addstr(MENU_PROMPT);
    getyx(stdscr, echoy, echox);    /* save coords of item # echo area */

    refresh();                                     /* display the window */

}
```

LISTING 8.9 rmenu2.c *continued*

```

/****************************************************************
 * draw_item():
 *  Display a single item (the current item) of the
 *  specified menu, using the specified video mode.
 *  Display assiciated help text only if "dohelp"
 *  is TRUE.
 ****************************************************************/

Void draw_item(M2p, item, vid_mode, dohelp)
MENU2 *M2p;
int item, vid_mode, dohelp;
{
    ITEM *Ip = M2p -> Items[item];
    COORDS *Cp = &M2p -> coords[item];
    int j;

    move (Cp->ypos, Cp->xpos);
    printw("%2d.", item + 1);

    if (vid_mode == STANDOUT)
        standout();

    printw(" %s", Ip -> text);

    for (j = 0; j < Cp -> spaces_needed; j++)
            addch(' ');

    if (vid_mode == STANDOUT)
        standend();

    if (dohelp == YES)
    {
        move(HELP_ROW0, HELP_COL0);

        if (*Ip -> help)
        {
            addstr(" HELP: ");                 /* display help text    */
            standout();
            move (HELP_ROW, (80 - strlen(Ip -> help))/2);
            addstr(Ip -> help);
            standend();
        }
        else
        {
            addstr("       ");                 /* clear help text area */
            move(HELP_ROW, 0);
        }

        clrtoeol();
    }
}


```

LISTING 8.9 rmenu2.c *continued*

```
/****************************************************************
 * get_cmd()
 *  Get a command from the user.
 *  Arrow keys or space returns the appropriate K_ code.
 *  Pressing Enter returns the K_RUN code.
 *  Pressing ! returns the K_SHELL code.
 *  Entering a direct number returns K_DIRECT,
 *  and the sel_val is set (indirectly) to selection number
 *  (1-based).
 ****************************************************************/

int get_cmd(nitems, curr, sel_val)
int nitems;
int curr;
int *sel_val;
{
    int ch;
    int newval;
    int savy, savx;

    static int digits = FALSE;          /* true if digits being entered */

    move(echoy, echox);                     /* move to prompt location */
    printw("%d", curr + 1);
    getyx(stdscr, savy, savx);
    clrtoeol();
    move(savy, savx);
    refresh();

    while (1)
    {
        ch = getch();
        if (!isdigit(ch))
            digits = FALSE;
        switch (ch)
        {
            case KEY_UP:
            case '\b':              /* WYSE 60s send this for left arrow */
                clrtoeol();
                return KEY_UP;

            case ' ':
            case KEY_DOWN:
#if UNIX || XENIX
            case '\n':              /* WYSE 60s send this for down arrow */
#endif
                clrtoeol();
                return KEY_DOWN;

            case KEY_RIGHT:
                return KEY_RIGHT;
```

LISTING 8.9 rmenu2.c *continued*

```

            case KEY_LEFT:
                return KEY_LEFT;

            case KEY_RUN:
                return KEY_RUN;

            case 'e':
            case 'E':
                return K_EXIT;

            case 'x':
            case 'X':
                return K_EXITALL;

            case 'v':
            case 'V':
                return K_VERSION;

            case '!':
                return K_SHELL;

            case ESC:                               /* clear digits area */
                digits = FALSE;
                move(echoy, echox);
                clrtoeol();
                refresh();
                break;

            default:                                    /* handle digits */
                if (!isdigit(ch))
                    return K_UNKNOWN;

                if (digits &&
                    (newval = *sel_val * 10 + (ch - '0')) <= nitems
                        && newval > 0)
                {
                    addch(ch);
                    refresh();
                    *sel_val = newval;
                    return K_DIRECT;
                }
                else if ( (newval = ch - '0') && newval <= nitems)
                {
                    digits = TRUE;
                    move(echoy, echox);
                    addch(ch);
                    clrtoeol();
                    refresh();
                    *sel_val = newval;
                    return K_DIRECT;
                }
                else
                {
```

LISTING 8.9 rmenu2.c *continued*

```
                        digits = FALSE;
                        beep();
                    }
            }
        }
}
```

LISTING 8.10 rmenu3.c

```
/*************************************************************
 *  Program: RMENU Menu Interpreter
 *  Module: rmenu3.c
 *      Execute a Menu Item
 *  Written by: Leor Zolman, 7/91
 *************************************************************/

#include "cmenu.h"
#include "rcmenu.h"


/*************************************************************
 * do_item():
 *  Perform the action associated with a particular item.
 *  Default path is supplied as "path":
 *************************************************************/

int do_item(M2p, curr, path)
MENU2 *M2p;
int curr;
char *path;
{
    ITEM *Ip = M2p -> Items[curr];
    char newpath[MAX_PATH];
    int i, j;

    strcpy(newpath, make_path(path, Ip -> path));

    switch (Ip -> acttyp)
    {
        case ACT_CMND:
            do_cmnd(Ip, newpath);
            break;

        case ACT_LMENU:
            if (sub_menu(Ip->lmenunum, newpath) == EXITALL)
                return EXITALL;
            break;

        case ACT_EMENU:
            if (do_emenu(Ip, newpath) == EXITALL)
                return EXITALL;
            break;
    }
    return OK;
}


/*************************************************************
 * do_cmnd():
 *  Run a directly executable item.
 *************************************************************/

Void do_cmnd(Ip, path)
```

LISTING 8.10 rmenu3.c *continued*

```
ITEM *Ip;
char *path;
{
    char *cmd_line;
    int retval;

    cmd_line = make_cmd(path, Ip -> action);

    if (Ip -> pre_clear == YES ||
        (Ip -> pre_clear == DEFAULT && DEF_PRECLEAR == YES))
            clear();

    move(0, 0);
    refresh();

    if (debug)
        put_msg(0, "About to exec: %s", cmd_line);

    pre_shell();                              /* set up for shell call     */
    retval = system0(cmd_line);               /* make the shell call       */

    switch (Ip -> prompt)                     /* decide whether to prompt */
    {                                         /* or not after the command */
        case NO:                              /* explicit no is clear      */
            break;

        case DEFAULT:                         /* if unspecified, then...   */

#if (DEF_PROMPT == NO)                        /* if default is NO,         */
                break;                        /* then don't prompt         */
#endif

#if (DEF_PROMPT == ON_ERROR)                  /* if prompting on errors,   */
            if (!retval)                      /* but there wasn't any      */
                break;                        /* error, then don't prompt */
#endif
                                              /* else fall through to YES */
        case YES:
            puts("\nPress RETURN to continue . . .");
            (Void) getchar();
    }
                                              /* Upon return from shell,   */
    post_shell();                             /* restore everything        */
}


/******************************************************************
 * do_emenu():
 *  Run an external menu specification.
 ******************************************************************/

int do_emenu(Ip, path)
ITEM *Ip;
char *path;
```

LISTING 8.10 rmenu3.c *continued*

```
{
    char filename[MAX_PATH];
    int retval;

    if (nestlev == MAX_NEST - 1)
        fatal("Too many nested external menus (increase MAX_NEST)");

    strcpy(filename, make_path(path, Ip -> action));

    nestlev++;
    retval = do_menu("", filename);
    nestlev--;

    return retval;
}


/************************************************************
 * pre_shell()
 *  Set tty mode for a shell call
 *  DOS only: save drive and path for later restoration
 ************************************************************/


Void pre_shell()
{
    push_path();
    tty_shell();
}


/************************************************************
 * post_shell()
 *  Set tty mode for curses
 *  DOS only: restore drive and path from before shell call
 ************************************************************/

Void post_shell()
{
    pop_path();
    tty_curses();
}


```

LISTING 8.11 rmenu4.c

```
/*************************************************************
 *  Program: RMENU Menu Interpreter
 *  Module: rmenu4.c
 *      System-dependent Utility functions
 *  Written by: Leor Zolman, 7/91
 *************************************************************/

#include "cmenu.h"
#include "rcmenu.h"

#if DOS
#include <dir.h>

static struct {
    int curdrive;
    char curpath[MAX_PATH];
} path_stack[MAX_PATH_STACK];

static int path_stackp = 0;
#endif


/*************************************************************
 * push_path()
 *  DOS only: save drive and path for later restoration, and
 *      select new drive based on new path
 *  Unix: a no-op, since sub-shells cannot affect parent path
 *************************************************************/

Void push_path()
{
#if DOS
    if (path_stackp == MAX_PATH_STACK)
        fatal("Maximum stack nesting reached");
    else
    {
        path_stack[path_stackp].curdrive = getdisk();
        getcwd(path_stack[path_stackp].curpath, MAX_PATH);
        path_stackp++;
    }
#endif
    return;
}


/*************************************************************
 * pop_path()
 *  DOS only: restore drive and path from path stack
 *  Unix: a no-op, since sub-shells cannot affect parent path
 *************************************************************/

Void pop_path()
{
#if DOS
```

LISTING 8.11 rmenu4.c *continued*

```
        path_stackp--;
        setdisk(path_stack[path_stackp].curdrive);
        chdir(path_stack[path_stackp].curpath);
#endif
    return;
}


/***************************************************************
 * tty_shell()
 *  Set tty mode for a shell call
 ***************************************************************/

Void tty_shell()
{
#if XENIX || (UNIX && OLD_CURSES)
        resetty();
#else
        endwin();
#endif
    return;
}


/***************************************************************
 * tty_curses()
 *  Set tty mode for curses
 ***************************************************************/

Void tty_curses()
{                                           /* set up tty modes     */
    raw();                                  /* ignore ^C, etc.      */
    nonl();
    noecho();                               /* do not echo input    */
    keypad(stdscr, TRUE);                       /* enable keypad    */
    return;
}


/***************************************************************
 * trans_slash():
 *  Translate forward slashes (/) into backslashes (\) in
 *  DOS pathnames.
 ***************************************************************/

static char *trans_slash(str)
char *str;
{
    char *cptr;

#if DOS
    for(cptr = str; *cptr; *cptr++)
```

LISTING 8.11 rmenu4.c *continued*

```
        if (*cptr == '/')
            *cptr = '\\';
#endif

    return str;
}

/*************************************************************
 * make_path():
 *  Construct new path based on old default path, old_path,
 *  and current incremental path, incr_path (which might be
 *  absolute)
 *************************************************************/

char *make_path(old_path, incr_path)
char *old_path, *incr_path;
{
    static char newpath[MAX_PATH];

    trans_slash(old_path);
    trans_slash(incr_path);

    if (*incr_path == '/' || *incr_path == '\\')/* If path is absolute */
        strcpy(newpath, incr_path);        /* then it is complete path */
#if DOS
    else if (incr_path[1] == ':')          /* drive designator? if so, */
        strcpy(newpath, incr_path);        /* treat as ABSOLUTE path   */
#endif
    else
    {
        strcpy(newpath, old_path);             /* start with old path  */
        if (*incr_path && *newpath)            /* add path delimiter   */
#if DOS                                        /* (if necessary)       */
            strcat(newpath, "\\");
#else
            strcat(newpath, "/");
#endif
        strcat(newpath, incr_path);            /* and append new path  */
    }
    return newpath;
}


/*************************************************************
 * make_cmd():
 *  Construct a system command string based on a given path
 *  and action string. If the path is non-null, generate a
 *  leading "cd" command to change the current directory.
 *  If running under DOS, then generate a drive selection
 *  statement as well to change the current drive.
 *************************************************************/

char *make_cmd(path, action)
char *path, *action;
```

LISTING 8.11 rmenu4.c *continued*

```
{
    static char cmd_line[MAX_CMD];
    char strtemp[10];

    trans_slash(path);

    if (*path)                                    /* select new path */
    {
        sprintf(cmd_line, "cd %s; ", path);
#if DOS
        if (path[1] == ':')                       /* select new drive */
        {
            sprintf(strtemp, "%c:; ", path[0]);
            strcat(cmd_line, strtemp);
        }
#endif
        strcat(cmd_line, action);                     /* action text */
    }
    else                                /* no new path: trivial case */
        sprintf(cmd_line, "%s", action);

    return cmd_line;
}


/****************************************************************
 * system0(): Execute a command via a system() call.
 *
 *  If Unix, just pass the command string to a shell.
 *
 *  if DOS, pass each sub-command (delimited by ;) to
 *          a command processor
 ***************************************************************/

#if UNIX || XENIX                            /* Unix version trivial */

int system0(cmd)
char *cmd;
{
    return system(cmd);
}

#endif                                       /* end of Unix version  */

#if DOS
int system0(cmd)
char *cmd;
{
    char subcmd[MAX_CMD];
    char savcmd[MAX_CMD], *cmdp;
    int i, retval;
    char *cp = savcmd;
    char c, lastc;

```

LISTING 8.11 rmenu4.c *continued*

```
    strcpy(savcmd, cmd);
    while (*cp)                             /* if more subcommands left */
    {
        if (*cp == ';')
            cp++;
        cmdp = cp;                          /* ptr to start of command  */
        while (*cp && *cp != ';')
            cp++;                           /* find end of subcommand   */
        lastc = *cp;                        /* save terminating char    */
        *cp = '\0';                         /* delimit subcommand       */
        retval = system(cmdp);                  /* pass it to system()  */
        *cp = lastc;                        /* restore last terminator  */
    }
    return retval;
}
#endif                                      /* end of DOS version       */
```

Index

!

A

B

E

Leor Zolman

Leor Zolman, a product of the computer counterculture, bought his first computer in 1975 while a high school student in Hollywood. Each new board meant about a month of after school shifts at McDonald's.

He attended MIT from 1976 to 1978, but dropped out when he found that he couldn't get an EE-CS degree without the EE. Instead of pursuing the degree, he joined the staff of MIT's Lab for Computer Science where he learned C and (in 1979) wrote BDS C, the first C compiler designed exclusively for personal computers.

BDS C was surprisingly complete and effective, allowing programmers to do serious development work on minimal Intel 8080-based CP/M systems. BDS C contributed significantly to the acceptance of C as the language of choice for microcomputer software development. Between 1979 and 1987 over 50,000 BDS C compilers were sold internationally. Leor resisted porting BDS C to the 80x86 family of processors, and the compiler died with CP/M.

After taking a few years off from programming, Leor joined the staff at R & D Publications, where he develops software for internal use and writes "Illustrated C" for **The C Users Journal** and "Tech Tips" for **Windows/DOS Developers Journal**.

He now lives in Lawrence, KS with his wife Lisa and their young daughter Katelyn.

SPECIAL OFFER

Companion Disk to **Illustrated C**

Don't waste your time entering the code from this book.

R & D Publications has created a Companion Disk to **Illustrated C**, available on either 5.25-inch or 3.5-inch MS-DOS format. This disk contains all of the source files from the book, plus PC Curses, a shareware function library. It is an essential resource for anyone who wants to forgo the drudgery of typing code (and the time required to find and correct those inevitable typing errors).

The Companion Disk to **Illustrated C** is available only through R & D Publications. To order, use the special reply card on the opposite page. If the card has already been used, send $10, plus $3.50 for domestic postage and handling, $4.50 for foreign orders to: R & D Publications, 1601 W. 23rd St. Ste 200, Lawrence, KS 66046, or call 913-841-1631 / FAX 913-841-2624. Please specify 5.25-inch or 3.5 inch format. Payment must be in U.S. funds. You may pay by check or money order (payable to R & D Publications) or by VISA, or Mastercard; please include both your credit card number and the expiration date. All orders are shipped within 48 hours upon receipt of order to R & D.

If you want to distribute the source code from this book you need a license. For licensing information, contact:

R & D Publications
1601 W. 23rd St. Ste 200
Lawrence, KS 66046.

YES send me a **FREE** catalog of all R&D Publications programming books

Name ______________________

Title ______________________

Company ______________________

Address ______________________

City __________ St. ______ Zip ________

Country ______________________

I'm particularly interested in the following:
(Please check all that apply.)

☐ C++ ☐ Object Oriented Programming
☐ UNIX ☐ MS DOS internals
☐ ANSI/Standard C ☐ Graphics
☐ Turbo C ☐ X Windows
☐ Windows ☐ Other ______________

I rate this book:
☐ Excellent ☐ Good ☐ Poor

I bought this book from a:
☐ Bookstore ☐ Catalog ☐ Advertisement ☐ Other

Comments ______________________

Illustrated C

Companion Disk to Illustrated C

YES... Please send me _______ copies of the Companion Disk to *Illustrated C* at $10 each...

U.S. funds only $________

Postage and Handling Charge

(Domestic) $3.50
(Foreign) $4.50 $________

TOTAL $________

Please check correct box ☐ 5.25 ☐ 3.5

Name ______________________

Address ______________________

City ______________ St ______ Zip ________

Country __________ Daytime Phone ____________

Payment:
☐ check/money order ☐ Visa ☐ MasterCard

Card# ________________ Exp ________

Signature ______________________

ILLUSTRATED C
Leor Zolman

ILLUSTRATED C
Leor Zolman

NO POSTAGE
NECESSARY
IF MAILED
IN THE
UNITED STATES

BUSINESS REPLY MAIL

FIRST CLASS PERMIT NO. 682 LAWRENCE, KS

Postage will be paid by addressee

1601 West 23rd Street, Ste. 200
P.O. Box 3127
Lawrence, KS 66046-9943

NO POSTAGE
NECESSARY
IF MAILED
IN THE
UNITED STATES

BUSINESS REPLY MAIL

FIRST CLASS PERMIT NO. 682 LAWRENCE, KS

Postage will be paid by addressee

1601 West 23rd Street, Ste. 200
P.O. Box 3127
Lawrence, KS 66046-9943

TEXT

913-841-1631

LISTINGS

913-841-1631